THE FUTURE OF AESTHETICS

THE FUTURE OF AESTHETICS

The 1996 Ryle Lectures

Francis Sparshott

UNIVERSITY OF TORONTO PRESS
Toronto Buffalo London

© University of Toronto Press 1998
Toronto Buffalo London
Printed in Canada
ISBN 0-8020-4426-3

∞

Printed on acid-free paper

Toronto Studies in Philosophy
Editors: James R. Brown and Calvin Normore

Canadian Cataloguing in Publication Data

Sparshott, Francis, 1926–
   The future of aesthetics

   (Toronto studies in philosophy)
   Based on the 1996 Ryle lectures, delivered at Trent University,
   Peterborough, Ont., on Mar. 11–14, 1996.
   ISBN 0-8020-4426-3

   1. Aesthetics.   2. Aesthetics – Study and teaching (Higher).
   I. Title.   II. Series

   BH39.S62 1998   111'.85   C98-931121-X

University of Toronto Press acknowledges the financial assistance to its
publishing program of the Canada Council for the Arts and the Ontario Arts
Council.

Contents

Preface

This book is based on the 1996 Ryle Lectures, delivered under the present title at Trent University in Peterborough, Ontario, on 11–14 March 1996.

The present volume expands the text of the lectures and supplies a mass of elaborative annotation. The format of a series of lectures delivered to a specific audience is maintained.

The Ryle Lectures were established by the Philosophy department of Trent University in 1977 in memory of the late Professor Gilbert Ryle of Oxford University. They are made possible by a grant from the Matchette Foundation and by funds from an endowment established by a group of members, alumni, and friends of the Department of Philosophy. Ryle is someone to whom I am deeply indebted, and whom I greatly admired and esteemed. It is an honour to have been invited to speak under his auspices.

I am most grateful to Trent for its invitation, for its intellectual receptivity, and for the generous and friendly hospitality with which I was welcomed at Peterborough. I am grateful to my audiences for their indulgent attention, and for the thought-provoking questions and comments that helped me on my way.

Thanks to Dr R.M. Schoeffel, and to other colleagues and friends at the University of Toronto Press Incorporated, for advice and encouragement.

Introductory Note

The aim of these lectures was to explain why aesthetics is a permanent concern of philosophy, and to consider the prospects of aesthetics as an academic discipline in our time of intellectual and cultural turmoil.

The outcome, as will be seen, is a threefold exposition of the core of aesthetics as a philosophical discipline, embedded in a fourfold account of the intellectual setting within which aesthetics has been, is being, and may or may not continue to be carried on. It follows that the titles of the lectures cannot correspond precisely to the actual divisions of the subject matter. But I trust that the order of exposition will prove clear in practice.

'Our Court shall be a little Academe,
Still and contemplatiue in liuing art.'[1]

The extensive annotation is designed to elaborate on the text of the lectures, rather than to document it. Publication of fact and opinion on such matters as the current state of post-secondary education and the future of the global economy is so abundant and so tendentious that nobody can keep abreast of it. During the preparation of such a book as this, authors have to close their minds at different times to different kinds of input. Nothing in this book pretends to be authoritative or up-to-date. It is intended, rather, to be illustrative of what needs to be borne in mind.

My reflections on the intellectual setting in which aesthetics and philosophy generally are carried on were previously the subject of my 'Aesthetics and the End of Civilization' (*Philosophic Exchange* 1993–4, nos. 24–5, 13–27). I also wrote and delivered, but have not published, an address titled 'Provincial Philosophy' to the annual meeting of the Ontario Philosophical Society in October 1993, and delivered but did not write down a talk, 'The Future of the University' to the Victoria Women's Association in March 1994. These are worked into the fabric of this book, as are some key themes of 'Art and Culture Today' (*Literature and Aesthetics* [Sydney, NSW] 4, 1994, 44–63).

THE FUTURE OF AESTHETICS

I Aesthetics and the Future of Philosophy

Before I can tell you about the future of aesthetics, I had better explain what aesthetics is. If we can speak of the past, present, and future of aesthetics, as plainly we can, there must be something called 'aesthetics' of which there can be a past and a present and a future. That is, there must be a traceable continuant – not necessarily or probably a persisting essence or describable constancy, but at least something that can be recognized as having (or being) a history.

If aesthetics is a part of philosophy, its history must be part of the history of philosophy.[1] That is, it must consist of people saying and writing things, asking and answering questions, disputing and explaining, within the context of philosophical activity, which itself is somehow recognizable as a distinct context of people saying and writing things to each other and after each other, asking and answering questions, disputing and explaining. For these recognitions to be possible, there must be a certain cohesiveness that confers identity on these contexts at any given time, and a comparable cohesiveness through time. And it would be surprising if nothing could be said about these cohesions, even if everything said was open to qualification and contradiction.[2]

Aesthetics, as philosophers use the term nowadays, is all that part of philosophy that is concerned with beauty and the arts. Such problems had occupied philosophers since classical antiquity, but the idea that aesthetics should be a distinct branch of basic philosophy was the work of one man, Alexander Gottlieb Baumgarten, in 1735.[3] Just as logic studies the criteria of sound reasoning in argumentative discourse, he contended, there ought to be a discipline to establish the criteria of excellence in non-discursive thought – in effect, in the imagery of poetry and the fine arts. After all, arguments are made up of propositions, and propositions are combinations of terms; and terms can be at the basis of sound arguments only if they have content. Baumgarten's idea was that a unified work or image in the fine arts occupies the same epistemological position in the structures of human knowledge as a term in a proposition does. Such terms, taken by themselves, are called concepts. An image is comparable to a concept, but is not quite the same. Technically, the difference between such an image and a concept is that a concept stands for a clear and distinct idea: that is, it has a definite content (is *clear*), and is defined by contrast with other concepts (from which it is *distinct*). A poetic or artistic idea, however, is clear, but not distinct: it has a definite content, but it is not defined – not contrasted with anything in particular. We simply perceive it as what it is. Thus, concepts can enter into well-formed propositions and hence into structured arguments, but poetic ideas combine in a less analysable way into perceptual, imaginative, and artistic wholes. Aesthetics, accordingly, could be defined as *scientia sensitive quid cognoscendi* – the science of perceptual knowledge. Baumgarten's notion could hardly have been entertained much earlier than it was, in the age when Descartes, Leibniz, Locke, and their followers had revolutionized philosophy by basing it on 'ideas,' basic mental contents – a way of thinking that itself could be formulated only in the post-renaissance age of individuals and markets.[4]

Baumgarten's inspiration does not, unfortunately, go anywhere much – I, at least, have never managed to derive any sustenance from his writings on aesthetics, nor have I ever met anyone who claimed to do so. Some decades later, however, that giant among philosophers Immanuel Kant, who used to lecture on Baumgarten and called him the greatest metaphysician of his day, worked a version of his basic idea into his own third critique, the *Critique of Judgment,* and thus installed aesthetics securely in the philosophical repertory. No philosopher can avoid Kant's first critique, and Kant has an argument (which also cannot be avoided) to show that the first critique is disastrous without the second. Kant then argues that the first two critiques together make no sense without the third, the starting point of which is aesthetics. Most contemporary philosophers would dearly love to ignore this argument, but cannot do so without an uneasy conscience, so aesthetics cannot be dislodged from its foothold on Parnassus.

Some people still maintain that aesthetics is perennially what Baumgarten conceived it to be: the study of how such indivisible mental contents as those of the fine arts enter at a foundational level into episte-mological structures and make aesthetic beauty a matter of central philosophical concern.[5] Aesthetics, as thus conceived, is suspect in some quarters, on the ground that it encourages aestheticism, the severing of all dynamic relations between art and practical life; and this severance is stigmatized as a familiar strategy of conservatism.[6] And so it may be; but those thus censured may retort that the stigmatizers really only resent the way artists evade the bureaucracies of police states, and believe that people have no right to enjoy themselves until the last window is smashed and the last bourgeois hanged.

Guardians of the sacred Baumgartenian flame are rare these days. In practice, both in Kant's day and later, what is done under the name of aesthetics results from the confluence of three streams of thought, none of which is very close to Baumgarten's concern, and none of which incurs the supposed stigma of aestheticism. First is the status of beauty among values; second is the logic of taste, the nature of the arguments used in literary and art criticism; and third is the part played in the economy of the mind by works of imagination. These are very different inquiries, each with its own dynamic; but in practice they cannot be kept apart. It is this uneasy relationship that both guarantees aesthetics and the philosophy of art a place in philosophy, and makes the subject abhorrent to tidy-minded philosophers.

The triple focus of aesthetic inquiry is already evident in Kant's *Critique of Judgment*, though many readers either fail to find it there or ascribe it to simple confusion. The underlying idea of aesthetic judgment, for Kant, is the simple affirmation of beauty, an emphatic harmony between the demands of the free mind and the orderliness necessarily assigned to the world of experience. The way this is worked out is inseparable from the mechanisms of Kantian philosophy, but it is developed out of a definition long familiar in philosophy, from Plato to Aquinas:[7] what we find beautiful is that of which we find the value simply in the experiencing of it. Kant's main point is that to judge that something really *is* beautiful goes far beyond merely enjoying or appreciating it: it is to judge that every competent observer *must* experience that value. In fact, the sense of that necessity is an essential part of what we enjoy. But actually, though Kant never says so, such imputation of *necessary* pleasure is really at home nowhere else than in art criticism, the business of establishing and applying valid standards of taste – that is, standards that apply to everyone. There is no point in laying down the law to nature, because nature has her own laws and pays no attention; and there is no real point in establishing standards for the appreciation of nature, since nature is massively there anyway. Art criticism, by contrast, can aspire to guide real choices in practice, purchase, publication, and display. But the practice of art criticism cannot be effectively carried on otherwise than within recognized arts, art forms, and genres. Artistic beauty is thus, to a large extent, contextualized beauty.[8] Kant's argument, grappling with this very tricky idea, draws into its scope not only the theory of beauty developed in classical and medieval metaphysics, but the mass of critical theory being produced by his own contemporaries, especially in Scotland.[9] A consideration of beauty, a kind of value without which, Kant shows, we would be unable to come to grips with the world at all, thus turns into a theory of the fundamentals of art criticism. It could hardly do otherwise, because art critics are the only people who find it practically necessary to clarify the fundamental issues that are involved whenever we find beauty in a complex world of functioning and interrelated systems.

If we are considering the principles of art criticism, though, we cannot ignore what art is all about. And two apparent truths about art had been widely received in the circles to which Kant and all his readers belonged. First, works of art not only give exquisite satisfaction to our sense of order (the beautiful), but are the source of profoundly moving experiences, experiences of the power and magnitude of creation (the sublime). And second, works of art are not mere sources of this or that sort of valuable experience, but function as a means of education for the young and as a mainstay of a civilized way of life. So Kant explores the limits as well as the powers of the mind's capacity for order, providing a philosophically sophisticated version of the long-established contrast between the sublime and the beautiful, and then moves into a rather baffling system of the arts that purports to show how the main types of artistic practice can and must enter into the formation of polite society. This last move is awkward, but inevitable. It is only in the arts that beauty (as philosophy must understand it) is cultivated, and the immediate value of works of art does lie in their beauty; but people would not spend so much effort and public money on the arts unless they felt that the arts somehow sustained the fabric of the society in which art and philosophy both flourish.[10] What gives aesthetics its peculiar status in philosophy is that these transitions among topics are as awkward and uneasy as they are inevitable.

It is usually agreed that the discipline of aesthetics as such is a discovery of the eighteenth century, and the form it takes is a function of the peculiar social, political, and intellectual history of that and the two preceding centuries. But the confluence of three streams of thought is not new. It is already present in Plato, whose fourth-century B.C.E. synthesis has been accepted in most succeeding ages as providing philosophy with its perennial agenda. The relation in the arts between the sheer value of beauty on the one hand and the educational and social values of artistic practices on the other is notoriously subjected in his *Republic* to a critique that seems to most readers to be compounded of profundity and perversity, though few trouble themselves to unravel its complexities; a series of dialogues culminating in the posthumous *Epinomis* assigns to the fine arts a determinate place among the organized uses of civilized mind;[11] the *Symposium* teasingly but compellingly argues for the place of beauty among fundamental values;[12] and the *Greater Hippias* plays subtly and satirically with the concept of beauty as it functions in the rough-and-tumble of the art world.[13]

It is something of a puzzle why this constellation of concerns has sometimes seemed important to philosophers, sometimes not, so that a Ryle could despise what a Plato or a Kant had vexed their brains with. Part of the explanation may simply be that in some intellectual contexts it is the physical world, in other contexts the human world, that seems to pose the more challenging problems and presents the most promising opportunities for investigation. Another part may be that at some places and times it is the procedures of technical investigation that seem more problematic, at other times and places those of humanistic education. Plato himself, preoccupied as he was by the differences between a well-run Greek city and such chaotic conurbations as Babylon, was pre-eminently the philosopher of general education (though it is not nowadays the fashion to describe him in those terms); and Kant's essay on Enlightenment shows a comparable concern with his own times as the Age of Criticism.[14] But in the end we have to say that it is a matter of historical accident – or historical necessity, which comes to the same thing. No explanation is to be given why the permanent possibility of this threefold inquiry should be realized in the philosophical practice of a particular epoch, other than specific turns of events at particular junctures, or the recurrence of typical forces that are themselves explicable only by their specific histories.

We may simply have to accept it, then, that it is in Plato's writings that the threefold inquiry first appears, though it has escaped comment, partly because he does not thrust it on our attention.[15] As there could have been no Baumgarten much before Baumgarten, so there could have been no Plato before Plato. Why not? The whole history of philosophy up to his time contributes to the answer, and much of the social and political history as well. Or we should rather say: if the threefold inquiry was formulated before Plato's day, it formed part of a history all memory of which has been lost.

The Power of Beauty

In Plato, the three streams of thought appear dispersedly, in various relation to one another and to other topics. That is because he had never heard of aesthetics (no Baumgarten before Baumgarten!) and had no reason to emphasize, even in his own mind, the unity of what would later be the specific complex of its concerns. In the philosophy of education that preoccupied him, a different set of emphases and connections comes to the fore. In Kant's construction, by contrast, the point of origin is the distinctive value of beauty. As we saw, it is the intellectual domestication of this value, comparable to the domestication of truth in formal logic, that Baumgarten had fastened on as the possible focus of a new philosophical discipline. Before Baumgarten got his hands on it, though, discussions of beauty had their home in a different area of philosophy: the discipline of value theory or axiology. Any general theory of value must itself be grounded in metaphysics – what is to be valued depends on what there *is* to be valued – even if our convictions about the nature of reality are actually determined by what we actually find valuable. And the place of beauty in such a relationship was most firmly determined by medieval 'scholastic' philosophy, in which all reality and value must be derived from the super-reality of a creative deity in whom all values must be super-realized (realized *eminenter*).

Scholasticism, identifying beauty as such as a distinctive kind of value, defined the beautiful as that which gives satisfaction simply in our being aware of it. Such a definition takes for granted a scheme of values in which all the possible ways of giving satisfaction are enumerated and classified,[16] though I am not aware that anyone consciously formulated the task of compiling such a scheme, much less carried it out. Be that as it may, the scholastic theory went on to enumerate three aspects or necessary conditions of beauty as such.[17] First is the sheer splendour of it. Second is perfection, freedom from deformity. And third is completeness, nothing missing.[18] All these, the scholastics argued, must belong supremely to God, Who (i) is object of the beatific vision, (ii) contains in Himself the source of all forms (and hence, of course, the forms themselves *eminenter*), and (iii) is free from all defect. The reference to God is not merely a pious gesture: it makes a difference to the whole axiology. If God is supremely beautiful, whatever that means, beauty as such obviously has nothing to do with perception, especially not with sense perception, but must be the object of apprehension and cognition quite generally. The object of such cognition would not necessarily be appearance as opposed to reality, but whatever is cognizable. God really is beautiful, I suppose, because, not being perceptible in relation to an organic sensory system, He can be cognized only as He really is. On this way of thinking, however, beauty generally, wherever we find it or think we find it, is not (as it is in God) the radiance of actual super-goodness itself, but the sign of *apparent* goodness. It is, as it were, the promise or (as Kant called it) the *symbol* of goodness.[19]

The scholastic way of thinking about beauty, which seeks to identify it and relate it in a determinate way to a goodness that is metaphysically conceived, goes back to a somewhat different line of inquiry pursued by Plato and Aristotle. Again and again we find them raising a question they never formulate, and which I am at a loss to find precise words for – in fact, I am not sure it is always exactly the same question. It was obviously a standing topic of discussion in their circle, one that kept coming up in different forms and different contexts. Roughly, the question is this: what are the basically different sorts of reasons people have for doing or preferring things, and how are these sorts of reasons systematically related each other? Can they ultimately be reduced to each other? If not, can they be reconciled? And, if they cannot be reconciled, how are we to accommodate them all in our lives? For each of us has only one life to live, into which everything has to be fitted. Rather oddly, considering how every aspect of their society differed from ours, we usually find it quite easy to follow what Plato and Aristotle are saying about this, and their reasons for saying it. This fact may too readily persuade us that they have got something right, are saying something that is timelessly true and equally applicable to their own way of life and to ours, whereas it could be only that centuries of repetition have made their ways of seeing and saying things familiar. However that may be, in any given passage in which this topic comes up we are likely to find both of these authors confronting us with three alternative kinds of reason among which we must choose: what is neither *a* nor *b* must be *c*. But the sets of three options are not always the same. Something proposed is neither good nor pleasant, so it must be (thought to be) just; something chosen is neither beautiful nor pleasant, so it must be (found to be) useful. Nor do the six contrastive terms always keep their connotations unchanged, so that (for instance) usefulness when contrasted with pleasantness almost seems a variant of (functional) goodness, whereas, in discussing friendships, an association based on utility would come closer to one based on pleasure in that both would be essentially contrasted with one based on goodness of character. The terminology has a sort of dynamic plasticity, taking its contours at any moment from the tensions and vectors of whatever matter may be under discussion.

In the end, what the axiological discourse of Plato and Aristotle amounts to is a recurring topic rather than a reiterated doctrine. If we extract the triads from their contexts and put them all together, however, we seem to be left with six options in all. One does and chooses things either (i) because one enjoys them, or (ii) because they confer some advantage on one, or (iii) because they are useful for some purpose, or (iv) because they are good of their kind or in relation to the situation at hand, or (v) because they are lawful or right, or (vi) because they compel one's admiration, one finds them fine or beautiful.[20] Beauty is what is sought out simply because it extorts love or respect simply as and for what it is, without regard to anything one hopes to gain from it or any advantage one sees in it, any good it may do. The pursuit of it is, as the eighteenth century was to say, disinterested.[21] It functions as an ideal. Plato and Aristotle agree that some motivation of this sort has to be recognized if we are to account for all the ways people behave.

At this point, monoglot English-speakers need to be reminded that in Greek, as in French and German but not in English or Latin (or, if Tolstoy is to be believed, in Russian),[22] the word we translate as 'beautiful' is a short, common, everyday word, like the English words 'fair' and 'fine,' not a dressed-up-looking polysyllable like the word 'beautiful'; and it is in Greek, French, and German that most serious philosophy has been done. Those among today's Anglo-American philosophers who system-atically rely on the everyday usage of the English vernacular are, for good or ill, cutting themselves off from the mainstream of philosophy. In the native languages of Western philosophy it comes quite naturally to make beauty a kind of value functioning as basic in our everyday evaluations as well as in our theoretical lucubrations. In English, it may require some violence to our usual ways of speaking, in which 'fair' and 'fine' share the work that 'beautiful' might have done.

The general philosophical question that Plato and Aristotle were deal-ing with can be put like this: Can a complete list and classification of kinds of value be compiled and justified? Is only one such list defensible, or are alternative analyses of value possible? As part of this inquiry, one has to ask the more specific question whether any such list has to find a place for the sort of idealism that words like 'beauty' represent; and, if it must, whether there is only one such value, rather than a cluster of such values, that would prove on reflection to be radically distinct. It is an immense topic; and one must bear in mind that the concept of 'value' is itself indeterminate in meaning, and must remain so until the task of enumeration and classification is plausibly completed.[23]

The complexities of what Plato and Aristotle themselves have to say about their six basic kinds of value and their relations, whatever their intrinsic interest, are relevant here only because, in classical Greek philosophy, discussions of beauty are embedded, not in Baumgarten's epistemologically motivated and artistically oriented discipline of aesthetics, but in general value theory, a wide-ranging problematic in practical philosophy. From this point of view, something like beauty is a value no less in ethics than in aesthetics. This is nowhere more notoriously evident than in Aristotle's ethical theory. What makes virtuous people virtuous, he argues at great length, is that their dominant motivation is always to make the best choice for their situation in the light of their understanding of that situation and their overall beliefs about what is good and bad. When choice and action thus motivated have become second nature to anyone, though, their *immediate* reason for performing such an action is always simply that it is a fine thing to do. They perform the action on account of its 'beauty' (*tou kalou heneka*).

There is no idiomatic way of saying quite that in English, but the facts (or ideologies) in moral psychology are familiar, especially from religious texts in which we hear of people hungering and thirsting after righteousness.[24] The same thought, though not the same language, is present in Kant. The good person acts out of reverence for the moral law, which functions as a compelling ideal; the moral law within us, like the starry heavens above us, evokes a never-failing awe.[25] This 'sense of duty' is a fundamental moral motivation that clearly functions in exactly the same way as the beauty that Aristotle spoke of. Kant speaks of it as a well-known fact about the motivation of idealistic youth, even though the rationale he provides for it is something new.[26] (Aristotle, be it noted, provides no rationale at all, that I know of.) For Kant as for Aristotle, the compelling power of the ideal, once formulated, is independent of any attractiveness there may be in the substantive grounds for action which enabled us to work out in the first place what would be the right thing for us to do.[27] We see the moral law, as we see the starry heavens, before our very eyes; it is this directly apprehended beauty that moves us.

Kant, unlike Aristotle, is in no position to use the word 'beauty' for the reverence-inspiring aspect of the moral law.[28] The beauty identified in

Baumgartenian aesthetics is essentially the object of a judgment of taste, and it retains this connotation in Kant's more general theory of aesthetic judgment. The invention of aesthetics *as a discipline* thus effects a massive reorganization in our conceptual scheme. In fact, it is not immediately clear how beauty conceived in its terms can be related to a general axiology at all.

In the classical axiology, perceived beauty acts as a compelling power – a power most tellingly expressed in Plato's *Symposium*. In Kant's critical philosophy, this compelling power is retained in the sphere of ethics, where the feeling for the beautiful takes the form of the sense of duty ('Duty! stern daughter of the voice of God!' – but adopted by the Enlightenment, and forbidden to speak to her birth mother). But in the domain of aesthetics, this power seems to be lost. What we *judge* to be beautiful submits, as it were, to our judgment – though this is not something that Kant himself would ever say. The necessity that he ascribes to the pleasure involved in aesthetic judgment is a logical inevitability rather than a practical coerciveness. And yet that compelling power of beauty, so vital in the Platonic and Aristotelian scheme, is conspicuous in the arts as we know them. A notorious case in point is the 1956 international architectural competition for an opera house in Sydney, Australia.[29] The competition was most carefully organized, the specifications spelled out, an expert panel of judges chosen – but the judges forgot all about the rules, and awarded the prize on the basis of little more than a sketch, which simply overwhelmed them by its breathtaking profile. They were like adolescents falling in love with a photograph. Not surprisingly, the building could not be built as designed, could not fulfil its requirements, and cost a preposterous amount of money; but in the end, after delays and debates, up it went, and there it is to this day, an architectural pin-up almost as famous as the Taj Mahal. The old myth of the artist starving in a studio pays homage to the same compelling power of beauty. No doubt such artists do dream of fame, riches, and sexual triumphs, just as Freud said.[30] But what explains their specific career choice cannot be any of those, which every artist realizes could be more reliably secured by other courses of action; it can only be the ideal of what Plato's Socrates in the *Symposium* called giving birth in beauty. And I suppose workers in all the arts know the moment when the work begins to reveal its final form, and its promised beauty takes over, demanding to be completed no matter what, to the despair of the artist's family.[31]

The sixfold classical spectrum of value terms – the pleasant, the profitable, the useful, the good, the right, the beautiful – can still strike us as somehow familiar, natural, and even persuasive. Suitably interpreted and stretched, it may be made to cover all the alternatives we can easily propose. And then, since philosophy can hardly dispense with axiology altogether, and any axiology that accommodates beauty is already dealing with one of the constitutive elements in aesthetics, and in aesthetics any element leads to all the others,[32] aesthetics seems sure of a niche in any likely development of philosophy. As Aristotle remarked of philosophy itself, once you have let it in you can't get rid of it, because all the arguments against doing philosophy are themselves philosophy.[33] Arguments against aesthetics work by explaining away the phenomena with which aesthetics deals, and in cultural studies to explain something away is simply to explain it. These things are like mildew; they lurk in the cracks, burrow in the crevices, only waiting for a rainy day to sprout again.

The ancient essays in axiology that issued in the sixfold scheme were not followed up. In recent years especially, the whole subject has been rather neglected. One has the impression that most of the little that has been done, though often shrewd and precise, has been inadequate to its task – narrow, reductive, inflexible.[34] Part of the reason for this may be that the prevailing orthodoxy in university philosophy departments has tried to construe all values in terms of 'interests' assumed to be *self*-interest, treating Descartes' methodological solipsism as if it were a substantive solipsism. This assumes that *Homo sapiens* is not a social animal, especially not one in which the newborn are for many years unable to survive outside a nurturing group, but consists of individuals that spring mysteriously into being in isolation and fill in the *tabula rasa*, the wiped slate of their minds, by accumulating and classifying the inputs from their sensory apparatus. The attempt to construct systematic knowledge on this 'empirical' basis is a valuable exercise, but an exercise is all it is. Neither individuals nor societies can construct their beliefs and information systems otherwise than in language-sharing communities. Even more obviously, the attempt to construct value systems on the basis of the perceived interests of individuals who are, initially and in principle, non-interactive is, at most, of academic interest.[35] In the end, one has to say that the philosophers' taste for assigning explanatory priority to the self-preoccupation of an isolated individual is just a thoughtless application of the mindless reductionism that contemporary scientism adopts in all fields without even trying to make it work.[36]

Whatever the actual state of axiological inquiry, nothing since Plato and Aristotle strikes me as having such an air of intelligence and profundity.[37] In saying this, however, my indoctrination by an old-fashioned classical education may have made me too easy a victim for an antique glamour. After all, since it is hard to say just what the question was that they were answering, one cannot readily determine the parameters of its solution.

No less important than the nebulous nature of the axiological inquiry of the ancients, to my mind, is the suspect nature of its origins. Ancient philosophers were mostly male, rich, slave-owning, and socially privileged – the autonomous individuals of enlightenment ideology. That being said, it becomes obvious that there are two things to question in what they were proposing.

First, just as Augustine said that the virtues of the heathen were really no more than splendid vices,[38] Christian philosophers can argue that the Platonic values exclude love – specifically the generous, self-giving love, *caritas* or *agape*, that seeks nothing from its object.[39] It is not that Plato and (especially) Aristotle were not aware of such a thing;[40] it is rather that their discussions make a separate topic of it, excluding it from the menu of fundamental motivations. Christian philosophers have often followed Augustine's lead and opposed the morality of love to the whole of worldly or secular ethics, rather than weaving it into the fabric of the human condition; but not all have.

A second questionable thing in the ancient axiology is forced on our attention by the deep challenge of feminism. Even if we discount the conflicting polemics of feminist dogmatisms, we cannot nowadays get rid of the suspicion that *all* accepted philosophy may reflect the (suspected) gender bias and (supposed) hierarchical structure-building of male-made history. Even if no item in the spectrum of accepted (by whom?) values is overtly slanted toward one sex rather than the other, there is no way of telling what male predilections are enshrined in the spectrum of identifiable values itself; or even, more disconcertingly, whether the whole idea of *value*, the way of thinking it represents, might not need to be supplemented or even replaced by some different perspective. As I remarked before, the concept of value is indeterminate, standing for an as yet unascertained horizon within which human action as a whole is orientated. The very word 'value' is borrowed from economics, and seems slyly to insinuate that life is a market. Even if we repudiate that suggestion, the language of value may still seem to suggest that all our being and doing are directed to the achievement of goals, rather than, perhaps, fulfilled in the mutual sharing and nurturing of a common life within which we are immersed and engaged.[41] Within the spectrum of values, beauty, even if not something to be enjoyed and possessed, is still envisaged as something external to its beholders, to be contemplated as an object; and it is notorious that in the seductive imagery of Plato's *Symposium* the love of beauty is envisaged in terms of male sexuality.

What alternatives does a feminist questioning open up? Many years ago, a Korean graduate student sought to work out for me what she claimed was an oriental view of aesthetics, centred, not on the joy in beautiful objects, but on the euphoria of being alive in an unspoiled landscape on a fine day.[42] In the same spirit, perhaps, there is a whole literature of 'environmental' aesthetics, in which beauty is found not only in physical surroundings, but in the intelligible totality of ourselves in nature – deep ecology, the interrelations of species and populations, perceived stability or an order in change.[43] And in more direct response to feminist advocacy, scholars working in aesthetics are beginning to explore more deeply the dynamics of shared creation, emphasizing the arts in which what is primary is the quality of lived experience rather than the competition and self-dramatization centred on galleries, prizes, and biographies in glossy journals.

The tendencies just mentioned may be illusory or abortive. But the forms of society are evidently in flux. We simply are in no position to tell what the human world will be like if it ever settles down, or what forms intellectual and artistic life will take in it – that is, if anything in it will take the places that artistic and intellectual life are understood to have here and now. In a Christianized or feminized world, we could expect a complete restructuring, perhaps not of the basic thrust of philosophy (though that word 'thrust' may give us pause), but certainly of its institutionally fostered manifestations; and in such a changed situation we cannot tell what part, if any, will be played by whatever will have replaced what we have come to know as aesthetics. Two specific areas seem recognizably dependent on the vicissitudes of philosophical inquiry.

In the first place, the future of the concept of beauty, and of the value schemes in which beauty finds its determinate meaning, clearly depends on the future of philosophy. We cannot predict when or even whether axiology will play a part in future philosophy, or what it will look like if it does; we cannot tell whether any value in the area now occupied by 'beauty' will find a place or places in any future axiology; and we cannot tell how any such value will be related to what we now variously identify as beauty. But, as we have seen, it is on the philosophical viability of the concept of beauty that the discipline of aesthetics depends for its origin and credentials.[44]

The second obvious problem is as follows. Aesthetics as a fully fledged discipline requires, I have argued, the confluence of three separate lines of inquiry. But it is only if one pushes these lines very hard, to see where they go, that their convergence comes to seem part of an inescapable dialectic. And it is this dialectic that makes aesthetics what it is. It is thus only when the study of philosophy is carried on in a certain way and reaches a certain level of intensity that aesthetics can be taken seriously by philosophers. Most students of philosophy in North America are trapped in courses of study that virtually preclude any such pushing. That is largely because of the way our universities are set up. And they are set up that way because of the turn our civilization has taken.

The future of aesthetics, then, depends on the future of philosophy in general; and the future of philosophy depends on the future of the university; and the future of the university depends on the future of civilization. All these are the futures I am inviting you to think about this week. But first of all, what is the future of philosophy? That depends on what happens to the universities where philosophy dwells. And that provides the topic of tomorrow's talk.

II Philosophy and the Future of the University

I said yesterday that aesthetics as a fruitful field of philosophical thought arises from the convergence and divergence of three lines of inquiry. First is the part played in human thought and action by what we call 'beauty': that is, by the recognition that some actions and persons and objects are such that they demand to be brought into being, preserved, admired for their own sakes. This subject has been relegated to the sidelines of recent philosophy, perhaps partly because it has seemed to be a matter of individual psychology and cultural convention, and hence the perquisite of the behavioural sciences. But the philosophical issue is not purely empirical. The issue is one of the *recognition* of such value, the nature of such a demand and its grounds, its place among the reasons we can give for the ways we use our time, energy, and resources. An inquiry into the 'nature of beauty,' whatever that may turn into, is an essential and integral part of 'general value theory' – and this, despite the mustiness of the phrases I have chosen, is a central part of any inquiry into what it means to be a human being. The second line of inquiry is the logic of criticism and aesthetic judgment, inquiring into whatever rational basis there may be for establishing the relative merits of works of fine art. On the one hand, it must be true that 'there is no arguing about taste' – *de gustibus non disputandum* – which means that one cannot mount a formal scholastic disputation based on personal preferences; on the other hand, it is just as obvious that reasoned discussions of the merits of works of art and literature often do take place and sometimes arrive at a consensus, and some such discussions are better than others. Thus there is an obvious place for inquiry into the logic and rhetoric that should prevail in this area of discourse. And the third line of inquiry is the proper place of the fine arts as organized modes of practice among the arts and sciences of a civilization, or in the economy of the human mind. It might seem that a conclusion in any of these three lines should furnish a conclusion for both the others. And so, no doubt it does; but the question remains whether the conclusion thus furnished is adequate, or even on the right lines.

This threefold field of inquiry, I said, emerges casually both in the writings of Plato and Aristotle and, two millennia later, in those of Kant and his contemporaries. But it was only in the eighteenth century that aesthetics came to be recognized as a distinct branch of philosophy. The new discipline, however, was to be rooted in a possible epistemology of specifically artistic beauty: that is to say, of the integrated imagery of the poetic and artistic imagination. And this very special kind of beauty, despite its philosophical significance, excludes not only the general kind of beauty integral to a comprehensive theory of human motivation, but also the overall significance of the arts themselves. Thus, Hegel, introducing his lectures on aesthetics in the 1820s, complains that 'aesthetics' is really quite the wrong word for what he is going to do, which is the philosophy of the fine arts – but the misleading terminology has already become so firmly established that it is too late to change it.[1]

The threefold unity of aesthetics has not been generally noted. Why not? Partly because people mostly do not think long and hard enough about the issues for it to become apparent; partly because aesthetics in American universities is usually dealt with in one course in a single semester, so that its teachers become accustomed to taking short and shallow views; partly because the terms of contemporary discussion are largely governed by the art industry; but mostly because in the present state of philosophy and culture studies the topic is too vast and vague to be profitably addressed. But, however that may be, the 'future of aesthetics' is a threefold topic. It includes, first, the internal development of our three lines of inquiry, separately or together, as a dialectic or an unravelling of argument which, once achieved, remains a permanent part of the repertory of philosophy. It includes, second, the development of the actual discussion of these topics by actual thinkers, as the fashions of debate and intercommunication may determine. But it also includes, third, the development of institutions, academic and political, in which these discussions can be carried on.

What, then, does the future seem to have in store for aesthetics? General value theory, including the development of some sort of spectrum of values on which something like beauty appears as one or more bands, may or may not come back into philosophical fashion. Philosophy is probably condemned to triviality without it; but then, philosophy may be condemned to triviality. The future of aesthetics as the discipline that A.G. Baumgarten thought it might be, a sort of logic of imagery, clearly depends on the continuing intelligibility of the special sort of structured epistemology that was familiar in his own philosophical milieu. Whether that kind of theory has a future in philosophy is more than I can say, but, if it does, it can only be in a very academic sort of philosophy indeed. The logic of criticism is a topic I have not yet discussed; it seems to be a going concern, but it may be that people will soon get bored with it, discovering that everything interesting has already been said. The place of the arts in society seems to be a topic with a rosier future, because the more the arts are discouraged by the powers that be, the more determined their advocates will be to find arguments in their favour – and the more the arts are encouraged, the more arguments will be needed to justify that encouragement. And finally, the future of aesthetics as the study of three philosophical topics in intricate interrelation clearly depends on the future of philosophy as a discipline pursued energetically and in depth.

But what is it that has to be pursued with such depth and energy? I acknowledged yesterday that one could discuss 'the future of aesthetics' only if aesthetics were already enough of a recognizable entity that it could be meaningfully said to *have* (or not to have) a future. What I forgot to mention is that it is equally meaningless to speak of the future of philosophy, unless we have some idea of what it is that is going to have *that* future. Perhaps it seemed obvious. But is it? Not really. I suppose most of us have some idea of what is going on *here and now* in the name of philosophy – for some here, and for some now. That is, we can loosely identify some present place and time within which we can identify with a certain degree of confidence something we are prepared to call philosophy. But if we are to speak of the future of philosophy in general terms, we are going to need more than that. After all, we can take it for granted that much of what is being done in our 'here and now' in the name of philosophy is foolish and perverse; and the future of *that*, we hope, is that it has no future. It will fizzle out when certain irresponsible practitioners go to their reward.[2]

So, what *is* philosophy? For us as philosophers to ask that question is like us as human beings asking ourselves 'What is humanity?' – a question that, admittedly, we do sometimes ask. 'Man,' said Democritus, 'is what we all know.'[3] His answer was often ridiculed, but it is one of the right answers.[4] Humanity is *precisely* what we all know – what we know from the inside. It is what we know by being it, and also by not being it, by encountering other people who by their difference from ourselves reveal what we have chosen not to be, what we have not chosen to be, and the choices that in a different world might have been ours to make but never came our way. It is the full extent and depth of this lifelong and unplumbed intimacy with our own humanity that is, for us, what it is to be human.[5] In much the same way, for us who have at least the smattering of philosophy that has brought us to this room, philosophy is 'what we all know.' It is the sum of our own practice, of what we have understood of the practice of others, and, not least, of what we as philosophers might have done instead: what we have grasped of the alternative possibilities that we have chosen to repudiate. It is the totality of this practical understanding that is, for each of us, the best answer to the question of what philosophy is. It is this that guides our own speech, and our understanding and reading of what others say and write. We know this, I said, in 'much the same way' as we know what humanity is. But we do not know it in quite the same way, because nothing in our knowledge is external to our humanity, while it may be that a great deal of what we know and think and feel and are is external to our philosophy – even if we cannot quite tell where the boundary lies. What is surely true is that this 'what we all know' of philosophy by being philosophers (by being just as much philosophers as we are) is something that extends beyond all possible definitions. It is what governs all our words about philosophy, so that it cannot itself be put into words. Or rather, sometimes it can; but only provisionally and partially, and probably not always into the same words.

In a mixed group like ours here tonight, where speaker is stranger to listeners, and the scope of our mutual understanding and misunderstanding is still uncharted, saying that philosophy is 'what we all know' is more honest than enlightening, and more enigmatic than either. It might be more realistic, though hardly more instructive, to say: philosophy is what philosophers do. More precisely, philosophy is all and only what philosophers do when they are doing philosophy. And who are these 'philosophers'? There are different opinions about that, and different ways of deciding; but not all opinions are equally responsibly formed, and not all decisions are equally well based. But in any case, philosophy is something done by people who do it. And how do we know when they are doing it? You will just have to ask them, or the people who have to do with them. Philosophy is a practice with practitioners, and subject to the variabilities and constancies of practices: these are not matters to be put into a sentence, but to be explored.[6]

It is important that any explanation of what philosophy is needs to take indirect and indeterminate forms such as I have been describing. But it is just as important that we really do need something that can be put into words, a formula or slogan that can then be expounded and to which subsequent elaborations and explanations can be referred.[7] For such a formula, we could do worse than say that philosophy is the attempt to establish the most fundamental and general principles of knowledge, whatever they may turn out to be – not forgetting that a large part of that inquiry may consist of trying to get clear about just what, if anything, words like 'general,' 'fundamental,' 'principles,' and 'knowledge' mean.[8] And there are lots of other phrases in circulation (for instance, there is an old scholastic definition: 'the study of things in their causes') – all helpful, all proving on examination to be tendentious in one way or another, all useless unless accompanied by protracted explanations. In any case, if we adopt the formula I have suggested, we should bear in mind that to say that philosophy is '*the* attempt' to establish these things may be misleading. It may well be that different attempts will set out, independently, in different directions. In that case it might be more realistic to speak, as many do, not of philosophy as a unitary sort of undertaking, but of philosophies in the plural. Not only that, but there is an ambiguity in our inquiry into what philosophy (whether as 'what we all know,' or as what philosophers do) is. We may be asking about an actual tradition of inquiry in our society as broadly conceived – roughly, in 'Western civilization'; or about a possible kind of inquiry, with its own ideals and standards, which that tradition (perhaps imperfectly) exemplifies; or about any inquiry that plays in its own society the part that what we recognize as philosophy plays in ours. In the last case, what we have in mind would vary according to the analogy we were using – most commonly, the 'philosophy' of a society would be either its most basic principles of establishing truth, or its most deeply entrenched modes of thought.[9]

The things I have been saying are all exceedingly general – too general, in any case, to articulate a curriculum. At different times, accordingly, it has seemed that all philosophy really comes down to something much narrower. The purport of such restrictions is not usually made quite clear, and there are several possibilities. One thing that could be intended is a repudiation of the general scope claimed for philosophy, in the name of a narrower and more specific agenda; another possibility is that the requirement of generality is accepted, but it is felt that the requirement is best fulfilled by some specific method or procedure. And no doubt there are other possibilities, but I do not know what they are. Whatever the purport may be, the 'something much narrower' preferred by some philosophers is logic, the critique of arguments in knowledge claims;

according to others it is conceptual clarification, the elucidation of what we really mean by whatever words we use; to others again, it is the construction of a system that will unify the intelligible world; to yet others, it is self-knowledge. Clearly, the fate of aesthetics as a division of philosophy would be governed by exclusive emphasis on any one of these. In the long run, though, none of these versions of what philosophy 'comes down to' will quite do. Even so one-sided a philosophy would have to include a critique of the process by which its chosen emphasis became exclusive. Without that critique, the claim to be truly fundamental could not be admitted; and without that claim, I would argue, philosophy has no reason to exist.[10]

Another way of putting the upshot of the discussion so far is to say that the fundamental project of philosophy is to promote the securing of truth and the avoidance of error in the most comprehensive way possible.[11] Its aim must accordingly be to replace our ordinary human condition of careless confusion by a different condition, one of enlightenment, an ideal condition for which the traditional name is 'wisdom.' But such replacement amounts to nothing less than the remaking of our humanity, and if it became general it would really amount to the replacement of mankind by a different species.[12] And it is not evident that that is possible, or would be desirable if it were. To *whom*, after all, would it be desirable? Socrates' famous claim that an unexamined life is not fit for a human being to live is deeply ambiguous:[13] he forgot to remind us that part of our examination of life will no doubt teach us what is best left unexamined, and what examinations, once made, are best forgotten. That means that existential philosophies and strategies of deconstruction must claim a certain precedence over science and system. (We do science; science does not do us.) But system and science will not go away. (Our discoveries dispel our daydreams.) In the end, then, we find that we cannot, after all, say in quite what way philosophy is the pursuit of truth and the avoidance of error, except that it is the unstable and indeterminate field of thought in which questions that sound like this keep arising in new ways and with new urgencies.[14]

In addition to these perplexities of principle, our practical understandings of what philosophy is also keep shifting. They shift, first, as the paradigms of our knowledge change, as new standards in science and history modify our ideas about facts and theories. They shift, second, as the rise and fall of fashions in inquiry generate new disciplines, new internal organizations and divisions of labour among philosophical workers. They shift, third, as our fundamental questionings penetrate to ever greater depths – some questions cannot even be asked until a great deal of philosophical work has been done and assimilated. They shift, fourth, as traditional ways of directing our inquiries come into question: unchallenged starting points cease to seem obvious, choices that once seemed forced on us no longer seem to be worth making. They shift, fifth, as philosophical systems that once held magisterial authority come to seem arbitrary or inconsistent. And, sixth, if we assume after all that philosophy is cumulative, so that all the doubts and discoveries ever made remain in principle perpetually available – we are left with too much to do. Since we do not have time to do everything, but must somehow collectively come to a tacit agreement about what to discuss amongst ourselves, certain questions and ways of proceeding will become salient for no reason that anyone can explain. Fashions in philosophy simply change. Quine or Adorno is the colour of the month.[15]

Obviously, the future of aesthetics depends on these shifts in perspective and fashion; and the different aspects of aesthetics will be affected differently. Let me recapitulate what I said at the beginning of tonight's lecture. The general theory of beauty requires a lively pursuit of the general theory of value, a critique of the basis of practical philosophy within the general domain of philosophical anthropology; and it is vulnerable to subversion of the whole notion of values and value theory if and as we move into a new feminist (degenderate?) phase of human history. The theory of criticism depends on the salience of logical studies, and is favoured by emphasis on the structure of confirmation – an emphasis encouraged by the American 'mainstream' vogue for information-handling machines, but repugnant to many devotees of philosophical reflection. Aesthetics in its original sense, the critique of imagery, requires the vitality within logic of a kind of speculative epistemology associated with idealism and romanticism; and, as I said before, this part of the repertory of philosophy has no secure place in today's curriculum. Consideration of the place of the fine arts on the map of knowledge, if it is to go beyond the pronouncements of journalistic culture-criticism, requires willingness to take seriously a global view of intellectual activity, a self-confidence of which philosophy has only fitfully shown itself capable. And, finally, the maintenance of aesthetics as a complex threefold inquiry requires the extensive and intensive cultivation of philosophy as a comprehensive system. Such cultivation depends on the maintenance of an appropriate organization of systematic studies, which in practice makes aesthetics dependent on the future of the university – a topic that will engage us shortly.

Clearly all the foregoing have been, and potentially still are, within the scope of philosophy. But I have already remarked on the tendency among Anglo-American philosophers who felt they could locate themselves in the 'mainstream' to confine professional philosophical studies to the first of our named possibilities, logic. This tendency no longer has the dominance it had thirty years ago, but in many departments and journals it still constitutes the normal view, the bread-and-butter view, of what professional philosophy is. On this view, the philosopher is a parasite, lying in wait until someone else has said something, and then pouncing on the utterance to explain and criticize its logical grammar. One obvious advantage of this view is that it makes philosophy teachable to children without talent, without knowledge of the world, without wisdom, without long attention spans, without intellectual passion, and without the habit of reflection – that is, to undergraduates fulfilling a compulsory course requirement. Only on such terms, after all, can philosophy be a manageable discipline.

On these terms aesthetics becomes an impoverished study; and it may seem that on the same terms all philosophical studies are impoverished. But, on the one hand, many philosophers, including Socrates as well as Gilbert Ryle, welcome such impoverishment – human wisdom lies not in the attainment of recondite truth, but in the elimination of pretentious nonsense and confident flatulence.[16] And, on the other hand, one has to recognize that philosophy as a discipline never accepted this confinement to logic. In principle, as I remarked, it could not do so without compromising its claims to be a foundational discipline. And in practice, logic was always supplemented by history and the study of classical texts.[17] Those texts, written in bygone days of courage and hope, are broadly speculative, thrillingly uninhibited, and rich in suggestion. What would be the point of trying to do their work over again? Our consciences, armed with centuries or millennia of disillusioned acumen, would not let us do so even if we shared their abilities. We do better simply to read and reread them, discounting their fallacies and acknowledging that our own minute and careful studies are mere correctives and supplements to their bold initiatives. A large part of their value, in fact, lies in their very sloppiness; their obvious and tempting errors keep provoking us to attempt the surprisingly difficult task of correction. Above all, we must remember that nothing is new to experience, but to innocence everything is new. In the history of philosophy, the most obviously important tasks were tackled first. To today's philosopher none of this is new, it has been done already. But to the student it is all new: it has been done in history, but it has not been done in the student minds of each generation.

The trivialization of today's academic philosophy, in fact, if it really exists, is not entirely due to the academy's subordination to the requirements of its least interested and capable members. There is something to be said for the late George Grant's contention that contemporary thought is inevitably dominated and trivialized by rampant technology.[18] But what Grant never admitted was that big efforts can be made nowadays only by small and insensitive minds, because the changes in the shape of the lived world are too complex and continuous for anyone to cope with honestly or adequately. The big issues are no longer real to us; if we are honest, we can only divide our days between the historical revitalization of times when the issues seemed within our grasp, and the honing of our technical skills on artificially restricted problems.

Meanwhile, philosophy's claim to foundational status, a claim that the fundamental tendency of its inquiries keeps insinuating, has no foundation in contemporary reality. The dominant institutions of international science, industry, and commerce sprawl too widely to need any foundation and are too massive to undermine. The prospect is rendered more bleak by the fact that philosophy today has no real home outside the university. The corpus of its accumulated methods and doctrines is too formidable for amateurs to assimilate. And academics are not professionally inclined to passionate profundity. We of the professorate are mostly nice people, because nothing in our work tempts us to violence or encourages us in cupidity; and, despite what the novelists say, the ones I have met are more given to cooperation than to competition. But we who found employment in universities were chosen for docile cleverness, good at our school exercises, too timid ever to leave school and take a proper job, and conformist even in our nonconformity. Passion and idealism are things we contemplate from a distance. Any philosophy cultivated by people like us is likely to tend toward manageability. And the fury and disreputability supposed to be endemic in the arts, with which aesthetics must come to terms, are a rebuke to the academic lack of passion.[19] Professional philosophy has always found aesthetics embarrassing.

Well, I don't know that I really believe that. But in any case, you may be wondering, is it not perverse to insist that the future of aesthetics depends on that of philosophy? Why not put it the other way round? What can philosophy be, after all, if not simply the resultant of all the things philosophers do? And some of what some philosophers do is aesthetics.

That being so, the future of philosophy is determined by the various developments in aesthetics, no less than in any other branches of philosophy. True; but it also remains true that the future of philosophy *in general* is the overall climate within which choices can be made. There will always be eccentrics, marginal people who pick up neglected possibilities from the ragbags of the past. The climate of philosophy does not silence such people. But the climate does govern what will be attended to, what will be reviewed, what will spread, what will be quoted, and, above all, what gets into the curriculum. And the curriculum will typically be that of a university.

I have been spending a lot of time on very general reflections on philosophy at large, and its prospects in a world so inhospitable that it hardly seems to matter, as though we were worrying about the blood pressure of a man drowning in mid-ocean. At the time when I first met Gilbert Ryle, my newly-assigned supervisor for the B. Phil. degree, I was already much possessed by these issues, and asked Ryle how much time he thought I should give to them rather than to the specific topics and writings of my research. Without hesitation, he responded with his typical gruff grunt: 'About fifty-fifty.'[20] I am sure he referred, as I had, to my immediate plans for graduate study, but I seem to have kept to his formula pretty well all my life. Meanwhile, let me bring this particular bout of rumination to an end by recapitulating what I have said about the ambiguities lurking in my avowed topic, 'the future of aesthetics.' That future is, first, the future of the internal developments and interactions of three branches of inquiry, and whatever patterns of inquiry may come out of those. In this sense, aesthetics is a cumulative inquiry, except that some vantage points may become practically inaccessible to all but the most single-minded devotees of intellectual archaeology. But the future of aesthetics is also, second, the actual deployment of intellectual effort in pursuing such inquiries within the scope of philosophy as that develops with its own internal logic. And that logic, let us remind ourselves, includes the transformation of philosophy by the successive developments and departures of autonomous sciences.

The future of aesthetics, then, on one interpretation depends on the future of philosophy. But that future in turn may be understood in two ways. It may be, first, the internal development of philosophical arguments and methods which, once articulated, become permanently accessible as part of the overall repertory of philosophical thinking – except that, again, some vantage points may become so intellectually remote from current concerns that almost nobody can spare time and energy to get back to them. But, second, the future of philosophy may be equated with what actual philosophers are going to do when they are philosophizing in the context of the university and other ambiances where philosophy can flourish.

It thus comes to seem that on one interpretation the future of philosophy depends on that of the universities (and other such places) in which alone philosophy can survive. But that future in turn can be understood in two ways. It may be, first, the development of the idea of a university as a place where studies can be pursued; and this development is cumulative, as every change is made in the light of an accessible history. But it may also be, what it is more usually thought of as being, the future of universities as actual uses of human and material resources by historically situated societies.

Is there a further step? Is there an ambiguity between the future of societies as the development of the envisaged possibilities of human sociability, and the empirical future of how people are actually going to live together on this planet? I think there is. But I am not going to take that step just now.

The Map of Knowledge

I have been talking about the future of philosophy as it affects the threefold complex of aesthetics overall, and as it affects the theory of beauty, with an eye to how these futures depend on the university as their normal setting. The place of aesthetics in philosophy, and the place of philosophy in the life of learning, in general or at any given time, sound like the sort of thing that would be best shown on a map – that is what maps do, show places in relation. And the place of the fine arts among systematic uses of the mental powers of humanity also sounds like the sort of thing a map might show – presumably the same map, or one very like it. And now we recall that the place of the fine arts on the map of knowledge was one of the three main topics that aesthetics has to deal with.

Where do the fine arts fit into a map of knowledge? One might suppose that that place would be determined by the consideration that the 'fine' arts are the arts in which the dominant value is that of beauty. This would be a matter of definition, since 'fine' in this connection is a mere synonym of 'beauty' (it is only in English, not in French *beaux arts* or German *schöne Kunst*, that this terminological variation occurs). But the supposition would be premature, since a map *of knowledge* would relate the arts to other uses of the intellect – no relation, no map. And until we know what the possible uses of the intellect are, we cannot tell what the possible relations might be. No doubt we should follow Baumgarten to the extent of conceding that the place of the fine arts should be something necessarily mediated by apprehensible qualities, but the bare possession of such qualities would probably not be enough. The kind of knowledge such qualities *immediately* afford is what philosophers once called 'knowledge by acquaintance,' and a place on a cognitive map would be determined by how such acquaintances entered into the system or systems whereby our minds accommodated our world and ourselves. After all, not every object of admiring cognitive acquaintance is a work of art – at least, not always.[21]

It is not necessary that all the fine arts should occupy the same vicinity on a map.[22] There is no authoritative list of the fine arts, and no natural unity among them. In the days when the fine arts came to be regarded as constituting such a unity, the reasons for linking them to each other were a mixed bag, and of unequal strength. The arts most often named – music, poetry, sculpture, painting, architecture, and sometimes dance – tended to be linked in pairs, for heterogeneous reasons. Painting and poetry, for instance, can both represent the same scenes and actions, by depiction and description, respectively. Poetry and music are joined, not by analogous function, but by being united in song. Dance and drama are partly parallel and partly complementary, as the silent and speaking arts of gesture. Drama itself can be read or recited instead of acted, and is then treated as a division of poetry. Painting and sculpture and architecture are all arts based on drawing – *arti del disegno*, in a fifteenth-century phrase – and are thus entangled with one another while remaining distinct. And so on. In all these linkages, philosophical argument and traditional practice have sometimes reinforced each other, sometimes worked against each other. Putting them all together, theorists have been equally receptive to arguments for thinking about all the arts as variant forms of a single sort of practice, called 'art,' and to arguments for thinking about them as fundamentally diverse professions. The unity discovered, by those who have found any, has been at least sixfold: formal, functional, pedagogical, historical, and, in the end, economic and administrative. And those who find no such unity have discovered radical diversity in precisely the same six ways. This set of facts, in all its ramifications, makes the placing of the fine arts on a map of knowledge a rich topic.

I said just now that theoretical and practical approaches to such cartography sometimes conflict and sometimes cooperate. That means that the mapping may be a priori or a posteriori: one may assign functions to the arts on theoretical grounds, or one may simply observe functional congruences in operation. But a priori groupings, once established with sufficient authority, may become a posteriori, for a classification may found an organization. A nation that establishes an 'arts council' to fund activities defined as 'the arts' tends to produce a de facto unity among those arts, when they find themselves in a common relation to the funding authority – and an art deemed ineligible for funding may find itself increasingly disassociated from those more fortunate.[23]

The supposed unity of art and the fine arts is a topic on which I have written at very great length.[24] Here are some of the things I said. In an attempt to enumerate and classify all the arts of their civilization, that is, all the uses of the mind in organized production, Plato's circle identified a group of 'arts of imitative play' or 'playful mimesis.'[25] The idea was that . in putting on a play, or reciting a story, or painting a scene, artists put our regular means of communicating information to a use that is non-serious, in the sense that it is primarily meant to be enjoyable rather than informative. Instead of saying or showing (or purporting to say or show) something about something that has really happened, or that should happen or be prevented, the artist says or shows something of the same form of which the interest lies in what is said or shown itself – not in what is represented, but in the representation.[26] When the philosophy of art became an object of concentrated attention in the eighteenth century, theorists generally picked up this idea and began by calling the fine arts 'arts of imitation.'[27] But the initial determination of artistic representations as not (in the obvious way) serious raises the question of why civilized people should take them so seriously. Why do we spend so much time and effort on them? The interest must lie in the ways in which things were said or shown, not in the fictive content itself. Consequently, an alternative line of thought developed the idea that the arts gave truthful accounts, not of the sorts of things that happen, but of the ways we humans experience them as happening: our subjective attitudes and feelings toward human experience, and our ways of interpreting it. As thus understood, the fine arts were redefined as 'arts of expression,' to be taken seriously as revealing ourselves to ourselves in our most refined humanity. Other theorists reflected that this interest in *how* things were said or shown must, more fundamentally, be an interest in the forms and methods of communication themselves, so that the fine arts are really the arts that explore and expand the possibilities of structure, codification, and form. As such, they are to be taken seriously as extending the boundaries of possible cognition, and, hence, of human possibility in its most fundamental aspect. Yet another line of thought, reflecting on all these possibilities together, decided that the fine arts are, most significantly, the arts that celebrate and cultivate the general human capacity to envisage alternative possibilities – in a word, arts of *imagination*.

These alternative ways of thinking about the apparent unity of the fine arts (which, in honour of the fundamental nature of the unity we seem to have established, we now designate by the single word 'art'), fastening as they do on different aspects of art as most deeply significant, all imply different maps of knowledge, different ways our civilization can and does organize, classify, and understand its ways of making, doing, and thinking. Even the primitive Platonic definition 'arts of mimetic play' could be taken two ways, as saying either that art is basically a recreation, one that happens to use the means of communication, or that it is basically one of our uses of the means of communication, namely, the playful use. Plato himself showed in *The Sophist* how a practice or profession could be variously defined, and how its redefinition could identify it with quite different ways of life and theories of society.[28] And history shows how the other definitions of art I mentioned answer to different views of life, different conceptions of humanity, and different selections and evaluations of artistic data.

The account I have derived from my earlier writings, however, has gone altogether too fast. It was untrue to its Platonic origins. Of course, this does not matter in itself, since the eighteenth-century reconstruction was equally hasty; but I have been at some pains here to claim for aesthetics a legitimate ancestry in classical tradition. And the fact is that it has not yet been made clear why the fine arts should be assigned a place or places on a map of knowledge at all. Arts in general are certainly assigned such a place by Plato and Aristotle, for whom the concept of an art (*technē*) was fundamental to their theory of knowledge. The concept is implicitly defined in the first book of Plato's *Republic* (340E–341E, 346A–E). An art is, approximately, a body of principles defining a teachable body of practice whereby a determinate set of operations working on a determinate subject matter produces a determinate sort of change defined within the art and in the context of human life as an improvement (in the ideal case, a perfection). That is the way in which production in general is organized. But in Plato's *Statesman* we are offered a summary presentation of how a society's work is organized, in which it is not clear that what we should call the fine arts are arts at all, and the idea of a 'non-serious use of the means of communication' is nowhere in sight. The 'Foreigner' who has been laying down the law in this dialogue is enumerating the prepolitical production that gives the politicians material to 'weave' into their polity. After specifying four basic kinds of product – tools, containers, means of transport, defences – he says (with interjections by 'young Socrates'): 'In the fifth place, then, would we want to put what has to do with ornament and writing/drawing, and whatever makes use of that plus music to produce representations, worked out merely for our pleasures and rightly to be summed up in a single word?' – 'What sort of word?' – 'I suppose it's called a kind of game (*paignion*).' – 'So what?' – 'This one word will fit, then, if we apply it to all of them. None of them are done for the sake of any serious purpose, but all for play.' – 'I understand that too, sort of' (*Statesman* 288C–D). The entire passage is weird – the unexplained classifications, sequences, and designations presumably refer to some discourse into whose secrets we are not to be admitted. But the bit that concerns us seems to envisage some loose association of practices akin to that of our fine arts, and combined in something like an operatic performance (such as Greek tragedies were). Be that as it may, the common name chosen for them is strikingly belittling. *Paignia* are not simply games or amusements; they are mere toys, playthings, trivialities. But this is plainly not the status they had in Plato's Athens, nor is it the status assigned to them in Plato's own *Laws*. Aristotle would later find a word for occupations that were economically unproductive but valued for their own sakes: they are arts that 'contribute to the course of life' (arts *pros diagōgēn*, *Metaphysics* A 1, 981b18) And, for Aristotle, this was no small matter: he thinks the quality of experience throughout a lifetime is precisely what defines 'the good' for human beings. On the face of it, in any case, 'representation' does merit location on a map of cognitive functions: it is a basic cognitive tool, perhaps *the* basic tool. Our own contemporaries, building on the tradition of philosophy that goes back to Descartes and Locke, and beyond them to Plato's own *Theaetetus* and to Epicurus, often take cognition to be founded on the formation of subjective equivalents for (representations of) the information processed by our sensory apparatus. Accordingly, the use of our cognitive or representational powers, not to convey information but to exercise and develop those powers themselves, has a place already reserved for it on many maps of knowledge. The name of that place is 'imagination.'

All the definitions of art I mentioned a little while ago are historically and philosophically important, but the equation of the fine arts with arts of imagination deserves (as the guidebooks say) a detour. Aristotle, whose basic ideas are so thoroughly ingrained in the commonplaces of our philosophy, already identified imagination, the ability to envisage possibilities beyond present experience and without regard to their realization, as essential to all complex animal action (*On the Soul* III 3). To take action, one has somehow to envisage how one's action might make the world different, and that is the work of imagination. But imagination in humans is more than that. We differ from other animals in that our ways of life, and hence our actual selves, are cultural constructs, continually being reinvented. In a sense, the ways we live in our cultures are products of a sustained work of collective imagination. In practice, indeed, culture becomes second nature. We experience our practical lives as a tissue of apparent necessities. But this is a mistake, a matter of self-deception, though it is a deception without which we could not sustain our actual lives.[29] So there is an obvious place for a set of organized activities in which these necessities are denied, and the essential freedom of the mind to create alternative realities is constantly re-emphasized and celebrated.[30] A map of knowledge on which the fine arts figure as arts of imagination and occupy an important place is by no means absurd.[31]

It seems that, in a way, what the arts primarily do is present alternatives – objects or experiences that are significant as being different from the everyday world in which we live.[32] If so, their basic function must simply be to pry us loose, to prevent our minds from being prisoners of the way things are. More fundamentally, what they do is cultivate the faculty itself of envisaging alternative possibilities. But it is important to remember that this is not their only possible place on a map of knowledge. By making vivid the vitality of culture, they may reinforce the orderliness of social order; by making alternatives vivid, they may hasten the breakdown of an overstrained polity. Many people accordingly prefer to draw maps on which the arts are placed within the domain of political thought: as auxiliary devices of conservatism, or of revolution. Such maps have their uses, especially within specific historical contexts. But we have to ask ourselves whether what they show is how art necessarily functions, just because it is what it is, or whether they show how art may be put to use in a particular context because it is already doing something else – for instance, simply keeping human cultural creativity alive. In the latter case, we have to ask whether this additional use has become (for some purpose, for all purposes) the true function of art, or remains (in some ways) secondary.[33]

One more thing needs to be said here. Suppose we place the arts on our map as arts of imagination. We then have to face the possibility that what really occupies that place is not the specific phenomena that have preoccupied aesthetics, but something wider. In that case, aesthetics might find itself replaced by some other discipline: perhaps by semiotics, the study of the use of codes and signs, or by structural anthropology or a general philosophy of culture, or even by that favourite of today's computerized philosophers, cognitive science.[34] Well, up to a point, so it might, and so it has been; but only up to a point. The epistemic cartography of the arts is only one of the three concerns whose interplay constitutes the domain of aesthetics. While the nature of aesthetic value and the logic of art criticism remain as perennial concerns, aesthetics cannot be completely superseded.

So much for the identification of the fine arts as the arts of imagination, and their possible place on maps of knowledge. It is high time we looked at that phrase 'map of knowledge' itself.[35] I have been talking as though there really were such a thing as a map of knowledge, and we knew what it was. But is there? And do we? On reflection, I am not sure it is more than a phrase I just find myself using – expressing, perhaps, an uncriticized feeling that the ideal totality of knowable reality must fit together somehow, and all my activities as a professional academic must stand in some definite relationship to all other such activities. Am I lost? If not, where am I? What I need is a map, showing the size and shape of the world of knowledge and enough detail that I can find where in it I am.

What are maps? First, they show spatial relations, where things are, not in sequence but in multiple relations to one another. The 'things' in question are represented under classifications, to which the mapmaker provides a key: churches, marshes, bridges. These classifications must first be chosen, to meet the intentions and needs of the cartographers and their public.

Second, maps show not only where things are, but how to get there. Routes are marked out; if no routes are in place, the map gives the data (contours, isotherms, surface permeabilities) from which routes can be worked out. The kind of map I use most often is a road map, showing inhabited places and the presence and quality of the roads that have been constructed to join them.

Mapping is as tendentious as any other way of selecting, ordering, and presenting information. What is mapped? What gets into the map? How is it related to the rest of the map? How is it presented? Lucy Fellows says that 'every map is someone's way of getting you to look at the world in his or her way.'[36] Well, obviously; and yet, in those maps I most use, road maps of states and provinces, I find myself at a loss to say who is trying to get me to see what in what way of their own, as opposed to providing me with information about routes that I want to have for my own purposes. And these are purposes I share with most users of the road system, which includes a large proportion of the population.[37] I would feel very clever if I could see how I was being manipulated, but I doubt if the extent to which I am a victim of manipulation is really that great.

Another thing to note about maps is that they are static. They are good for showing geographical features, though even there they may be thrown out of date by volcanoes and earthquakes. But the world of knowledge is, necessarily, in constant change as new informations and corrections call for reorganization. Maps (in a historical atlas, for instance) may include arrows to indicate vectors of change, but are essentially inert; they can indicate a field of force, but are not really good at showing situations whose elements are essentially in tension with one another.[38]

There may be many maps of the same terrain, on different projections, to different scales, giving different information, representing different points of view. If they are all true maps of the same terrain, it seems almost to follow from the definitions of 'true' and 'same' that all can be related to one another. In fact, their differences should not be problematic or puzzling, provided one understands the cartographers' materials and methods. But does it follow that all such maps can be mapped onto one another? Not without further information, one supposes. And even if no further information is required, so that for any two maps there is some process of transformation whereby one can be mapped onto the other, I can think of no reason why such a process should in all cases be easy to carry out. In short, the logic of mapping is not familiar to most of us; we have no reliable hunches as to what is and what is not practicable. And that suggests that the use of the mapping metaphor in speaking of 'maps of knowledge' is not really helpful.

Why, then, I ask myself, am I so fond of this metaphor? Is it just that I like maps of all sorts, as designs in themselves or as promising possible terrains? Perhaps it is, because I do like them – I have books of them, put them up on my walls, and so on, more than most people do. But my preference also relates to a deeper cognitive orientation. Whatever I am inquiring into, I like to get clear about its place in the overall scheme of things, whatever that scheme and those things may be. And my inquiry itself more often than not turns into such a 'scheme of things' itself, rather than answering a straightforward question within a framework that is taken for granted. I seem always to be seeking the completion of a *mappa mundi* rather than the elaboration of a *periplus* – that is, my objective is more often a domain within which possible routes and voyages may be traced at will than a network of itineraries that may be retraced without reference to any hinterland. Routes and locations may be laid out for us to see, without constraining us to follow or visit them. A world map, unlike an itinerary, does not indicate how it is to be used.[39]

What I have been calling 'maps of knowledge' are really not at all maplike. They are simply classifications of all the material that falls within a certain domain. And in practice one is more likely to start with a heap of stuff to be sorted than with an overall classificatory scheme within which pigeon-holes may be established a priori. When a heap becomes too big for us to scan its individual members, we may divide it into two or more smaller heaps, and these smaller heaps as they grow may themselves be subdivided. The ancestry and present condition of such a system of subdivision is best represented by a branching diagram – most famously in the system of bifurcation once familiar as 'Porphyry's Tree.'[40] Such branchings may follow one principle throughout (as Plato and Aristotle thought would be nice) or switch over to some different principle, often ending up in simple alphabetical listings. Their forkings may be, and often are, plotted as tree graphs, and can then incorporate maplike elements – branches can be of different widths and colours, and items within the branches may be quasi-cartographically related to one another.

The earliest example I know of what I had in mind as a 'map of knowledge,' the systematic classification of arts and professions in Plato's *Sophist*,[41] is in fact a set of trees. Plato's interest, as I have said, is that of a philosopher of education, for whom the city is primarily an educational system, and his map's conscious articulation is a sort of mixed critique of and project for Greek civilization. Later 'maps,' less single-minded, were compiled or envisaged in Hellenistic and medieval times, as libraries grew and had to organize and shelve the accumulated records of their intellectual heritage. They could not adhere to any educational agenda, but were constrained by a variable history. In the sixteenth and seventeenth centuries, a later generation of encyclopedists had to synthesize this antique corpus with the proliferating insights and data of modernity.[42] And as the modern mind acquired confidence the great encyclopedias of the eighteenth century were introduced by synoptic reviews of how the unified sum of knowledge was to be organized.[43] Now at last the organization of the totality of knowledge could take on something of the nature of a *mappa mundi*; it is hardly a coincidence that in the same period the blank spaces in the map of the globe were being filled in.

None of these mappings, or whatever they should have been called, are definitive, but all have made their mark.[44] Not having actual determinate classifications at their disposal, people have carried on as though they had some rudimentary filing system in mind, often based on fragmentary classifications that had become traditional. It is as if we all had the same map of our mental world, even if we could not draw it, in the same way that we understand one another's accounts of our travels because we share a sort of mental map of the world, however sketchy our geographical information may be.[45] But the analogy is deceptive. We behave rather as if we had been using our discoveries to fill in a map of knowable reality, in the same way that voyages of discovery filled in the gaps of what had long been known to be a finite and measurable globe. But 'knowable reality' is not known to be finite and measurable. It makes little sense to speak of our ignorance as consisting of 'gaps' to be 'filled in.'

The idea of the fine arts as occupying (contiguous or overlapping domains within) a common place on a comprehensive map of mental activities, an idea that encourages us to think of 'art' as a single sort of activity carried on by people called generically 'artists,' is radically at odds with the no less compelling idea that each of the arts forms a distinct practice, with its own media and techniques and traditions and practitioners, its own public, and its own institutions of training and marketing. Both of these ideas correspond to well-entrenched and thoroughly familiar realities.[46] In either case, it is possible to allocate a definite place or places to art or the arts among the uses of the mind if there is some map, either one actually drawn or one that we are confident we could draw if we had to, which lays out a determinate system of those uses. A cartography of the arts in general, of the systematic practices of productive thought, could be based either on institutional organization and recognition, or on practical interactions of method and collaboration, or on the common function assigned to a complex of practices, or on some mix of these. But by the middle of the eighteenth century it had already been pointed out that, in an industrial age and a society in flux, the very idea of an art as a determinate complex of production has limited application.[47] Instead of the sort of craft to which one might be apprenticed and of which the lifelong practitioners might form a guild, small constellations of mutually linked skills would become temporarily conjoined in specific industrial practices which would dissolve and re-form, merge and split, as needs and markets changed.

In general, once the identity of arts ceases to be a matter of unreflective tradition and becomes self-conscious, it is open to practical challenge, hence flexible. In such a climate of thought and practice, cooperative ventures and interdisciplinary studies flourish, and themselves breed new disciplines and institutes, many no doubt transient, some probably not. And if this state of affairs continues, institutions of teaching and the division of labour, together with the power relations that govern them, will cease to reflect a map of knowledge and look more like a wilderness survival kit.[48] Neither the arts, nor the disciplines that study the arts, will retain any functional identity.

I have heard university administrators of great experience and intelligence say that the fluid situation I have described is becoming the institutional norm, at least in the hard sciences. Scientists still retain professorial appointments in their home disciplines, but will in fact be seconded (on a temporary or part-time basis) to specialized units with their own budgets, students, websites, and labs, which will exist only so long as a specific research program is in place.[49] Researchers thus seconded will in fact be functioning as generic 'scientists,' just as in the sixties many artists who retained the name of 'dancer' or 'musician' or 'painter' were in fact operating as generic 'artists' within ad hoc collectives. Important as such developments may be, however, it is not clear that they represent the shape (or shapelessness) of the future. The new flexibilities that burgeon and proliferate do not have things all their own way. Arts and disciplines are curiously tough. The synapses governing the flow of information in our cultural world are hardened by long use.[50] Except under the pressure of some specific project or problem, cooperative and interdisciplinary ventures tend to be unstable and ephemeral. The connections never come to seem natural and require constant effort to maintain.

However that may be, it is quite generally true that the idea of a map of knowledge charting a determinate system of arts and disciplines requires two things. First, ideally, it requires a historical economy in which culture has become nature in a conceptually stable society. The civilization mapped must be in something like a 'Pareto-optimal' condition, that is, one in which no specifiable change would be a clear improvement for anybody, even if the conditions prevailing overall are not the best possible for anyone. And second, practically, knowledge to be teachable must form a system of organized curricula. This is what Plato and Aristotle both saw: beyond a certain point of intellectual development, a society's stock of knowledge cannot be sustained without organized systems of recording, transmission, and development. What makes 'maps of knowledge' possible also makes them necessary. Just as, we saw, Plato's maps sketched the teaching program for a well-ordered city conceived as basically an educational system, so the great encyclopedias that formed the world-map of knowable reality could be best conceptualized as *what there was to be taught* – the curriculum of an ideal university. Maps of knowledge are about the practices and programs of real and ideal institutions of learning – of higher learning, that is, because what every citizen should know does not figure on the map, any more than a geographical map shows that the whole mapped area is blanketed by the atmosphere. Just as the future of the practice of philosophy in general, what philosophers do and how they do it and how much of it they do, depends on the future of universities, so, too, any map of knowledge that shall assign to the philosophy of art a determinate subject matter depends on the future of real or ideal universities. After all, whatever the place of the fine arts is, its identification clearly depends on there being decipherable and reliable maps on which places can be located;[51] and the most likely place to find such a map would be a university calendar. And since scholars, whether students or teachers, move quite freely from one university to another,[52] it would not be surprising if their maps showed a certain working congruence, even when they were not identical.

So now we have to ask: what is the future of the university? But that raises the prior question: What is a university? For us here, in the midst of a university, many of us spending much of our lives in universities, the question is a baffling one, in just the same way that 'What is philosophy?' baffled us before. And it calls for the same answer, based as before on Democritus's answer to the question 'What is man?' The university is – what we all know. It is all around us and inside us, a many-sided environment, performing many functions for many groups of people. It is a source of income for a local economy, a centre of prestige for a municipality, a marriage market, an absorber of surplus labour power, a place for tomorrow's professional and business power to form. But all these purposes can also be served by social arrangements that do not involve universities. What we want to know is why universities came into being; or, if those purposes have changed over the years, the purposes for which universities would need to be reinvented if they did not already exist. (These may be many such purposes; our present interest is confined to those aspects of universities that have to do with maps of knowledge and with the possibility of sustained, extensive and intensive study in such fields as philosophy.)

How, then, did universities come to be? Histories are many and long and quite beyond our scope here. Besides, the facts would only confuse us. What we need is something more like a creation myth, to make us feel reassured when we are wondering what universities are all about. Fortunately, such a myth is widely circulated.

The original form of the university myth, as I see it, stems from Plato, was shaped by Aristotle, and has been gift-wrapped by later commentators.[53] It goes like this. Universities start from a general split between what people want to know and what they can pick up in everyday life or by asking around.[54] Geometry in Egypt, mathematical astronomy in Babylon, were developed by priests and surveyors as part of their profession. It was among the Greeks that it dawned on people that such studies could be carried on without regard to ritual or practical occasions. This novel idea came about at a time of political upheavals, in which traditionally unsophisticated social groups needed to acquire political and rhetorical skills. Their need gave rise to a professional class of general adult educators, called 'experts' or 'sophists': skills that had previously been incorporated within the unsystematized traditions of privileged classes were analysed and made amenable to systematic pedagogy.[55] Something like the university begins to take shape as soon as people formulate a general distinction between, on the one hand, experience acquired and remembered and handed down, and, on the other hand, *research*, the quest for principles and general explanations.[56] The fateful step is taken when this difference in principle is consciously generalized into a distinction between truth and tradition in *all* fields. This generalization yields the idea of universal science, of which the scope is unrestricted, the methods tested, and the results corrected and cumulative. Such science requires the formation of an archive, and of a body of people who can add to it, use it, and expound it. That calls for a fixed centre where the archive and its users are housed and can be visited. And such a centre is already at least the germ of a university. It is already in place when the young Aristotle lectures on rhetoric in Plato's Academy; as he grows older, Aristotle formulates some of the basic structures and starts the systematic building of archives of knowledge.[57] The idea catches on, and a couple of centuries later we find the system in full blast, when the young Roman Cicero, at the university of Athens, attends philosophy lectures that sound horribly familiar from our own undergraduate days, and later publishes popular books on philosophy based on his old lecture notes.[58]

Such a university involves a three-tier system – one already in place, in fact, in Plato's original Academy. A core of research scholars explores and expands the frontiers of knowledge; a band of initiates aspiring to be their successors serves as their acolytes and disciples, as graduate students do among us; and a wider circle of outsiders who are not committed to contributing to the enterprise, and may have no intention of ever doing so, attend lectures in which the experts explain as much as they can of the nature of the archive and how it is developed.

Up to a point, today's universities recognizably do the same sort of thing in the same sort of way as those ancient institutions. But the medieval European university, of which today's Western universities are the more immediate successors or survivors, took on a somewhat different character, arising from basic discontinuities in the transmission of the archive. In the religions of the Book, which then prevailed, priestly lore is bound up with hermeneutics, the understanding of authoritative texts in dead languages, so that priestcraft and theology become inseparable from scholarly research in philology, and perhaps in history and anthropology.[59] And among the descendants of the peoples who had invaded the Roman empire from the east, the practice of law and medicine, which are pre-eminently practical and hands-on undertakings in themselves, was carried on in the shadow of ancient researches, with their partly recoverable archives, salvaged from the vastly more sophisticated though often ill-informed achievements of the civilization that the invaders' ancestors had partly obliterated.[60] So the medieval university acquires a different structure: partly autonomous, and partly alienated from the society around it; partly concerned with present reality, and partly oriented toward the past – a past of which the relevance was partly a daunting discovery and partly a matter of faith.[61]

The eventual outcome of the complex origins of medieval and post-medieval universities is an overall structure on four levels.[62] There is a primary education, without which a person cannot function other than menially in a literate society; there is a secondary level, the studies without which people cannot understand the supposed origin and functioning of such a society;[63] there is a tertiary level at which one is indoctrinated into the specific methods and special archives of the learned professions; and there is a fourth level on which the depth and breadth of the world's understanding and knowledge are increased.[64]

An important aspect of the medieval and post-medieval university is its tendency to lateral integration, the fact that studies of all sorts come to be carried out in the same place and under the same institutional auspices.[65] Partly this is because, historically, all studies used to require the same preparation in the learned languages and access to overlapping classical archives; partly it is because of the crossover of relevant skills;

partly it is because scholars share a way of life that sets them off from their philistine neighbours and imposes common requirements for accommodation, administration, and policing; and partly it is to enable neophytes to discover their intellectual and professional vocations without leaving town – for the integration was taking place at a time when transport and communications were difficult, dangerous, uncertain, and slow.[66]

According to the myth I have been expounding, the post-medieval university is a rather ad hoc congeries of studies based on the heritage of classical antiquity. But the European university has another transformation to undergo. The distinction between experience and research is, as I said, universal in scope; and this universality becomes an object of conscious aspiration around the end of the eighteenth century. Science as science, history as history, systematically purged of superstition and ancient pieties, are the invention of that period, in which the disciplines as disciplines come into their own and become professionalized. In part, this revolution must have been prompted by the discovery of the New World, with its flora and fauna quite unconnected with the hallowed lore of antiquity.[67] In any case, the ideal now clearly formulated is that every aspect of reality shall become the object of appropriate systematic scrutiny. All systems of belief and enquiry shall be subsumed in what will now be called science, and on which the rest of the world, partly in mockery and partly in envy, sometimes bestows the German name *Wissenschaft*. The model of a complete research university, the bureaucratized temple of *Wissenschaft*, was indeed German: the University of Berlin, founded by Wilhelm von Humboldt and his colleagues in 1809. Belatedly transplanted to North America with the foundation of Johns Hopkins University in the 1870s, this model still underlies the most ambitious universities in North America today.[68] In a university thus conceived, with its implicit claim to universal scope, the study of philosophy in its widest sense must clearly have a place. And, since philosophy is in principle the most critical and fundamental of all studies, that place should in principle be a central one, whether it actually fills that place or not. And in philosophy as thus understood aesthetics is sure of a small but sufficient and significant place.

Tomorrow, we must look at what the future seems to hold for the research university. But, before I leave you, I must confess that the story I have told you is not the whole story. Myths, after all, never are.

When John Graves Simcoe became the first lieutenant-governor of Upper Canada in the 1790s, he conceived it to be his duty to preserve the colony from republicanism and democracy. 'Liberal education,' he wrote, 'seems to me ... to be indispensably necessary; and the completion of it in the establishment of a university ... in my apprehension would be most useful to inculcate just principles, habits and manners, into the rising generation; to coalesce the different customs of the various descriptions of settlers, emigrants from the old Provinces of Europe into one form.'[69] Simcoe was writing, of course, before the research university got under way. But nothing in the myth of origins that I recounted prepares us for Simcoe's idea of what a university could be or should do. What, indeed, was that idea, and where did it come from? His words may remind one, in part, of Squire Brown's ruminations on what he hoped Dr Arnold's Rugby School would do for his eleven-year-old son, in Thomas Hughes's *Tom Brown's Schooldays*.[70] In part, they are reminiscent of Second World War pamphlets on 'The British Way and Purpose.' But what has all this to do with the idea of a university? Some light is shed by the dismal condition of Oxford University before the mid-nineteenth-century reforms, where Simcoe had spent a couple of years, and which seems to have functioned as little more than a social club for the Anglican gentry.[71] And Simcoe's educational ideal seems akin to that of Bishop Berkeley's 1725 proposal to set up a college in Bermuda to convert the savage Americans to Christianity.[72] I really do not know. But I suppose it is natural that, once universities exist and admit undergraduate students, the wealthy and powerful will want to send their children there. Obviously, such parents will have no interest in the world of learning, but will simply want their children to learn how to go on being wealthy and powerful. And so, since the wealthy and powerful are, by definition, the people who get what they want, that is a large part of what the universities are going to be.[73] But what has *that* got to do with the future of aesthetics? That is another thing we will have to think about tomorrow evening.

III The University and the Future of Civilization

Yesterday I talked about the rise of the research university, as perhaps embodying the final and most comprehensive 'map of knowledge' on which philosophy and aesthetics, as well as the cognitive enterprises represented by the fine arts, might be most authoritatively located. The potential significance of such an institution is hard to exaggerate. From the point of view I attributed to the Platonic Socrates, it would represent the highest achievement of reinvented humanity. In Aristotelian cosmology, ascertained scientific knowledge is simply the self-knowledge of the universe, and the university is the only location that systematically aspires to such knowledge. Such high-flown language is out of style, and such pretensions would sound ridiculous if one were to make them. But one hardly sees what serious alternatives there are. Though our science is in a sense conjectural, confirmed only piecemeal and with qualifications, it cannot plausibly be denied that the massively embodied systems and results of modern science are approximations to truth.[1] And surely it is mere stupidity that prevents us from being astonished and bewildered, as Plato and Aristotle were already bewildered, that science should be possible within the universe.[2]

If we prefer to avert our minds from the astonishing spectacle of a universe in which science exists, we may limit our reflection to the undoubted fact that science does exist, and that the research university both depends on that existence and promotes it. And we were considering some ways in which the future of aesthetics was bound up with its future. But what is that future? The university may be regarded as the central institution of our civilization, with its Hellenic and Roman origins modified by the Religions of the Book.[3] If so, the future of such universities may depend on the future of that civilization – though it may not, because what is central in one civilization may survive to be the glory or the embarrassment of its successors. I will get on to that presently. But first I must say something about the prospects of the research university as such.

The research university is in fact self-destructive. Its originating idea depends on the notion of a single world order that is fixed and finite, and hence graspable. That is the way Aristotle saw the world; and Hegel's system of philosophy around 1820 updates it and adapts it to the new age of Enlightenment and science, by providing a scenario for all possible future developments within a comprehensive world-order that is in principle complete and hence limited. But the idea of *Wissenschaft* that actually governs the research university knows no limits. Its freedom of learning and teaching *(Lernfreiheit* and *Lehrfreiheit)* has no ideal unity beyond such coherence as the ambitions of scholars and their publics may chance to have.

In a self-contained society, such as the polite society of the Enlightenment in post-Christian Europe seemed to be, a single intellectual order could be sustained by, and taken to be what in its turn maintained, the social order.[4] In a multicultural society, however, such as ours seems to be, the politeness of polite society is no more than one set of mannerisms among others. Other social forms are considered as alternatives, and the sum of things as they are is envisaged as evolving toward a future that we cannot as yet even conceive. In such a society, no intellectual order can sustain or be sustained. The map of knowledge is useless, because signs on every highway read UNDER CONSTRUCTION.

Research, then, becomes an uncontrolled growth. The proliferation of studies becomes unmanageable, and its unmanageability generates a comparable burgeoning of university administrations. Just look at the lists of participants in Canada's annual 'Learned Societies' conferences: year by year, more and more of them are nothing but conclaves of managers. And let me read to you just an inch or two of one column from one page of the degrees awarded in one winter evening at the university I come from:

Master of Laws; Master of Studies in Law; Master of Museum Studies; Master of Library Science; Master of Information Science; Master of Information Studies; Doctor of Music; Master of Music; Master of Science in Forestry; Master of Architecture; Master of Science in Planning; Master of Industrial Relations; Master of Health Science; Master of Nursing; Master of Science in Biomedical Communications; Master of Arts in Teaching; Master of Science in Teaching; Master of Applied Science ...[5]

Well, as Humpty Dumpty said to Alice, 'The question is who is to be Master, that's all.' No wonder all our universities constantly complain of underfunding; since every solution generates a host of new problems, and every discipline spawns a cluster of new disciplines, no funding can be anything *but* underfunding.[6]

From this overflowing smorgasbord, each university piles onto its plate a large and partly random selection. It would be nice to offer courses in everything: after all, you never know when a student of science in forestry may need a course in nursing, or whether museum studies may not find it advantageous to teach a joint program with information science.[7] But life, money, and human resources are all too short.

The ideal of *Wissenschaft*, in any case, is that all possible research should be carried on; but it does not require that it should all be carried on in the same institution, or even in the same country. Science is science and scholarship is scholarship, and the civilized world is one world. Not all universities *can* research everything, and probably not all can research or even teach in all established disciplines. Even if they can, they need not. In fact, the ideal of *Wissenschaft* as such does not even require that any given country have universities at all, any more than it requires that every village should have a community college.[8] In short, the idea of the complete research university has both centripetal and centrifugal tendencies: centripetal, because all knowledge is interconnected; centrifugal, because the ideal of inclusiveness exceeds what any one institution can manage.

The situation I have just described poses practical problems that resist tidy solutions. But not all such problems are equally serious. It is often said, for instance, that today's scholars know more and more about less and less. One sees what is meant; but all that complaint really comes to is that, as the body of knowledge accumulates at an exponential rate, any one individual's knowledge must necessarily be an ever smaller *proportion* of the totality of what is known. Certainly the sum of knowledge is beyond any individual's capacity and has to be distributed among a host of knowers. But it is not distributed in the damagingly simple way that critics seem to be suggesting. Most individual scholars develop their own unique selections of data and competences, overlapping other people's selections in unpredictable and often surprising ways.[9] So the dispersal of learning does not bother me: knowledge is not so much fragmented as laminated.

A problem that seems to me more serious arises when we ask ourselves what someone like Cicero would do today. Marcus Tullius Cicero could go to Athens, somewhere around 100 B.C.E., and pick up a fair proportion of what was then knowable by way of general education, what his civilization called *paideia* as opposed to the sort of technical training that smiths and doctors acquired in forges and surgeries. But the sort of research university I have been describing is in principle inhospitable to such aspirations.[10] They are more easily accommodated by institutions where options are artificially restricted to something like Ciceronian proportions.

In nineteenth-century America, especially, the research university was accompanied by a separate and different institution, the liberal arts college, where young people could be indoctrinated in genteel accomplishments. But these institutions hardly attempted the task of tempering the rigorous winds of science to the shorn lambs of a freshman year. The accomplishments inculcated in such colleges had little to do with the real intellectual work of the sciences, except that they had to provide for studies preparatory to engaging in the learned professions (law, medicine, the church). And this initiatory mission had as much to do with acquiring smooth manners and useful contacts as with anything bookish. It was certainly not conceived as affording any sort of entry into a world of serious science or scholarship.[11]

I touched on this theme in yesterday's talk, which I ended by remarking that John Graves Simcoe deemed it important that Upper Canada should have a university to convert the local peasantry into Anglican royalists, but I could not see why he thought a university would bring that about. Similarly, when John Strachan eventually got a charter for a provincial university there, it is something of a mystery what he thought a university was for, except for one thing. By limiting access to the professions to university graduates, and then stipulating that only subscribing Anglicans could be university teachers, it would render positions of power and influence less accessible to dissenters and Catholics.[12] No intellectual skills or knowledge seems to be of specific importance. Nor was this attitude confined to the Anglican establishment. My college at Toronto, a Methodist foundation, has an old song from those years which begins, 'My father sent me to Victoria, determined I should be a man'; but as to what the singer's father thought he was up to, and what he meant by being a man, the song offers no clue.[13] The emphasis clearly was on character development rather than mental stimulation.[14] In fact, a historian of the period remarks that the principal aim in mid-century Upper Canada was to instil earnestness under the aegis of evangelical Christianity, even the natural sciences being taught less to interest students in the laws of nature than to show how those laws fulfilled the will of the Creator.[15]

The underlying feeling of these Victorian architects of Ontario colleges is perhaps that persuasively formulated by Cardinal J.H. Newman in his 1852 proposals for a new Catholic university in Ireland. Something must be taught, he argued, or it will not be a university; it must be knowledge, for why teach error? But it must not be research, for students are learners, not researchers. So it can only be the content of the traditional learning – and the only tradition commanding the necessary authority was that of authoritative religion.[16] His basic idea, as Pelikan interprets him, was that a university is 'an institution that was dedicated ex professo to learning and to ideas, and therefore to first principles.'[17] Yes, but Newman, whose precise and powerful mind chose to operate within limited areas, did not consider what Aristotle asked us to ask: 'Are we on the way from, or the way to, first principles?' What is primary in human experience (*quoad nos*) is not the same as what is primary in its own right (*per se*): first principles in the sense of logical premises for a deduction are not the same as first principles in the sense of the principles that should govern our search for such premises. A Thomist devotee of orthodoxy might well be committed to the rational faith that we are already in possession of the first premises of our most basic sciences. But not everyone shares such faith, and Pelikan's sympathetic rethinking of Newman would base the university on principles of inquiry, not principles of dogma. 'To set forth the right standard, and to train according to it, and to help forward all students towards it according to their various capacities, this I conceive to be the business of a University,' says Newman;[18] and Pelikan concurs, but would make the 'right standard' one of intellectual virtue, notably the virtues of free imagination and intellectual honesty.[19] And from this it follows that 'the whole world and all of humanity are the only appropriate ultimate context of scholarship'; so the teaching university must after all be, as Newman denied, a research university or ancillary to one.[20]

Charles J. Sykes in his diatribe against today's research-ridden universities invokes the name of Newman to support his idea that young people go to college to absorb the traditions of their culture.[21] But what are those traditions? Not those of the Catholic Church, since the United States is not (as Newman's Ireland was) a predominantly Catholic country. What, then? Sykes, like many others, notes that Newman intended his new university to be a model for the world. Like everyone else, he notes that the university that was actually founded in Dublin never served as a model for anyone. It has been common to blame the blindness, malice, and poverty of the Irish hierarchy for betraying Newman's vision. But the vision itself was myopic from the start, in the ways that Pelikan has sought to remedy.

Newman's failure to work out a practicable model for college education in his time has left us without any clear alternative to the unmanageable juggernaut of the research university. At one time, as I said before, the more venerable and authoritative part of the traditional archive was composed in dead languages, which had to be learned. But all that has withered away; and evangelical earnestness is uncongenial to the prevailing powers of a consumer society. What has replaced those unquestioned and largely inarticulate pieties that a Simcoe and a Strachan could take for granted? Nobody quite knows. At the publishers' booths at the Learned Societies Conference last year, contributions to old-fashioned humanist scholarship were relegated to the background; the books displayed were tracts on feminism, multiculturalism, environmentalism, and other reformist isms, all emphasizing scepticism or downright hostility toward traditional learning, rather than contributing to that learning itself. In the setting of such a conference, this emphasis represented a quite startling repudiation of the disciplines, an apparent turning away from the universities and colleges themselves to which the publishers' clientele all belonged.[22]

So what, finally, is today's Cicero to do? Post-secondary education offers him and his sister many options.[23] The research university is accompanied by democratized survivors of the old liberal arts colleges; but also by community colleges, in which the provision of more practical, popular, and non-traditional forms of skill and knowledge is concentrated; by seminaries where religious sects at least pay lip-service to the traditional call for an educated clergy;[24] by polytechnic institutes, where the advanced technologies and their supporting sciences are developed and imparted; and by agricultural colleges where immigrants with no farm background learn how to raise unfamiliar crops from unfriendly soils in unpredictable climates.[25] But all of these tend to turn into each other. Polytechnics aspire to the dignity of universities. Universities want a piece of the agricultural action. Agricultural schools, in revenge, sprout liberal-arts appendages.[26] And so on, as the specific requirements of the local geography, history, and economics may dictate. Government, industry, and commerce, meanwhile, where the power and the money come from, exert an unthinking but remorseless pressure to reduce all educational establishments to the status of training schools for their own workforces.[27]

The result is a sort of mitigated chaos. Within this chaos, little bits of philosophy, tattered shreds of aesthetics, get taught here and there; and what is taught tends to be governed by what the available teacher learned at school rather than by any coherent notion of what philosophy and aesthetics could and should be, or how they are best developed and presented for the situation at hand. Besides, conditions of employment being what they are today, a great mind who should be changing the face of philosophy from a professorial chair in a metropolitan school may be doing his or her best to change it as a teacher of remedial English in the back of beyond, while the chair in question is occupied by an entrenched mediocrity in whom the effects of senility have been hardly noticeable.

This chaos, in which aesthetics somehow contrives to lurk and flounder, is, however, mitigated. The real needs and desires that have shaped post-secondary education are definite enough that we could construct a myth of college education in America to set alongside our myth of the total map of knowledge.[28] The myth might go something like this. At first, when the American settlements were culturally colonial extensions of the Old World, classical colleges were set up to instil upper-class gentility and traditional lore.[29] (The 'sabbatical year' was instituted to enable teachers to cross the Atlantic and recharge their batteries with the intellectual energy that only Europe could generate.) But the immense westward expansion that followed Independence and persisted throughout the nineteenth century created a new situation and called for new measures. In the occupied territories there would be no gentry and no recourse to old sources of knowledge. The settlers would have to carry their own intellectual resources with them. Especially after the Land Grant Act of 1862, tracts of land were set aside in the new settlements to finance all-purpose educational institutions with the main stipulation that their offerings would include agriculture and engineering. It is these foundations that have persisted and developed as what we still recognize as state universities, and which remain the norm well into the present century. They are a compromise between giving the Ciceros what they need and giving an undeveloped territory what it needs. Their isolation, their scale, their relative wealth, encourage them to develop as multipurpose institutions with varying emphases. It is the needs of a mixed population in a strange and challenging land, with a traditional archive that is part treasure, part encumbrance, part challenge, and part opportunity, that form a new and subtle locale for collegiate study.[30]

Like the land-grant colleges, today's state universities, which are their successors, represent an autonomous learning that is perpetually faced with the temptation of isolationism. According to my myth, America was woken from this dream by the shock of Sputnik. It was this shock, with the realization that there was a world of learning in which America risked falling behind,[31] that led to the dominance of the long-established but hitherto little-regarded ideal of the research university. The new aim of the university was not to prepare people for life in America generally, but to train recruits for science, the professions, and business. But the world has changed again, and what we are now seeing (or being shown by our myth) is the rise of the corporate university, in a world in which international rivalries have been swallowed up by an international corporate marketplace. What this will turn into remains to be seen; all we can be sure of is that the age of the land grant is over, and that governments will be less and less inclined to do anything about higher education except grumble at it.

What my second myth tells us about is not so much the way things are as a partly intelligible core in the mitigated chaos I described before. It is this chaos that is 'what we all know' as the university. And within it, fragmented, diluted, compromised, oppressed, distorted, but perpetually regenerated, the dynamic that regenerated the comprehensive research university persists undiminished, still recognizable and still invoked among all the multiplicity of our preoccupations and frustrations, and gives them an underlying intelligibility that they would otherwise lack.

Chaos, however, mitigated or unmitigated, is encountered only by theorists and historians – and, by exclusion, mythmakers. Real organisms exist in relation to specific environments which they draw into the principles of their own organization. Cicero and his sister are historical individuals in a specific situation variously manipulated by an assortment of real powers, all of which are in their different ways solicitous to accommodate them. What we took for chaos was really the diversity of powers, clients, and possible destinies that called for specific treatment – a structured multiplicity of mutual adjustments among organizers and the organized. And in fact, even in today's big universities the new Cicero and his sister can get on quite well, if they keep their heads. What they need is the sort of street wisdom necessary to find one's place in the structure or the interstices of any big institution – big-city skills, as opposed to small-town skills. Such skills are widely distributed among the young, and not impossible to acquire. More people, after all, make their lives in big cities than in small towns. Cities and villages offer different threats and opportunities to the bashful, as they do to the confident: the familiar rhetoric that emphasizes the 'alienation' of the novice on the big campus addresses a condition that is common but not universal. Level-headed young people are likely to find that the uproar of conservatism versus revisionism within disciplines, surrounded by enclaves and annexes of undisciplined lore, and associated with professional schools of comparable complexity, makes many choices available, ranging (within limits) from almost random sampling to single-minded concentration on specialized inquiry. It is important that these diverse patterns of study are pursued side by side by students who can observe and discuss one another's strategies, both in their substance and in their dynamics. Perhaps even more important, they are in a position to learn the variety of the life-choices these strategies embody, their ways of fitting curricular and extra-curricular pursuits together and of relating the whole package to life before, during, and after college.[32] As Gilbert Ryle once said to me, 'We expect the undergraduates to educate each other';[33] and this interchange of strategies may have been what he had in mind. This is what my father should have sent me to Victoria for, determined I should be a man:[34] to be humanized, not by absorbing earnest piety, whatever the Victorian founders thought, but by acquiring a deep and intricate insight into how people find their ways through a world in which study and research are variously possible but are never the whole of life.[35]

A great deal is going on, then. But meanwhile, knowledge is what is known, people can teach only what they know, and what they know is what they once learned. So universities, though the main sources of intellectual innovation, are inevitably conservative in their overall tendencies. The research university, accordingly, with its intimidatingly massive archive, though in a way it remains the paradigm and ideal, evokes a vigorous opposition in our age of the 'information explosion.'[36] Acceleration in the growth of knowledge and the means of its communication has become terrifyingly swift and abrupt. So much new stuff keeps coming in that the old archive functions as mere dead weight.[37] We continually hear it denounced as not 'relevant.' Old-fashioned scholars take offence at this, but it has a serious meaning: that the maintenance of the old is obstructing access to the contemporary, which is what we urgently need to know. So universities are under attack by governments all over the Western world: their uncontrolled accumulation of unusable junk is a real threat to the intelligent conduct of human affairs.[38]

Perhaps we can generalize that a little. Why are universities in the modern world always hated? For two reasons. First, they have to teach what is known, and hence is becoming obsolete and hence irrelevant; and, second, they have to teach what is really new, hence what is not understood in relation to existing problems and for *this* reason irrelevant. What is 'relevant,' in the eyes of the media, is only what immediately responds to what is already obvious and conspicuous. What is always tiresomely and unchangingly present, and what is alarmingly but as yet invisibly imminent, is what chiefly concerns those who must grapple with reality and what the media despise. Perhaps the basic objection to universities, though, is their inevitable inertia overall. Before novelty can be accommodated, curricula have to be worked out, and personnel engaged and trained. That takes a lot of time. Almost as important an objection is the enormous waste involved in all intellectual and creative work. Waste is inevitable because important success involves real risks. Economy is an ideal of engineering, 'applied science' in which only what is ascertained is put to use. But somebody has to do the ascertaining. You'd think the media people and back-bench politicians would be smart enough to figure that out. And so they would be, if they thought about it. But they don't want to; their lives are based on their clientele being at least as ignorant as themselves, so they carefully avoid anything that would injure their ignorance. Consequently, the waste inseparable from real achievement is assumed to be a product of muddling incompetence.

Where does this leave us? We have seen how the development of the ideas of knowledge and research culminates in the ideal of a complete research university in which the self-knowledge of the world is preserved and furthered without restriction. We have seen how the fragmentation of this idea from its own excess and from external constraints leads to a miscellany of vestigial and particularized manifestations. And we have remarked the growth of a secondary ideal, that of the New World university synthesizing and distributing the intellectual equipment people need and can use in a novel and unfriendly environment. The resulting totality offers many points of access, many routes, many selections – and many understandings of the choices that consequently confront the student. This multiplicity is generating a new phenomenon, the consumer university, which from another viewpoint is the university as commercial enterprise in a world where only consumer values are effective. Those who recognize this phenomenon usually speak of it as a perversion of the original university ideals. I am not sure that it is; but it is certainly a very powerful solvent. However, in spite of everything, the archive remains, and maintains its irresistible growth. The ideal of perfecting and supplementing the archive is one that will not go away: not to complete the totality of knowledge, which is neither possible nor desirable, but to fill in gaps and remedy errors as they are revealed.

That is all I have to say about the future of the university in general, and in North America especially. But what about the future of the university in Canada? Though I have already adverted to the topic incidentally and anecdotally, a more pointed treatment would be in order. But is there anything special to say about it? Presumably not, if the university is the central institution of the civilization in which Canada is a component. But in what sense is it a component? I sometimes feel that there is something odd about civilization in Canada. If we look at Canada's history we see that it was settled by trappers and traders in the service of transatlantic managements, by refugees from lands where they left their hearts behind, by trainloads of peasants evicted by landlords or fleeing from despotic armies – never by autonomous colonists aspiring to found free nations of their own in a new world.[39] To such people, the trappings of civilization must be an incomprehensible embarrassment.[40] Universities, like opera and ballet companies, are things we suppose we have to have, but we really don't know why.[41] A.B. McKillop differentiates Canadian from United States university policies by saying that

> [a]ll university founders, regardless of their religious affiliation, saw the fundamental purpose of their institution to be the continued preservation of a social order that because of its British and Loyalist origins was more conservative than that of the American colonies ... Yet overlaying this ethic of concern for tradition ... was an acceptance within British North American society and its fledgling universities of the liberal tenets of a capitalist market economy that took substantial shape in Canada precisely in the years when the universities of Ontario were founded ... [I]n this way colleges and universities founded to train clergy, educate a professional and citizen elite, and ensure stability also took up the ethic of material growth central to commercial and industrial capitalism.[42]

Well, I suppose so. But, as I said at the end of yesterday's lecture about Simcoe's ruminations on the theme, it is hard to see how this generates a vital course of studies. One cannot help noticing that McKillop does not find it necessary to say a single word about knowledge, civilization, science, or anything like that. It may be the lack of any basis for a real educational agenda that accounts for the vacuum in Ontario educational policy and what a recent critic has described as the stupefying and extravagant homogeneity of its university scene.[43]

Internally, since the universities have to be staffed by adepts in the intellectual achievements and standards of the international civilization, the universities are bound to envisage themselves as transplanted bastions of that civilization; but perhaps it is only stubborn insistence from within the universities, where professors indoctrinated elsewhere search their memories for what universities in the rest of the world are all about, that keeps up the pressure to maintain in our cold and pragmatic clime these exotic representatives of anachronistic pretensions. Of course, in Canada, connections to international civilization and the world are the official prerogative of the federal government anyway, while the provinces attend to the parish pump; so the assignment of universities to the provincial sphere of interest seems almost to guarantee that universities will receive no encouragement to be anything other than prolongations of the secondary education with which provincial governments feel more at home.[44] Learning, research, scholarship are not within the purview of a provincial government; all a province needs by way of teachers is good communicators who can keep one chapter ahead in an imported textbook. Well, as I observed before, nothing in the idea of the research university requires that it shall be exemplified in every political unit. It could be that one of the reasons Canada is regularly proclaimed to be one of the world's happiest countries is that it has never been really taken in by the delusions and discontents of civilization.[45]

But all this is mere caricature. Tom Symons, in his epoch-making report on Canadian Studies, proposed a sophisticated and elegant solution to the problem of how a provincial university can fit into the international world of science and scholarship, and his proposals were incorporated in the original organization of Trent University (of which he was, as I hardly need to remind this audience, the founding president).[46] In general, Canadian universities and artistic institutions flourish, and could not do so if they were not, in reality, actively supported by society at large; while it is really obvious that in every country in the world there is at best an indirect and uneasy relation between the institutions of official culture and the everyday lives of real people.

In any event, we must distinguish three things. First, there is a case to be made against universities in general, as a type of institution no longer appropriate to the worldwide conditions of information exchange that are developing today. Second, there is the case that a specific polity and economy might develop against universities as inappropriate, either to the specific local ethos or to an impoverished society in which scarce resources should be deployed in other ways. And neither of these is the same as the case to be made against the values and practices of the whole civilization on which the flourishing of the international university system depends. This third possibility is something we have yet to examine.

So much, then, for the future of the university. To recapitulate: we have seen how the ideal, central to our civilization, of a comprehensive map of knowledge breaks down in a chaos of proliferating quests that can be neither curbed nor controlled; how the ideal system to which the research university owes allegiance is accordingly matched by a succession of alternative structures and a host of makeshift expedients in which whatever can be taught is adjusted to the local requirements of whoever can learn; and how it is still the ideal of the research university alone that gives coherence to the whole. But the research university as reflecting the ideal of total knowledge is, I was saying, arguably the central institution of 'our' civilization, with its cumulative archive, its historical traditions, and its ideology of enlightenment; while the actual condition of our universities presumably reflects the nature and condition of the civilization we can more honestly claim as 'ours' – that of the United States and Canada today. The scattered and fragmented knowledge of the research university must represent a scattered and fragmented civilization – not 'multicultural' so much as chaotic in a mitigated way. Our humanities colleges are those of a civilization whose traditions are in tatters; community colleges are proper to a civilization of pragmatic pieties. Universities in the 'land grant' mould belong to a civilization always in transit, confined to its travelling kit. What the consumer university and the corporate university tell of our civilization does not need telling. And the usurpation of the universities' traditional tasks and prerogatives speaks of a civilization where process has succeeded substance, where the archive has dissolved into a handling of information in flux.

Let us return to our starting point. Aesthetics and philosophy, just as we know them, are obviously inseparable from universities as we know *them*. In a slightly more general sense, they are unthinkable apart from our civilization in which universities are a central institution. Traditionally, we have thought of that civilization as based on esteem for book-learning, critical thinking, and science. But the fragmentation of the university, I was just saying, corresponds to a fragmentation of our civilization. And as soon as I say that it occurs to me that I have no right to say it, because I have not explained what I think civilization is. What do I mean by this word?

I cannot now use the same ploy as I did with philosophy and the university, saying that 'civilization is – what we all know,' because what we can be sure of relevantly knowing is only the totality of our way of life in a presumably civilized society. We have, at the moment, no way of telling what part of that totality is civilization, what part is distinctive of *our* civilization but not of civilization in general, what part belongs to our local culture or lifestyle but not to our civilization as such, what part is generically human, what part is simply mammalian or vertebrate, and what part is mere moonshine. As Kant said, an age of enlightenment need not be, as a whole, an enlightened age.[47]

So, what is civilization, *exactly*? When I ask myself that, I find that I honestly don't know. The word suggests to me, first and foremost, a way of life that is self-conscious, deliberately maintained, relying on literacy. But whose is that way of life supposed to be? That of an elite, or of the educated classes? Or of an influential minority? But even elites and pundits may have passages in their ways of life that do not reward close inspection. In some ways, civilization is not so much a quality of day-to-day living as a characteristic of one's 'best behaviour.' One might go further: civilization is less a manner of behaving than a feature of public life and a dominant set of formal relationships, to which appeal may be made. But then it may be retorted that in a *truly* civilized community everyone really would behave, think, and feel like that.

The locus of civilization is, in any case, not the conduct of individuals in isolation. Etymologically as well as functionally, the word is connected with cities, which are complex artificial communities with elaborate and permanent dwelling places, communities based on status and function rather than on familiarity and ethnicity, relying on a network of intertranslatable languages. Since Aristotle, it has been a commonplace that civilized life is impossible otherwise than with reference to cities.

All these factors are part of the idea of civilization. What may be just as important is that civilization is conceptually linked, not only to cities, but to civilizations. Civilizations are united by the common recognition of an extensive history; a civilization is the largest internally recognized, regularly interactive, multigenerational human grouping, ill-defined and without institutional identity, but distinctive. Our own post-Christian civilization has ragged edges, but it is clearly distinguished from other civilizations: the Indian, the Sino-Japanese, the Mayan, the Islamic.[48] Recognition (and, hence, recognizability) is the key: a civilization is, in the first instance, an object of reflection, not of experience, but what it presents to thought is throughout a complex of very real experiences which then itself becomes an object of experience. Foreigners travelling for the first time in Egypt are besieged by a mass of flavours and strangenesses, which are united by the awareness that one is in Egypt.

Gradually their knowledge about Egypt, both theoretically and practical, coalesces with the continuing mass of impressions to form an experience *of Egypt*. And if we use the term 'civilization' of what it is that we are then experiencing, it is by way of recognizing that, at some level, what is being done is the outcome of a sustained system of choices guided by reflection on how things ought to be done.

Particular civilizations, however, do not necessarily exemplify civilization in general. One way of looking at the matter is exemplified by a speech given by Mustafa Kemal Atatürk in 1925, on the occasion of his first wearing a panama hat:

> The Turkish people ... are civilized; they are civilized in history and reality. But ... they must prove in fact that they are civilized and advanced persons in their outward aspect also ... A civilized international dress is worthy and appropriate for our nation and we will wear it. Boots and shoes on our feet, trousers on our legs, shirt and tie, jacket and waistcoat – and of course, to complete these, a cover with a brim on our heads. I want to make this clear. This head covering is called a HAT.[49]

We have to understand the symbolism here. Atatürk's scandalous sartorial gesture is the repudiation of the official dress, the fez and frock coat, introduced a century earlier by the Sultan Mahmud II, a debased compromise between the historic reality of traditional Ottoman civilization and the pragmatic reality of the upstart civilization of Europe. The choice of the non-traditional European dress is to symbolize a choice between civilizations. What the panama hat symbolizes, though, is not just one civilization, but civilization itself, *international* civilization. What Atatürk is saying is that this is now the only game in town. And such exclusiveness also is part of the idea.

The idea of civilization, evidently, harbours tensions and contradictions that make it hard to pin down. Atatürk's use of the word appeals to a consensus:[50] it implies the existence of a cluster of preferred features, including the sartorial as well as the functional and moral, which together would constitute a paradigm of civilization. But we cannot say precisely what these are: which features are taken to be diagnostic, and which are paramount, will depend on the context of discourse. In a moment I shall be citing an article that names a specific, value-laden nexus of alleged properties; but that nexus itself may derive its coherence less from the ineluctable dynamics of human development than from the presuppositions of the article's expected readership. The concept of civilization no doubt owes this spurious conceptual unity to the fact that we inherit it from days when its users knew less of world history than we do; and, since what *they* did not know is also what *we* do not always bear in mind, talk about 'our civilization' or 'Western civilization,' and hence about civilization in general, has an obvious and obtrusive meaning, which in our everyday usage escapes a scrutiny that it might not survive. James Boswell, in 1772, when the word was newly coined, wanted Samuel Johnson to include it in his dictionary.[51] Johnson demurred, because he thought the correct term was 'civility,' but he knew exactly what Boswell meant: he meant the opposite of 'barbarity.' And barbarity is the opposite of civility. So that's all right, then.[52]

The contrast between civilization and barbarism, which seemed so plain and simple in the eighteenth century, was plainer still in France, which knew itself to be the heartland of civilization – a claim definitively staked out in the *Encyclopédie.* The history of term and concept in their French manifestations has been laid out in a magisterial article by Jean Starobinski.[53] It was a unifying concept, he says, which 'drew together ... such notions as improvements in comfort, advances in education, politer manners, cultivation of the arts and sciences, growth of commerce and industry, and acquisition of material goods and luxuries.' In other words, it was a combination, not felt to be adventitious, of economic progress, scientific advance, and refinement of manners; but in many authors it is the last of these that predominates.[54] Obviously the idea of general progress is central here, and the word is often used with a suggestion (or affirmation) of specific stages to be passed through. Starobinski says that this is first spelled out in British sources: it was Adam Ferguson around 1760 who defined the succession of four stages: savage, nomadic/pastoral, sedentary agricultural, and industrial/commercial – a succession, we may note, in which the improvement of morals and manners is either ignored or taken for granted. A crucial point here is that the same word is used for the process of history and for the end point of that history as contrasted with a hypothetical primordial state – primitive barbarity as opposed to the present civility of Johnson and Boswell. It only remains to add (as Mirabeau did) that the stages identified are not bound to a single historical development but are successive phases in what could be a cyclical process. But, since we do not really doubt the uniqueness of eighteenth-century enlightenment, to speak of 'civilizations' in the plural tends to imply a veneer of civility over a persistent underlying barbarity.[55]

Unfortunately, we are neither in France nor in the eighteenth century, and a more directly useful insight into the archaeology of our idea of civilization, giving us insight into what the word meant when people thought they understood it, comes from the eleventh edition of the *Encyclopaedia Britannica*, the last edition to come out before the First World War.[56] A long article on civilization, by Henry Smith Williams, M.D., B.Sc., gives an unselfconscious version of what survived from the conceptual evolution that Starobinski traces. It purports to describe a unilinear development through three distinct stages of savagery and three stages of barbarism to the stages of civilization, all in the direction of permanent housing, elaborate technology, refined artistic practices, complex political institutions, and international peace. The process is not so much a single worldwide set of developing forms as a single way in which practices and institutions improve by cumulative learning: through discoveries of what works, what is more efficient, and what is more humane. Since these are real discoveries and real improvements, the author does not envisage that this process, whatever its specific cultural content, could ever be reversed. If civilizations decline and fall, presumably, it must be through some catastrophe. Dr Williams, apparently, does not envisage catastrophes; but others have.

The idea of civilization as a normal condition of perfection, repeatedly achieved and repeatedly lost through natural disasters, goes all the way back to Aristotle, and is supported by his cosmic view.[57] But that view, in which the fixity of a basically timeless and spatially limited Earth precludes evolutionary change, was dead wrong, and without it the idea of normal progress somehow lacks conviction. When I read that old *Britannica* article, with its weighty reliance on the achievements of nineteenth-century sociology and anthropology, I feel that it ought to be true but cannot be. What makes me uneasy is its assumption that there can be no legitimate standpoint from which some or all of the obvious and real discoveries and improvements could prove after all to be mistakes and disasters. But what is wrong with its argument *as an argument* is less its cultural complacency than its assumption that local improvements, made in the light of immediately perceived inconveniences, must add up to a way of life that will be better overall. What is most fundamentally amiss, however, is that the word 'civilization' is simultaneously used as a value term and as descriptive of a specific sort of praxis.[58]

The embarrassing difficulty of saying just what we mean by civilization and exactly what is good about it does not prevent it being clear enough what *sort* of difference there is between civilization and its opposite.[59] And perhaps we can say that the idea does always involve some notion of improvement based on conscious critical reflection.[60] If so, perhaps we can add that without such reflection there can be nothing like a university; that without *something like* a university philosophy as the pursuit of wisdom cannot flourish; and that aesthetics can take shape only as part of a flourishing philosophy. This will be true even if *something like* aesthetics can exist without philosophy, *something like* philosophy can be carried on where nothing like a university exists, and *something analogous to* a university can exist in cultures that do not qualify as civilizations. (These might be, respectively, unsupported, unanalysed, and unguarded generalizations about 'art' and 'beauty'; portentous orotundities, smartass quips, and comfortable platitudes about humanity and the cosmos; and seminaries for instilling approved hatreds and prejudices.) However that may be, it is also clear that *our* civilization would not be what it is without our universities, nor our universities without what we know as philosophy. And our philosophy would not be philosophy as we know it if aesthetics (as we know *that*) were not at least a possibility within it.

The Logic of Criticism

At this point, I have to step back a bit. My attempt to understand the idea of civilization has left my wheels spinning in the mud. To get where I want to, I need to say something about an aspect of aesthetics that is directly bound up with the idea of civilization in a way I have yet to discuss. By a fortunate coincidence, it is the only one of the three topics that make up the philosophy of art (the others being the ones connected with systems of values and maps of knowledge) about which I have not yet said anything. This third topic is the rational basis of art criticism.

Art criticism is directly related to the idea of civilization in two ways. First, the distinction between civility and barbarity is enshrined in a contrast between polite taste and uncultured preferences in the arts, so that this contrast has to be explicated and made to seem defensible. Second, the development of critical tradition and method in general is often said to be an essential ingredient in any civilized system of general education, and the very idea of criticism is native to the discussion of the arts.[61] And art criticism raises specifically philosophical problems. On the one hand, the arts are organized modes of activity in society, involving teachable skills; and, on the other hand, the immediate values of art are subjective, lying in personal pleasures based on personal appreciations. Philosophical reflection is needed to determine what modes of justification are appropriate to these two aspects of art, if any are, and how they are to be reconciled, if they can be. The teachable skills and their associated values may be such that their outcome is unavoidable: knowing how to produce involves knowing how to appreciate, and at a given historical juncture this knowledge may necessarily take a given form. But the consumers of the expert product are not themselves experts, and lack the knowledge that formed the practitioners' taste. I don't care how good Boulez's music is, so long as I don't have to listen to it; and I don't care how bad the music I love to listen to is, so long as I can get to hear it. Obviously, the value space within which this divergence can arise requires to be articulated.

As so often in philosophy, the problem is ultimately one of assurance; in this case, the need for certainty in public evaluation and security in private judgment. Public certainty is needed to protect investment against the fluctuations and conspiracies of the art market;[62] private security is needed to defend the texture of one's own experience and commitments from such external onslaughts as indoctrination and fashion.[63] As always in philosophy, reflection may lead us to conclude that no such defence and protection are available, or that none are necessary – or even desirable, for some would argue that it is better to stand up for one's loves and convictions without cavil or question. But that is a possible outcome of our inquiries, not an initial justification for failing to inquire.

Art criticism as a distinctive practice hovers uncertainly between two poles. One of these poles is represented by the concept of criticism in general, as a special kind of argumentative discourse; the other pole is what art critics actually do. Criticism in general, at the one extreme, is discourse grounding the evaluation of any action or thing that can meaningfully be said to be well or badly done or made.[64] Now, anything at all that is made or done may be made or done more or less well or badly, and it is always potentially a matter of interest which it is; but usually the practical context is so complex that organized comment is pointless or impossible. We exist, as it were, in a continuum of commentary that barely rises to the level of consciousness. The organized discourse of criticism, apt to ground evaluation, is possible if and only if one can identify some purpose or function that the object criticized is to serve or fulfil. A work of art is typically subject to criticism in this sense, but no more and no less than the policy of a government or the baking of a pie. Philosophical discussion nowadays generally holds that such discourse has three phases: description, interpretation, and evaluation. One has to identify and describe what one is talking about, explain what is going on in it, and establish its worth as thus described and explained. But the relations between these three prove to be endlessly discussable.

That threefold discourse that underpins evaluation in general, in the subtle forms that it takes when applied to the arts, is one of our two poles. At the other pole, 'art criticism' is just the name we give to what the people called art critics actually do in the exercise of their profession. And that, it turns out, is simply to say anything about a work or an artist that interests them, or their editors, or their readers. The whole point of works of art, for their producers and for their consumers, is that they are totally engrossing objects. People's actual enjoyments and appreciations in art accordingly involve their complete selves and all their involvements in the world; and into the works that are thus enjoyed the artists must have put themselves no less completely. So why should art critics exclude any part of that totality from their professional discourse? In fact, they do not. This openness, however, is not much help to curators mounting an exhibition, or to teachers in a creative writing class. At the other extreme, the logic of criticism as such, with its stipulation of precise functions and purposes, threatens to reduce artistic creation to a technical exercise.

Reconciliation between the two extremes is not impossible. On the one side, it is recognized that not everything that might be said about a work is acknowledged as equally relevant to the interests people find it possible to take in it. Granted that works of art are comprehensively engrossing and involve the whole of life, such involvement is not unstructured. Not everything is involved to the same extent, or in the same way. On the other side, one makes the function assigned to art a very general and variable one, so that invoking the concept of art leaves art criticism a wide domain within which it has a lot of freedom to construct its arguments. It is true that the location and limits of the domain thus established for art criticism are uncertain, depending on what maps of knowledge are available, so that the appeal to the concept of art may amount to little more than a claim to significance and privilege.[65] To claim for something the status of art is then to give it the benefit of all possible doubt (and, one sometimes feels, a lot of impossible doubt as well).[66] The result is that the earnest question 'But is it Art?,' the serious meaning of which is to ask whether criticism of a given object can properly be carried on within this privileged domain, turns into a joke. But art critics are not all fools, individually or collectively, and the functional domain of art is one in which one can learn one's way around.

However these questions turn out, aesthetics as the philosophy of criticism plainly has plenty to do. Its mission, I was saying, is provided by the underlying need for certainty and assurance in judgment and appreciation. But when is such a need originally felt? Presumably it is only when there is some gulf between one's life experience and the domain in which judgment and evaluation are to be exercised, whether this be art or any other form of practice. Otherwise, there is no room for systematic doubt, and the supposed need reduces to a personal foible.

When do such gaps open up between experience and judgment? For one thing, they must be endemic whenever there is no direct connection between private satisfactions and public successes. In large and complex societies, this easily happens. It can happen when there is simply more going on than one can keep up with; more specifically, when practice runs ahead of one's own experience. This must happen in any professional practice, especially when traditions of practice divide and diverge.[67] And gaps of a rather different kind occur in multicultural or historically extended societies, in which one may well be tempted to extend one's knowledge and love to times and places other than those in which one is native.[68]

Reflection on the different ways in which gaps may occur between people's actual experience and the demands on their judgment has suggested at least five functions of criticism, or five aspects of critical reason. There is, first, the induction of appreciation, in which we show each other how to discover and respond to what we ourselves have found rewarding (or repulsive) in a particular work. There is, second, the more general demonstration of how kinds of works may be appreciated by relating them to the traditions to which they belong. Then there is, third, the public ranking and evaluation of specific works, as for a market or competition, in which the analysing and balancing of pros and cons among a given population are carried out and justified. Here, the question whether there really is in some relevant sense an operative market or competition needs to be considered. Fourth, more modestly, there is what the daily reviewers do, talent scouts who save people's time by identifying among the torrent of new work what is likely to reward whom and why.[69] Fifth, at the other extreme, there is the exploration of the grounds of convictions based on personal knowledge. And to these five Northrop Frye at least would have added a sixth – the only one, he thought, deserving of the name 'criticism' – the explanation of how a work relates to the totality of all possible works in its art.

You can see that the philosophy of criticism confronts a dense tangle of problems, quite enough to preoccupy it. But there is an aspect of aesthetics that this agenda leaves unexplained, and it was primarily to highlight this anomaly that I went into as much detail as I did. The fact is, there is a strong tendency among writers on aesthetics to take as their preferred terrain, not the whole range of artistic practice in which such questions arise, but only masterpieces, the sorts of things one finds segregated in museums.[70] Why is this? Great achievements do not dominate discussions in this way in ethics, or in the philosophy of science. So, why do they in aesthetics?

There are several good answers to that question. To begin with, it is convenient to be able to refer to a small range of examples with which everyone is (or can soon become) familiar. In art, as in all skills, discussion naturally concentrates on successes, not failures; and a masterpiece is simply an undisputed success.[71] So the small range of examples cited will obviously be confined to the most uncontroversially successful works. If this explanation leaves one unsatisfied, one may reflect that it is in masterpieces that the compelling power of beauty, the philosophical importance of which I stressed in my first lecture, is clearly evident. But this topic is too unfashionable for much to be made of it. One could also argue that in discussing cultural phenomena it is only the richest, most advanced, most complex examples that clearly exemplify what is at stake. And in the special case of the fine arts it has been influentially contended that the success to be achieved is of a very special kind, a seamless unity that is rarely achieved in an unalloyed form.[72] Even if one rejects that thesis, one may respect it sufficiently to use as one's illustrations the sort of work that is most often said to support it, and this will again be the uncontroversially accepted masterpieces of art.

I find the 'good answers' I have just been deploying persuasive, but they leave me uneasy. Might it not simply be that we are weighed down by the classical baggage that, for good or ill, our humanistic studies still carry on board? Histories compiled in antiquity, from Aristotle to Pliny and Plutarch, relate how a fine art proceeds by progressive discoveries of techniques and effects, and trace its development through a series of innovative practitioners and their canonical works. Perhaps we unreflectively model our thinking after those hoary exemplars.[73] The underlying idea would then be that of progress in civilization, of which I was speaking a little while ago. But no, this won't quite do. A masterpiece is typically an *old* master, which retains its artistic authority despite its antiquity – like the Parthenon in Athens, of which it was written six centuries after its construction that it looked venerable as soon as it was built, and still looked new now that it was old.[74] A society that truly believed in progress would unselfconsciously prefer its own art to the primitive stuff it had superseded.

At this point, the historians bring us down to earth. Our idealization of museums is, they remind us, a tendentious myth. What art museums are full of is, in reality, nothing but loot, the spoils of national conquest and capitalist acquisition. Aesthetics, they imply, concentrates on these displays of power and privilege because the successors of the people who bought and displayed the masterpieces are the people who now pay the critics and professors. Aesthetics is the flattery of the rich and famous.

I am sure that is true. But it cannot be the whole truth. Loot is not looted unless it is thought worth stealing in the first place. A bank cannot establish its solidity by spending millions of dollars on a Van Gogh painting unless the people who are meant to be impressed already agree that a painting *might* be worth that much money, and that the painting purchased *might* be such a work.[75] A recent researcher claims to have discovered that, whatever the follies of today's art market, an artist who gets to be expensive and famous is typically recognized first by fellow artists, then by some serious critics, and only then by collectors and dealers and, subsequently, by the general public.[76] Besides, my earlier remarks on the successful exercise of skills were absurdly understated. We should never forget what everyone knows: that in any taxing and intricate complex of skills there are likely to be a few who find the activity more congenial, master the techniques sooner, grasp the principles more firmly, work harder and more innovatively and with more confidence and self-criticism, than anyone else; and their supremacy is not disputed even by those who find the practice itself artificial, and even arbitrary. Whatever you think of ballet and hockey, only Karen Kain is Karen Kain, and only Wayne Gretzky is Wayne Gretzky. Without this unmistakable dynamic of recognized achievement, the pride and greed of the museum-makers would have nothing to work on. That is true even if the fact that only the rich and powerful can command the highest skills means that the best talent is often warped in directions that the rich and powerful dictate or encourage. It remains true even when the true worth of achievement becomes exchange value in a corrupt market.

For a long time, I thought that this was all one needed to say about the seemingly disproportionate emphasis on masterpieces. It is simply an inevitable part of the dynamics of critical discourse as it works itself out in this or that historical situation. But eventually it occurred to me, what had no doubt been evident all along to my more sophisticated colleagues, that something essential was missing from this explanation. The very idea of a masterpiece, it seems to me now, is bound up with the assumption that among fine art practices some are to be singled out as 'high' arts: a restricted range of artistic work in which alone supreme efforts are called for and supreme achievements recognized and rewarded.[77]

The notion of a high art is, I believe, indigenous to the idea that I want to introduce under the name 'empire.' This is a rather vague and approximate sort of notion, but what I have in mind is the sociopolitical situation where a number of separately functioning sociocultural units are bound together in an administrative unity without thereby losing their vital identity. Such a unity exists as an apparatus of coordination and control; and that means that, first and foremost, it is an information system. To a greater or lesser extent in all sorts of political organizations, but most conspicuously in the great civilizations, such as the Indian and the Sino-Japanese no less than the Graeco-Roman and its successors, we find an officially recognized high art that is associated not only with the central organization of the political power but, more closely and relevantly, with an educational system into which those people are co-opted who are to be concerned with the body politic as a whole. If one is to move out of one's village one goes to a school in which one is indoctrinated in what passes current throughout the empire;[78] and this indoctrination is likely to include a recognized music and literature, which does not express the lived reality of any specific local or ethnic identity but passes current everywhere as an inculcated appreciation and an acquired taste. Thus in India the classical dance theatre is politically and culturally enshrined, not as one set of dance forms among others, but as the kind of dance that is proper to the spiritual and intellectual system that is officially identified with India as India.[79] In comparison with this, all other dances indigenous to the subcontinent are relegated to the status of ethnic or folk practice,[80] and either excluded from the educational system or taught as marginal or exotic.[81]

There are three reasons why it took me a long time to realize the specific importance of empire as the educational, cultural, and generally informational unity of a heterogeneous political conglomerate. The first reason is that I was confusing empire with civilization, which is what I was talking about before. Civilization is a level of cultural praxis, and *a* civilization is a domain within which such a level is spontaneously maintained and intercommunicated. But an empire is a political body with a common system of communication and control. Such a system requires a unifying educational apparatus, maintaining and maintained by a common system of informational exchange with its own unifying culture; but it is not to be identified with that culture. The second reason I overlooked the importance of empire is that, like practically everyone else, I thought of empire in terms of imperialism, and regarded imperialism exclusively as an agency of exploitation and tyranny. But imperialism is the will to unlimited expansion of empire, not empire itself. And the third and most important reason is that, like so many theorists until recently, I was just insufficiently sensitive to the extent to which organic and communal life is a matter of information exchange.[82] In any case, whatever my reasons for not seeing it sooner, the specific energies of writing in aesthetics are predominantly devoted to the recognized pinnacles of achievement in the 'high' arts, and these are the arts cultivated in and by the educational organizations of the empires that articulate the institutions of the great civilizations. The compelling power of the perceived beauty of those supreme achievements lends credence to the claims of those civilizations themselves to our esteem.

In my last lecture, tomorrow evening, I will flesh out these skeletal remarks about empire, and remind you of some familiar facts and beliefs about empire and civilization today. This material will put us in a position to say what has to be said about tomorrow's announced topic, civilization and the future of aesthetics. But then, finally, I must turn briefly to a subject about which I have somehow contrived to say practically nothing. I will have to say something about the future.

IV Civilization and the Future of Aesthetics

Last night, I recounted the forces making for the disintegration of the research university, and hence by implication of the civilization to which such universities are integral. But the reflection that civilization in general, and our own civilization most conspicuously, elevates critical thinking into a guiding principle reminded us that we had hitherto neglected one of the three lines of thought whose confluence and divergence constituted the discipline of aesthetics. That neglected line was the logic of critical thinking itself – a kind of thinking that may be applied to anything within the scope of purposive action, but takes its most refined form when applied to art.

A sketch of the aspects of art criticism that make it a topic for philosophy confronted us with an anomaly. Nothing in the nature and scope of criticism prepared us for the extent to which the actual discussions of aesthetics concentrate on the masterpieces of the most prestigious of the fine arts, what we sometimes call the 'high arts.'[1] I suggested some reasons, good and bad, why this should be so, but ended by suggesting that the significance of high arts everywhere is that they pertain, not merely to the refinement of civilized living, but specifically to the widespread sociopolitical phenomenon I called 'empire,' in which a unifying structure of information exchange is superimposed on a multiplicity of local cultures.

What remains for me to do this evening is to say something about how the vicissitudes of empire and civilization bear on the likely fate of aesthetics. My lectures conclude with the admission that, as so often before, their argument depends on the intelligibility of a familiar concept that turns out to need more explaining than it sometimes gets. This time, the concept in question is that of the future. I hope you will agree that the future is a good place for me to stop.

Before we come to the future, though, the concept of empire requires attention. The paradigm of an empire is something like the Roman or British empire, a semi-permanent super-nation with several (perhaps many) subordinate nations which it variously incorporates or dominates. And we tend to think of the empire as dominated by one originating nation – in our examples, Rome and Britain. But in mature empires no dominant nation can be readily identified; what persists is the structure of information, coordination, and control. And imperial structure can be identified at several levels: Canada, for instance, functions as an imperial power in relation to its provinces and aboriginal nations (on which it imposes a common educational and financial system), but was itself a part of the British empire, from which it has freed itself only to become part of the quasi-empire constituted by the sphere of influence of the United States.[2]

Thought about empire is further complicated by the fact that it has long been fashionable to discuss it exclusively in terms of imperialism, a Hobbesian 'restless desire of power after power' in which strong political organizations dominate and incorporate others.[3] But not all political powers attempt such domination, and it is not really clear why any should. The underlying reality is rather that different kinds of action require cooperation on different scales and with different degrees of integration. Rich personal life requires close familial contacts, but systems of banks, highways, and airlines, with provision for famine control and emergency relief, require permanent structures that do not call for that sort of personal involvement. It is the maintenance of such large-scale, durable structures, within which long-term cooperative endeavours can be set up, maintained, and safeguarded, that I take to be the central fact of empire.

The maintenance of an empire is first and foremost a matter of administration, and administration is primarily a matter of information exchange, which requires a common system of education in which the norms of such exchange are formulated. And that amounts to a common quasi-culture with its official forms of logic, rhetoric, sciences, and arts, superimposed on whatever culture may be native to the individual administrators.[4] But if we ask what this imperial information system is *for*, we have to say that it exists ultimately to facilitate integration of action. And such facilitation is a manifestation of power. Consequently, when we think of empire, we immediately think of power.[5]

When we think of power in a political context, we tend to think of oppression. But power is simply the ability to do things, and there is nothing inherently oppressive about such ability. Power facilitates as much as it coerces. In general, to be a member of a large organization enables one to do many things one could not otherwise do, but at the price of being constrained in ways in which one would otherwise not be constrained.[6] Whether this prevailing and surrounding power is experienced as oppressive or empowering depends on just what one is trying to do, and whether these endeavours are furthered or thwarted (or, annoyingly or blessedly, treated as irrelevant by) the 'powers that be.'[7]

Empires conceived in terms of power are typically conceived in terms of relations of dominance and exploitation between peoples of grossly unequal power who remain essentially separate from each other, forcibly held together by the military, economic, and bureaucratic control of the dominant group.[8] On such a view, it would be the arts – originally the ethnic arts – of this elite group that are classified as 'high arts,' their prestige being merely a manifestation of its oppressive power. This view is popular, persuasive, and easy to illustrate. But we have seen that it is deeply misleading, in two ways. First, because history is still mostly written in terms of kings and conquests, that is, of *events*, empires appear as manifestations of force. But power may be latent energy, rather than active force. Once a power system is in place, its inertia need exert no pressure. Local coercions, reluctances, resistances, usurpations of all kinds, frequent as they may be, are malfunctions of empire: the reality of an existing imperial structure, Inca, Chinese, Mogul, or whatever, is the administrative structure that supports its functioning. And this structure is in itself an information network, articulated in a unified educational and cultural system. Administrators have to talk the same language, both literally and figuratively; and this applies to all those who in any way participate in or relate directly to the overall sociopolitical structure, including anyone who is to enter into dialogue with it.[9] This is not in itself a matter of oppression, though it may be carried out or experienced oppressively.[10] It is a function of the need to communicate: one learns the languages one needs. If there is a central organizational system, groups must operate through agents who become effectively bilingual and bicultural as between their own ways and those of the system; the system itself can cooperate with them (or control them) effectively only if its agents understand the separate groups, but the only tools and methods by which *all* can operate are, of course, those of the single system. What determines social and cultural reality is the *specific* relation of any given phenomenon to the centralized structure, on the one hand, and, on the other hand, local structures that retain their independent form and dynamic.

The second way in which our common understanding of empire is misleading is that we tend to construe it primarily in ethnic terms, equating the imperial power and its information and educational system with one ethnic group exercising permanent power over others. But I have remarked already that racial and ethnic differentiation as such have no structural role in these relationships.[11] The mandarinate, the body of those whose common schooling makes them able and eligible to take part in public affairs, obviously cannot be open to all members of an ethnically dominant group.[12] The whole point of having such a system is that it should be open to the talents of all, whatever their social or ethnic background, and closed to those without the relevant capacities; and the very existence of the system, with the demands placed on it, guarantees that neither its membership nor its direction can coincide with those of an ethnic group as such.[13] It is the mandarinate as such that defines the proper public for the high arts of the empire, and it is they and those whom they sponsor who take part in the practice of those arts. They are the arts integral to the educational system that recruits and defines the mandarinate, whether or not they are formally promoted within the educational institutions.

The association of high art with the mandarinate is already clearly visible in David Hume's 1759 essay 'On the Standard of Taste,' glanced at last night,[14] which to my mind is still the shrewdest and subtlest investigation of how critical standards are established. The standard of excellence, he tells us, is the consensus of the best judges. But when we look at who these judges are, it turns out that they are people who have the same sympathetic sensitivity, scrupulous impartiality, breadth of knowledge, reliance on detailed information, and discriminating care that we look for in people who are to take responsible positions in law or bureaucracy.[15] Critical ability is not a mysterious faculty uniquely joined to aesthetic connoisseurship; good critics are simply people who apply to the judging of art the same qualities of mind and character that fit a person to take part in public affairs, the qualities we would wish to be shown by anyone who is to make decisions affecting our own lives.

Hume's essay also implicitly reveals a specific connection between high art and the educational system. The canonical works he cites, works whose perennially recognized excellence is to testify to the durability of the alleged standard, are such as the *Iliad*, which had been the staple of schooling in ancient Greece, Virgil's *Aeneid*, which acquired similar standing in Roman schools in its author's lifetime, and the handful of Athenian tragedies selected and edited for school use by the educational bureaucracy of the Byzantine empire. The high arts, it seems, around which the concept of the fine arts was being articulated in Hume's day, were those selected and endorsed neither by the artistically creative community nor by the wielders of political power, but by the framers of the curriculum, the educational bureaucracy that gave the civilization in question a common set of methods and references to orient itself by. An essential point for my overall argument, though it is one I will not follow up here, is that such systems, whatever the actual forces that shape them, do purport to be systems of education, not of indoctrination. They claim to discover rather than decree the value of what they teach. And the claim is, to a large extent, justified. As I suggested last night, the excellence of Karen Kain's dancing is directly observed and appreciated by those who have the appropriate familiarity with the high art of ballet. It is not a necessary part of the education that the art itself should be shown (or asserted) to be anything other than arbitrary; it is the dancers and their dances that are valued, the art itself need be assigned no value beyond the perceived excellences of achievements and achievers.[16] It may be simply an empirical matter that certain specific ranges of practice (arts, art forms, genres) have been developed within which beauty can be manifested, discerned, and appreciated.[17]

In the preceding paragraph, I have slipped from talking about the high arts of an *empire* with a mandarinate to talking about the canonical arts of a *civilization*. I did not at first realize that I was doing so. The immediate explanation is that Hume speaks for a *civilization* that regards itself as a successor to Christendom, itself the non-political heir to the Roman *empire* – a familiar feature of our history, of which I have made much in preceding lectures. It is, indeed, inevitable that empires should correlate rather closely with civilizations, because the common understanding that constitutes a civilization facilitates the active information exchange that characterizes an empire, and the common arrangements of an empire foster a common civilization. The correlation is by no means complete, for there are countervailing forces of many kinds that make for independence; but it is so strong that in what follows it is possible that I shall sometimes be found speaking loosely about 'empire' or 'civilization' or 'imperial civilization' without scruple or apology.

Empire, like other social forms, is seldom purely or completely exemplified. Every large-scale cultural and political organization is unstable, its living present haunted by its historical past and its threatening future. I began my discourse on empire by saying that the British and Roman empires were paradigm cases. But in fact both of these organizations changed continually through time, and at a given period included units of the most various sizes, with very different degrees of integration and autonomy, and bound to each other and to the central power by very different ties of sentiment and resentment.[18] And to the extent that any of these units had any degree of autarchy and autonomy they were themselves likely to manifest an imperial structure, with a central system of information exchange working through its mandarinate and relating to its continuing ethnic units – which themselves might be articulated as imperial metropolises in relation to the villages in which ethnicity was less compromised and diluted.[19] At the other end, we see today how in the worldwide network of mass transportation and electronic information exchange the most massively imperial entities are becoming variously entangled in alliances of continually changing scope and significance – the European Union, NATO, the U.N., organizations of African and American states – which themselves show incipient tendencies to congeal into empires. And the fact that this is a single recognizable worldwide phenomenon, though without any single organizational framework within which it formally operates, suggests the looming imminence of a sort of shadowy super-empire.[20]

In the days of Hume and Kant, European civilization was strongly unified by its educational system; it did not, however, constitute a formal empire, but (as I was saying) lived in the uneasy aftermath of the Roman empire, which seemed perpetually striving to reconstitute itself – and, to all appearances, still is. Its educational system was centred on the international university network of Christendom, through which ideas and teachers circulated, and which was largely governed by the inertia of its traditions. But the next century saw the triumph of the 'Enlightenment,' the growth of the exact sciences and the deliberate erosion of the limits on systematic doubt; and the undeniable successes of natural science and its associated technology caused the network to begin its expansion into the articulation of something like a world system, linked to a partial and informal order of international cultural organizations that has some of the features of a world cultural empire, akin to the imminent political super-empire I just mentioned.

Critics are at pains to distinguish the possible new world order based on the inescapably cosmopolitan network of scientific and technical information from the imperial expansion suggested by the use of United Nations and superpower force to resolve local conflicts.[21] The tendency of the latter would be to set up a single 'power to keep them all in awe,' an international force in which (like a Hobbesian sovereign at the national level) all force would ultimately reside; but the tendency of the former would be to establish a stable network of equal cultures, perhaps effectively united in lesser networks corresponding to the more radically opposed civilizations. But it is not clear that these are really separable. When one says 'network' one may be thinking of the interstices rather than the reticulation, concentrating on the pattern of the web and forgetting the toughness of the fibres that would be needed to sustain it. The difference in civilization that kept such a network from being an empire would require a singularly determined, dedicated, and agile mandarinate to keep the system going. On the other side, the idea of a superimperial force to keep the world in order is not persuasive either: its unification would be proportionate to its clumsiness, and (as I have been urging all along) such effectiveness as its unity had could only be that of an information system linking diverse local and specialized forces.

Modern science and technology are inseparable from an elaborate educational system, with its associated disciplines of thought and procedure. But they are not, in themselves, closely linked to any living culture.[22] Despite this lack of intrinsic connection, however, the way the science-bearing institutions move out into the world is shadowed by a comparable movement in the high arts of the originating civilization. The winner of a ballet competition or a piano competition, or the music director of a symphony orchestra, may nowadays come from anywhere in the world.[23] But, whereas the worldwide authority of the natural sciences rests on theoretical coherence and experimental confirmation,[24] the international spread of art forms rooted in European traditions has no visible ground other than the factual cohesiveness of the educational system that is centred on universities of the sort in which science is native.

Though every empire is likely to have its own high arts, then, it seems that high art today is art that happens to be institutionalized worldwide by way of an educational system that has no competitors, because it is the only established vehicle of the system of modern natural science, and that science is the necessary basis of a technology that has made itself everywhere indispensable.[25]

For the last few minutes, I have been building up the idea of today's international order as a sort of super-imperial hierarchy superimposed on or superseding all other imperial systems, articulated by an international cultural and educational system that carries along with it its own high art with its own procedures and canons. And this, to a large extent, is what aesthetics as actually taught has in view and implicitly supports.

Surprisingly little attention has been paid to how this works in practice – to how a worldwide quasi-empire emerges from and interacts with actual empires with their own articulations, and how the institutionalized communication networks and educational systems in which this is worked out subtend the informally organized cultural structures toward which we gesture vaguely with the concept of civilization in general and the idea of a civilization as a distinct grouping within which civilization is maintained in a distinctive way. That this intricate phenomenon exists we can, I think, see; just *how* it exists, what characteristic forms it takes, and just what other structures (such as international financial markets) go along with it, nobody quite sees, and nobody seems to be looking very hard.[26] It is easier to postulate and evaluate political and economic forces to drive whatever international order and disorder we think we see, without looking to see precisely what it is that is being driven and maintained.

My way of talking about interaction between two systems, the unified high art of empire and the diversity of ethnic tradition, may have reminded you of what I was saying last night about the philosophical problems of art criticism, with its implicit polarity of certainty in the public realm versus security in personal judgment. But such dualism, however modified by mutual fertilizations and contaminations, is not the way things are. Exclusive emphasis on antagonisms and oppressions, malfunctions and perversions, puts us in danger of misconstruing all the phenomena of our cultural world.[27] We merely diagnose them all as cases of oppressing or being oppressed, instead of trying to understand each one in its precise relationship to the flow of information. Ethnic and imperial traditions of training, production, and reception interact in subtle ways that insistence on the brutal dualisms of power ignores. I remarked previously that actual phenomena tend not to belong exclusively to the imperial or the ethnic, but represent specific locations on the scale between these extremes, and specific forms of their dynamic interaction. But the implied dualism is itself illusory, because in a hierarchy of incorporation what is 'ethnic' in one relation may function as 'imperial' in another. And the ways in which a superordinate relates to a subordinate vary widely according to the ways such relationships have evolved, their extent and scope, and how they are understood. If my experience is any guide, our understanding, appreciation, and practice of the arts place us among a variety of traditions and tendencies, roughly distinguishable as cosmopolitan, metropolitan, provincial, local, folk, popular, exotic, and so on.[28] The realities to which these terms refer cannot be hierarchically ordered or schematically diagrammed: they have intricate histories of their own, histories that have to be learned and lived.

The complexities of power and potency, of influence and adoption, to which I have been alluding, are complicated in real life by the sociology and epistemology of reception. Not only are works embedded in traditions determined by specific relations of isolation, differentiation, influence, and control, but the ways we as individuals relate to specific works show a comparable variation. To each one of us, some works are known as gossip and media events,[29] some as historical markers, some as cultural icons or fetishes, some as objects of our own special interest and affection, some as commanding a distant respect, some as uncovenanted epiphanies, some as ingrained in the textures of our own lives and circumstances.[30]

Use of such terminologies as these to distinguish traditions by their varying relations to empire, and to discriminate among different ways of relating to works and traditions, testifies to awareness of a dynamic order in the cultural world in which one lives. Failure to use them suggests a narrowness in the scope of one's vision. Imprecision in their use shows a coarseness of cultural sensibility – or, what may come to the same thing, conceptual impoverishment.[31] To the extent that the arts engross our attentive concern, we all develop an intricate wisdom in these matters, even if we never formulate it to each other or even to ourselves. Formal art history and criticism, in search of accounts that can be clearly stated and followed, tend to pass all these intricacies by, but in doing so they risk substituting for lived relationships a useless tissue of inert fictions.

If the reality of artistic practice and experience is the sort of intricate thicket of information transfer that I have been trying to suggest, are we to conclude that the apparent emphasis in aesthetics on the 'master-pieces' of the 'high arts' is mere ideology? Not really, because imperial and super-imperial structures, though far from being the whole of contemporary reality, are an important part of it and remain firmly in place. And the Enlightenment model of an ideal order of civilization, on which these structures rely for support, continues to beguile us, even while we feel its absurdity. It is because of the complex convergences among systems and forces I was alluding to before, of which we have some sort of inkling, that it is still possible to speak in general terms of 'civilization' even in our own disillusioned age. So we cannot successfully pretend to ourselves that we simply have no idea what high arts and masterpieces are.

The project of the eighteenth-century Enlightenment, after all, was ultimately to substitute defensible standards for mere local preferences in *all* areas of cultural and spiritual activity.[32] The key to its understanding is that the Enlightenment as it conceived itself admitted no competitor or rival. To accept the very idea of such rivalry was to concede that there was a competition, and to be in a competition is to accept that there are standards of success; and it was this acceptance itself that was the essence of the Enlightenment. So to compete with the Enlightenment was to join it. In principle, the Enlightenment was to be the hegemony of reason itself, the first and only fully self-correcting system of theory and taste.[33] The abstract idea of a high art and its masterpieces stands for this presumption of perfectibility in the procedures and products of all civilized activities.

What mattered was not the viability of the Enlightenment idea as a program, but its intelligibility. It never mattered how many mistakes were made in the name of civilization and progress, how many crazy projects were formed and abandoned. What mattered was that the mistakes were *mistakes*. The important thing about a mistake is that, in principle, it can be discovered, and when it is discovered it can be corrected.[34] As for the oddness and arbitrariness of the practices and preferences that actually flourished as the high art of the empire, I have already pointed out why that did not matter either. Just as good poems and good laws can be written in any of the world's languages, artistic success can be achieved within any system of conventions; and conventions there must be. Acquired tastes can be real. So long as an educational system retains its integrity, real prowess can be achieved and the compelling power of beauty can be genuinely experienced, in appropriate ways on appropriate occasions, by those whom the education has adequately prepared.

At the very moment, however, that the Enlightenment has finally triumphed in the establishment of a super-imperial order with its associated high arts and the educational scaffolding that supports them, the entire civilization to which they belong is being called into question. And its loss of conviction threatens to involve in its downfall the idea of civilization itself. Such scepticism has, of course, always accompanied the Enlightenment idea: one thinks of William Blake's fulminations against Locke and Newton, and the intransigence of back-street chapels and apocalyptic salvationism from that day to this.[35] Elizabeth Barrett Browning, in Book II of *Aurora Leigh* (1857), already felt impelled to complain of 'the world half-blind / With intellectual light, half brutalised / With civilization.' What is different today is that the staggeringly accelerating growth in the speed and scope of information exchange throughout the world seems suddenly to confront us with the lived reality that corresponds to what is now revealed to have been nothing but a daydream. It is the revelation of its power that makes its dangers plain; it was when its reveries were impotent that the lure of their fulfilment seemed irresistible.[36]

It is all very well to dismiss ugly realities as corrigible errors, partly attributable to the way that structural and technological changes have outpaced any possible adaptation in personal lives and relations. The fact is that what confronts us, perversion or not, is the only reality we know; and a vigorous demystification industry dismisses the pretended universalism of the overarching civilization as a sham, a conspiracy of bourgeois, white, elderly, European, and mostly dead males to do everyone else down.[37] Moreover, my claim that the empires and super-empires, to which the mandarinates with their high arts pertain, are a potentially benign supplement to the living ethnic cultures and economies within which most people continue to live out most of their lives is a delusion: the superstructure with its trappings proves to be not a support, but an impoverishing and destructive substitute, for spontaneous and responsive ways of living in an experienced environment.[38]

What is being rejected today, more or less articulately, is what is perceived as a misdirected holism and a spurious universalism. The idea of a universal research-based science is repudiated in favour of an empirical wisdom based directly on life as experienced by those who live it, with the accretions of their local lore; intrusive ecological and medical engineering, aimed at specific results without regard to their eventual overall outcome, are denounced in the name of skills and remedies discovered and used within a familiar working context that controls their use and limits their abuse.[39] The underlying conviction is that a planned and researched order, on a scale that goes beyond the control of a face-to-face community, simply generates a deeper and more widespread disorder;[40] and that this new disorder cannot be controlled or mitigated, as is suggested by those who say that only good science can remedy bad science.[41] The new disorder could be counteracted only by a countervailing force – that is, by an even more massive, and hence necessarily more destructive, intrusion.[42]

The general idea that there is a conflict between the values certified in the private realm by experience and those established in the public realm by institutionalized practice is one we came across before, in our sketch of the basics of the philosophy of criticism. But in the present context it gives way to something more apocalyptic. The very idea of a worldwide civilization within which humanity remodels itself into the truly rational animal through a universal science-based education – everything from Socrates and Pythagoras to UNESCO and the IMF – is repudiated as necessarily leading to something that our new worldwide research programs and information networks enable us for the first time to foresee, even as we encompass it: irreversible, worldwide, demographic and ecological disaster.[43] Our technology enables us to effect this catastrophe, our research enables us to detect its imminence; but we have no power to avert it.[44] Any power we could generate to reverse the trend would only be a yet more ruthless and crass concentration of the powers that humanity is misusing already. (Who, after all, would be the 'we' who could generate and wield this power? Not nice people like you and me, we may be sure.) Our only hope is that the few humans who survive the imminent destruction, if any do, will revert to something like the harmless impotence of the early Bronze Age.[45] All in all, it is no wonder that 'Enlightenment' has become a term of abuse, standing for the intrusion of heartless *reasoning* into areas where observant and sensitive *experience* should be our guide.

Not only is the idea of a world civilization widely repudiated, but the very conception of a specific civilized order to which we ourselves belong is becoming inaccessible. For example, at Stanford University a few years ago it was proposed to eliminate the compulsory first-year course in 'Western Civilization' in favour of a course in 'Culture, Ideas, and Values.' The aim of this new course, according to one of its advocates, 'was, and is, to broaden the concept of what constitutes "valid" intellectual history by including non-Western as well as Western perspectives on culture, society, history, literature and so on. Such a change necessarily involves a challenge to the formerly unquestioned dominance of the predominantly white, male, upper-class contributors to the western intellectual tradition.'[46] Note that the advocate is not challenging the old course's interpretation of Western civilization, but ignoring it altogether. Instead of a course on the basics of the international educational and cultural structure, the structure without which neither Stanford University nor the advocate's public could exist, we are offered a mass of material defined in terms of abstract generalities, the *only* stated merit of which is that it has no functional connection with that structure.[47]

My immediate concern is not with the merits of this curriculum change, to which I will return in a minute or two, but with the alarming insouciance of this specific defence of it. The defence seems completely devoid of any suspicion that there might be any such thing as an operative cultural system into which it would make sense to indoctrinate its neophytes – and outside of which, I must insist, neither the formation of the advocate nor the terms of his advocacy would even be thinkable.

The advocacy in question has no obvious connection with the practical world in which policies are framed and put into effect. What it represents is rather the world of disconnected appearances with which we are confronted by the electronic media. One of the things that is beginning to make the very idea of civilization generally invisible, or even unintelligible, is the way these new means of communication tend to eliminate structure. It is predominantly through their mediation that the public world nowadays reaches us; and they work through an egalitarianism of appearances. Whatever appears through them is necessarily shown as equally present, immediate, and actual, just as pictures taken by inexperienced or incautious photographers turn out to be pictures, not of what interested them, but indifferently of everything within the photo frame. A judicial verdict in a criminal case looks and sounds on television no different from a mere expression of arbitrary opinion.[48] Structure and hierarchy may be asserted by the announcer, but the assertion remains merely an assertion alongside the data to which it relates, and may always be countered by a denial. The denial, because it is equally audible and visible, has equal weight.[49] And this insistent destructuring, be it noted, depends absolutely on the elaborated technological and industrial system the effective authority of which it implicitly denies.[50]

Of course, we must not make too much of a single curriculum change, even in California.[51] Besides, as I was saying, what is alarming is not the change itself but the terms of the specific advocacy I quoted, which I found in nothing more authoritative than the correspondence column of a magazine. One could argue, for instance, that undergraduates need no introduction to the operative basis of their own civilization, because if it really is such a basis it can hardly escape their notice.[52] What they do need is precisely what the new course promises: to be aware of the vital alternatives to the imperial superstructure, and to be sensitive to the areas in which the emperor's clothes are thinnest.[53] In any case, historians tell us that these university introductions to Western Civilization were not spontaneous outcroppings of pedagogical conscientiousness. They were introduced in the United States, when that country entered the First World War, as a visible contribution to the war effort, in the hope that their defence of the American Way of Life against the evil ways of the Central Powers would convince government that university funding should not be cut as a patriotic economy measure.[54] They were, and are, self-serving and possibly pernicious humbug.

Once it occurs to us that 'basic civilization' courses may not represent a considered judgment of what incoming students need to know about the foundations of their spiritual heritage so much as what deans can tell politicians is necessary for keeping the citizenry loyal to whatever it is the politicians stand for, we may be in a mood to look less indulgently at their pretensions. It may then occur to us that what is being inflicted on the students is *someone else's* civilization. And if, as is not unlikely, the students are predominantly from a different economic or ethnic group than the professorate, they are being told that they are not merely less well informed but actually of a lower order of humanity than their instructors.[55] Besides, wherever such differences prevail, the official art incorporated in such courses is almost certain to embody and systematize insinuations of the inferiority of the students who are supposed to make it their own.[56]

Whether we approve or disapprove of the backlash against civilization, we should not overestimate its power. It is, after all, only in universities that these doubts are voiced and find a public; and they do so, to a great extent, as part of the ongoing business of the universities themselves.[57] To all appearances, then, the doubts are a sham. Similarly, so far as I can see, multicultural festivals and exchanges, which purportedly undermine the superimperial hegemony, always take place under the auspices of the super-empire itself, of which they are indeed a characteristic manifestation. What we are supposed to be seeing and hearing on such occasions is the authentic and autonomous expression of indigenous cultures that have preserved their integrity despite the homogenizing pressures of the international order. And we do see them – or something like them. But it is the super-empire that provides both the common understanding that makes them thinkable, and the practical arrangements that make them possible.[58] So the very concept of multiculturalism, which is sometimes thought to subvert or dilute imperial hegemonies, in fact endorses them. What multiculturalism means is the compresence of different vital systems within a unifying political and economic framework, and the compresence itself enters into these vital realities and reinforces the quasi-culture that the operation of the framework would itself tend to generate.[59]

Despite all these mitigating factors and built-in corrections, it remains true that the partial realization of world civilization has made it difficult to accept it as an unequivocally valid ideal. The tacky excesses of the

'New Age' amount to a protest against the claims of 'science' to usurp the place of lived experience, a continuation into adult life of the loathed tendency to suppress the *life* of children in favour of *school*.[60] The threat of such usurpation evokes a terror and horror that find realization in the more sentimental extremes of environmentalism, according to which every prospect pleases, and only man is vile.[61] But the truth is that the factors that contribute to that civilization, and the life we live under its auspices, are what we are, and, we suspect, part of what humanity – vile or not – inescapably is. The familiar sequence of economic revolutions – pastoral, agricultural, industrial, and such – is a manifestation of human physical and psychological equipment acting sequentially in situations it discovers and creates; the equipment is what we are, and could not exist without manifesting itself. Our pretended hatred of civilization is self-hatred. And self-hatred cannot usefully be pushed to the point of self-destruction; for, if it were, who would be left to do the hating?

Anyone who reflects on the world today is likely to trace and retrace a maze of pathways through some such drearily familiar but unavoidable mass of reflections as the foregoing. We are left to conclude that the likeliest outcome of our disillusion is a partial and fragmentary and perpetually contested realization of a world order and its associated culture, in varying and unpredicted relation to local cultures and ramshackle empires that are perpetually being eroded and perpetually revived.[62]

Let us cheerfully concede, then, the uncertainty of the future of civilization, and revert to our original question. What, finally, does the future hold for aesthetics? With the dissolution of the idea of civilization must also disappear the notion of high art, the unique symbolic order of imaginative achievement; and when the idea of high art loses its authority aesthetics as an ongoing discipline loses its original reason for being. That loss, however, has no practical consequences for professors of aesthetics and their students, because aesthetics is no less tightly bound up with imperial educational order than are the high arts themselves. The institutional viability of the discipline and the identity of its principal subject matter stand or fall together. The complete discrediting of civilization would, indeed, undermine the claim of aesthetics as we have known it to play an important part in the ideal order of humane learning, because the idea of any such order would have lost all its appeal, if not its intelligibility. Conversely, the survival of empire and the idea of civilization in a fragmented and contested form could be expected to be accompanied by the survival in a comparably modified or attenuated form of a set of high arts. And so long as a set of high arts remains in place, aesthetics as the theory of those arts is sure of its mandate.

But what if the high arts lose all their prestige? As I have already hinted, aesthetics must then yield territory to more democratically hospitable studies: to hermeneutic sociology, semiotics, structural and poststructural anthropology, and rampant deconstruction.[63] But these studies do not do all the work that was done by aesthetics, with its three intertwined lines of inquiry. The power of beauty, and the place of something like beauty among values; the function of the artistic activities of adornment, fiction, and play in the life of the mind; the logic whereby criticism gets from description to evaluation and back – these three deep, underlying problems seem certain to persist as recurrent perplexities for the philosophical mind, in one form or another, even if no discipline is devoted to them and no organized philosophy has a home prepared for them. And the three problems will continue to lead into each other, as they always have when people really think about them. So I suspect, as I said at the start, that aesthetics will always be with us, like a mildew that we scrub away but reappears every time the weather is wet and warm enough.

That really concludes my exploration of my announced topic, the future of aesthetics. So I could really stop here. But have I not left something out? What about doomsday, the imminent ecological apocalypse I mentioned in passing? How can I natter on complacently about the durability of aesthetics, when I have admitted that our colloquy is held under the shadow of death? Dare one just *mention* that human life on earth is about to end, destroyed by self-poisoning, population explosion and mass starvation, pandemics, or things that go bump in the nuclear night – and say no more about it? Actually, one dare. As individuals, we are all mortal; and the earth we all live on must in the fullness of time cease to be hospitable to life. These finitudes are common to all action and discourse. It is foolish to forget them, but useless to talk about them. If I were to do so now, I would be like those tiresome people who accompany all their promises with a caveat like 'God willing' or 'Unless I am run over by a truck.' But philosophers are never deterred by the thought that anything they say might be useless, and seldom refrain from being tiresome, and I did bring the subject up. So I must tackle the doomsday theme somehow.[64]

Thinking about doomsday is thinking about the future. (Doomsday is the future that has no future.) But what *is* the future? That is a conceptual question no less confusing and frustrating than the questions that have been baffling us all week: What is philosophy? What is civilization? But, baffling or not, we have to face it. If I opened my disquisition on the future of aesthetics by explaining what aesthetics is, I cannot bring it to a conclusion without saying what the future is.

But should not the question not rather be, what the future *will be*? No. Just as I could not say what aesthetics will be without saying what aesthetics is, so as to make it clear what I would be talking about, so there can be no question about what the future will be unless the future already *is* something.[65] But of course, the future isn't anything – that's the whole point. That's why I chose the *future* of aesthetics as my topic in the first place. Given that my overall topic was to be aesthetics and the philosophy of art, I could not talk about the present condition of the subject, since after my retirement I was no longer really in touch with that. And I would not talk about the past, because there is too much new stuff in the world for a serious person to be bothered with the old stuff. On the future, however, I have exactly as much hard data as anyone else, and by the time the audience discovered my errors I would be long gone. It remained for me to announce as my topic the future of aesthetics; and that is what I did.

Although my topic was the future, though, I found I had to start with the present, which is what it will be the future of. But that meant I had to deal with the past first, because cultural and scientific and philosophical manifestations are real only as transactions, as what people do; and everything people do they do as a modification of the past. But the specific past they modify is always the past *of the present*, just as biographies are always accounts of how people came to be what we already know they ended up as. The lives the biographies recount for us are made up of the possibilities that we see they failed to reject, and the fatalities that we know they failed to avoid.

From this point of view, it is almost a paradox that the past, which seems so definite because it is what has really taken place, turns out to be elusive because we have to *choose* which paths we shall trace back in time – how the biographies are to be written. The future, which is all up in the air, is more fixed, because it is not ours to choose. Aesthetics is just what it is, and its future is just what will become of that. But the paradox does not quite come off. The future *of aesthetics*, of which I have been speaking, is not what is actually going to happen: it is what present tendencies in aesthetics (and its environment) project. But tendencies do not project; they are projected by people. So it matters who is doing the projecting, who is identifying the tendencies and giving them salience: an old person or a young, a working academic or a spectator.

Projecting tendencies is one way, a systematic way, of predicting. And some predictions are confirmed and others are falsified by what indubitably happens, even if confirmations and disconfirmations are themselves often relative to standpoints and interpretations that not everyone would take or make. So let us brush all that aside (and, if we wish, sweep it under the carpet), and ask: seriously, what about the future?

The ways philosophers and other theorizers talk about the future usually make it seem to belong, together with the present and the past, to a symmetrical tripartition of time: what did happen, what does happen, and what will happen.[66] But the apparent symmetry is deceptive. One retains memories of the past, performs observations of the present, forms expectations about the future. But expectation differs from both memory and observation in that, in a sense, it has no external object. What one really remembers or observes is really there to be observed or remembered. That is notoriously untrue of anything one merely expects.[67]

When I was being instructed in the rudiments of Japanese, they told us that the Japanese language has no future tense: one doesn't say that something *will* happen, but that it is obliged to happen, or is likely to happen. But of course, though our instructor did not mention this, the same argument shows that English has no future tense either: we take the indefinite form of a verb, such as *die*, and prefix it with a verbal auxiliary: 'you will die,' 'you shall die,' 'you are going to die.'[68] If we are to deal with English as my instructor dealt with Japanese, we will have to say that the underlying meaning of these expressions is not a straightforward projection into the future, symmetrical with that of the past form, *died*, or the present, *die*. The English auxiliaries are anchored in present reality: something like present necessitation in 'I *shall* die,' present intention in 'I *will* die,' present tendency in 'I *am going* to die.' What we never have is an inflection of the verb form itself, such as we do find in Latin, from whose grammarians the idea of a future tense was lifted and foisted onto our vernacular.[69] So why bother with doomsday? The English-speaking world has no future anyway.

So much for words. What about facts? People have sometimes said that the future is indeterminate because, for one thing, we haven't yet made up our minds what to do. Will there be a sea battle tomorrow? Nobody knows; we will have to wait until the morning, when the admiral will make his decision after consulting the weather, the auspices, and his hangover.[70] It is through freedom that uncertainty gets into the world. So they say. But is that quite right? A year ago I *knew* I would be here tonight, because I could promise and commit myself. It is not my making of a commitment *then* that causes me to come *now*; but it is because I have kept my engagement continually in mind, and still hold myself bound by it, and have been free to bind myself so, that I am here tonight. Think of what will happen a year from today: so far from being unpredictable, the things that depend on human freedom include, short of astronomy, about the only things we can be reasonably certain of.[71] I can trace a single effective line from present to future. When I look at the past in the same way, though, it proves to be surprisingly indefinite. What I call *the past* is the past of the present as I now choose to interpret it; if I thought of my present differently, I would think of a different past for it, no less well-founded and convincing than the past I now remember.[72] I trace back into the 'dark backward and abysm of time' a sequence of what I can now distinguish as events and situations that seem relevant to what I take to be my present position; but it is only the sequence that gives them determinate reality.[73] I know that in the past there is infinitely more than I am aware of or interested in, stuff that is equally capable of constituting 'the past' for some present actuality that happens not to be mine. But the future has no assignable reality other than the promising and threatening sequences built from my present hopes and dreads – there is no real but indeterminate reservoir to make selections from. From the point of view of this analysis, the past seems more indeterminate than the future.

What has all this to do with doomsday? Well, a book called *Limits to Growth* came out in 1972 and caused a great stir. It calculated the dates at which the non-renewable resources of the planet would be exhausted; petroleum, for instance, would all be gone by the late 1980s.[74] But the computer program the authors used was too simple. It made little allowance for feedback; mostly, it projected present tendencies into the future. A few months later, some other scientists published a refutation.[75] They pointed out that as a resource became scarce it would be used more thriftily and intelligently, alternatives would be sought, it would become economical to look harder for new supplies of it and to use sources hitherto too expensive to exploit.[76] In short, as a situation changes, people begin to behave differently, in all sorts of new ways. These changes are unpredictable, continuous, and cumulative, and their interactions constantly produce new configurations. It is to these ever-new configurations that people react, not to bygone predicaments.[77] The tendencies and saliences that futurists projected a little while ago no longer exist – we cannot even remember what the world looked like back then.[78] So our predictions are stultified by a world we could not even have guessed at, or imagined.[79]

As imminent doom impinges by making noticeable changes in the conditions of some people's existence, they will behave differently because they will feel their situation as different.[80] And they will act, not in the light of the calamity as the futurologists predicted it, but in the light of the specific situation that impinges on them.[81] What that will be, of course, no one can predict, because no one can even imagine what they would be predicting *about*.[82]

The principle I am invoking here is that people always act on the pressures that they feel and perceive as impinging on them.[83] This is a tautology, because all it says is that people act on whatever motivations they have. So, if it is a tautology, how can it be important? Because people ignore it. Not that people deny it; how could they? They simply forget to take it into account. Those of you who, like me, belong to learned societies or similar professional groups will doubtless be familiar with what I have in mind from what happens at the general meetings of such organizations. We members all resolve with enthusiasm to follow some new policy. But, of course, we never do follow it. When we voted for the policy, we imagined ourselves in a future in which the priorities that preoccupied the conference would retain their salience. We simply forgot that when we got back to work we would be returning to the same demands, opportunities, obligations, constraints, and commitments that we had before, as well as to new urgencies that would unavoidably confront us. We did not remind ourselves forcibly enough that, among all these, the resolution we so enthusiastically passed at our conference, however important we might still think it, could not possibly be more than one of the factors we must take into account. It could absorb all our attention at the conference just because, in order to attend the meeting, we had to leave our everyday preoccupations on one side. Or again, consider a coroner's jury looking into a disaster, making perhaps a dozen recommendations for regulations by which similar disasters might be averted in future. Excellent recommendations, no doubt; but hundreds of earlier juries will have made equally excellent recommendations to avert other kinds of disasters.[84] The cumulative outcome is likely to be a book hundreds of pages thick, with thousands of regulations, each one of which is to be complied with whenever anything is done. Operatives confronted by this book cannot be preoccupied with the regulations guarding against any one kind of disaster. What is more, they cannot afford to be *preoccupied* with the totality of all the regulations together, since the overriding reality is that there is a job that must somehow get done.[85] Even if a government sets up a bureaucracy with an inspectorate expressly designed to stimulate such one-sided preoccupation by direct and continuous enforcement of the policy in question, it will prove unable to do so. The inspectorate, functioning in the real world, is certain to be subject to the same conditions of action as the operatives subject to its control: it, too, will be working in specific situations that exert other pressures that cannot be ignored. If I may say so without unseemly partisanship: our premier Mike Harris's commonsense revolution is anything but commonsense,[86] to the extent that it consists of policies that are to be followed in the light of a situation *as it was diagnosed long beforehand,* without regard to the developing situations with which the government and its unfortunate agents will actually have to deal. Politicians who insist on keeping election promises are a new and alarming breed ...

Practical policy makers often go wrong because they forget the tautology that people act on what they perceive as impinging on them. This includes the commitments they remember they have made, the obligations they acknowledge, the moral principles they adhere to, and the laws they live by, which impinge no less directly and sometimes no less urgently than their plans and desires, the emergencies that arise, and the specific demands that are constantly being made of them.[87] Theorists, on the other hand, often go wrong, not by forgetting our tautology, but by adding to it, specifying what the pressures have to be and how they are perceived and handled. 'People always act to maximize their own interests,' they say. Or, 'What people do shows what their principles really are.' Or, 'People always respond to the stimuli provided by the situation that confronts them.[88] Or, if they don't, they should.' It is as if these thinkers believed that by such pontifications they could somehow eliminate most of the substance of our lives from consideration, or reorganize it, or analyse it away. One sees the point and value of these theoretical concoctions, especially in first-year ethics classes when students have to be got into the way of standing back from the turbid stream of their lives and testing the water. I used to use them myself. But as soon as one gets away from the classroom context, what strikes one is the extraordinary silliness of almost all moral philosophy.[89] If I had another lifetime before me, and if by some mischance I were condemned to spend it in an academic environment, I think I might spend a decade or two on the hitherto unexplored problem of how to do ethics without being silly about it.

Now, how do all these reflections affect the argument I was developing? People, I am saying, act in the light of the considerations they find important in the situations they find themselves in, as they interpret them; and both the situations and the interpretations develop historically in ways that cannot be foreseen. All the things I have said about the future of aesthetics, and about the global tendencies that will affect that future, even though my generalizations are the outcome of a lifetime of study and reflection, are nothing but a residue, a froth that has come to the surface of my mind under the stimulus of a speaking engagement, working on a backlog of unpublished or uncollected papers, my recent reading, and the random churnings of my daily ruminations. But even if my memory were unimpaired, my powers of synthesis and analysis intact, my insight deeper, and my wit sharper, my best projections of a future for aesthetics would still be useless. No one can guess what things are going to be like. Come to think of it, neither aesthetics nor civilization is the kind of thing that can *have* a future.[90] Being deeply historical phenomena, they can only have pasts. But, you may be protesting, can't they have future perfects?[91] May there not be conditions which, from an even more distant future, will be seen to *have been* part of the history of civilization, or of aesthetics? Maybe. But in a radically changed world, how could any phenomenon then present be identifiable as what we now call aesthetics? Such identification requires that our descendants should be able to understand what our word 'aesthetics' meant. But if the changes in the world are radical enough, how could that be possible? The only hopeful answer has to be that aesthetics, like philosophy generally, is a rational pursuit, arising from a reasoned inquiry into the foundations of human thought. If that is the case, it will remain a permanent possibility, so long as its starting points are accessible – that is, not seen to be either false or self-contradictory. But those starting points may not be *readily* accessible (for instance, not without painful historical reconstruction), and there may be no point from which any substitute for them can be easily reached. And, if it could, it might not seem worth reaching. Philosophy, I said earlier, is intrinsically unavoidable, because a question opened and unsolved remains open. The history of philosophy seems to show this. Usually, a little study enables us to follow the developing history of philosophical debate and analysis. We can see the point of what was said, and the reasons for saying it remain as good as they ever were.[92] But the *practice* of philosophy is very easily avoidable; and for aesthetics that holds a fortiori, in spades, doubled. No doubt, at many future times, much will go on that we would now call aesthetics, and that could be fitted somehow into what I have been talking about. But what it will be, and when, and whether any of it will be given the name 'aesthetics,' and what the name will imply if it *is* used, is more than anyone can say.

Some weeks ago, as I was preparing this part of my lectures, I had a dream. In this dream I had left my family and friends in a predicament, and had gone to seek rescue.[93] But I lost my way. At last I woke up, or thought I did, because I said to myself: 'I must go back to sleep, and finish my dream, or my friends will be in their predicament for ever, with no one to rescue them.' Even before I came fully awake, I knew that what I was dreaming about was these lectures.[94] But I also knew it was all right really. You are not in my dream and do not need me to rescue you. And you certainly do not want to sit here while I tell you about my dreams.

So here we finally are, what's left of us, as we were on Monday, awake in the same room together, coming from our different experiences and our various preparations, in our varying relations to the tattered educational system of our part of the forest. One thing about the future is certain: that never, till the sun explodes, will we all meet in this room again. So it is time for me to remind you that whatever aesthetics may be, whatever philosophy may be, whatever civilization may be, they are all sustained, if they are sustained at all, by people like us: intellectual animals to be sure, social animals, but animals first of all, in the vicissitudes that carry our bodies from generation through nutrition and excretion, copulation and reproduction, through dissolution to death, through all the sensations and encounters and impacts, the acquisitions and losses and lettings-go – 'the sweet, normal, stolid matrix of the merely human.'[95] Aesthetics and the rest are real, perfectly real, as real as anything could be, because we do sustain them and they are sustained. But they are sustained by the likes of *us*.

And now, after all our labours lost and won, it is time for us to carry our diverse memories and understandings away with us as we disperse, you that way, I this way.

Afterword

The lectures have been moving toward their final sentences, the dispersal of the audience and their separation from the lecturer with the valediction from that enigmatic play *Love's Labour's Lost*. Our attention is brought back to our situation, the compresence of strangers at an academic discourse. Who has been talking? Whom was the audience hearing?

The Danish journalist-theologian Søren Kierkegaard notoriously wrote several of his books under 'pseudonyms.' The point of these was that they had to be recognized by the reader as Kierkegaard-writing-pseudonymously-and-pretending-to-be-pretending-to-be-someone-else. Naturally, he found it necessary to write an essay titled 'The Point of View for My Work as an Author,' to give a self-serving and disingenuous (or creatively fictive) explanation of this singular posturing.[1] The underlying assumption was that Kierkegaard was a terribly important person and it was terribly important for the world to understand what he was up to. The underlying assumption of this afterword of mine is not like that. It can only be that every academic lecture represents a real or simulated encounter between speaker and listeners, in which the speaker takes up an implied stance. Or rather, that such a stance must be being implied for each member of the audience.

A lecture is a real event, and a communication event, so there must be some real communication. Stances have to be taken in a real position. All lectures are made by some real person from whom they issue and to whom they relate, and are heard (and later read) by real people who receive them into their personal selves, and into whose reception some reading of the lecturer's stance must enter. Audience, lecturer, or both, may emphasize, or mask, or falsify, or ignore these quasi-personal factors, but they are inevitably present. In the slow process of composition,

or of revision for delivery, or of remodelling for print, as in the readers'
faster processes of listening, reading, rereading, and reflecting, changes
of many different kinds will take place in the stance being adopted, or in
the recollection and reconstruction of the stance originally intended or
revised, or ... What more is there to say?

I have increasingly come to view philosophy as a many-sided swarm
of discourse in which there are many conversational encounters: everyone talks to someone, no one talks to everyone, but the living mass of talk
has a history in which no voice is definitively lost and no voice dominates
for ever or without dissent. Out of this mass, trends emerge and are what
we recognize, permanently or for the time being, as history. On the
whole, the debate settles down into something reasoned and reasonable:
to understand philosophy, one has to be able to grasp the reasons that
have been given at different times for different positions. Ability to cope
with this massive interactive reasonableness is something that can be
nurtured and developed. That is what makes philosophy possible as a
living discipline.

All lecturers and all audiences are engaged in an interplay of imperfect
communication. My feeling about this matter is dominated by an image
that is often present to me: that of the earth, with its billions of swarming
humanity, a partially clouded spheroid as seen from an orbiting satellite.
As one approaches, one's vision encompasses smaller and smaller areas
until at last it is filled by the street where one lives.[2] In the end, I see
myself as a householder known to some but not to others of the neighbours among whom he lives and walks, and as one animal among so
many emerging from and returning to the mass of organic matter, just as
I am one academic voice emerging from and returning to the intermina-
ble discourse of reason.[3]

Alongside the image that has an eye zeroing in from outer space to
detect me at last as one human in an ordinary place among the members
of a numerous species, I have been haunted by the poet Langland's image
of *a fair field full of folk,* as he sees it in dream 'on a May morning on
Malvern hills.'[4] I have envisioned a field in which I make one among so
many. But what Langland describes is a field in which each takes his or
her own place, working or wandering: a field that makes distinct places
possible. Without some such map, one could not meaningfully claim a
place – there would be no places to claim.

Langland, awake or asleep, is not in the field. As poet of his poem, he
looks down on it from the hills. As a lecturer, for the time being, I cannot
maintain the stance of simply one person talking to other people on a

particular occasion. I implicitly claim a higher ground. I stand on the podium, they sit at desks. But what academic formalities represent is not the arrogance of this claim, but its modesty. I am an authority only in the classroom or on the library shelf, in a context that has no vital signifi- cance. My hearers and readers need feel neither threatened by my author- ity nor indignant at my presumption.[5] I can get out into the real world only by climbing down from the podium to the classroom floor, and leaving the classroom – and the school, and the schoolyard – by the same doors and gates as the rest of the class.

What is the point of view for my work as an author? The question must arise; but need it be answered? Unlike Kierkegaard, most authors accept that the viewpoint must show itself in the perspectives implicit in what is said. In the present case, though, a stance intruded itself insistently toward the end of the final lecture. Not only did the moment of parting inevitably call for a personal note that had to be suppressed if not acknowledged, but the concluding remarks had made it plain that dis- course about the future, more conspicuously than other discourse, must issue from a viewpoint. And the lecturer's viewpoint must have been emphasized when the lecturer was first introduced to his audience: that of a professional academic, once active but now elderly and well past retirement. Three things follow from that. First, being no longer subjected to the daily pressures of disciplinary practice, the lecturer is more in- clined to talk *about* aesthetics and philosophy than to engage in them directly. Second, by the same token, being no longer immersed in the reflective pedagogic conversation where words like 'civilization,' 'art,' and 'philosophy' have to be common coin, the lecturer finds himself less and less able to understand what that conversation was all about. And, third, the future spoken of is coloured by the future that more and more closely confronts the elderly: dissolution, impotence, and death. So the last lecture sees the future of aesthetics under the shadows of the end of our Western civilization, the end of civilization itself, the end of life on earth. It would have been dishonest to let this book go before the public without acknowledging that all these personal and public dissolutions are being used as, in a way, metaphors for one another. At the same, though, it has to be acknowledged that the lecturer's stance is also that of someone who has been invited to say his say, by people who must have known what his say was likely to be; so it would be no less dishonest to pretend that the implicit viewpoint must invalidate what is seen and said from it.

So much for the 'point of view for my work as a lecturer' on this occasion. But what about my work as an author? Is there anything that needs to be said about that? Perhaps not: academic work is an accepted way of making a living, aesthetics is an accepted academic specialism, and academics are expected to write about their specialisms. My specialism is what I was told to teach when I started work, and the nature and extent of my published output was determined by the gaps in that specialism that seemed from time to time to need filling.

That may be the only story we need, but it cannot be the whole story. Why was I so sensitive to those gaps, and so industrious in filling them? It must have been that I found the incompleteness, the fragmentation and deformity, the overall messiness, the inconclusiveness of the argumentation, offensive. In terms of the classical, scholastic definition of beauty I mentioned in my first lecture, I was offended by the intellectual ugliness of the philosophy of art and beauty – its lack of wholeness and coherent order, its lack of *shine*. Like all philosophers, I detested fallacies; like all professors, I abhorred all errors other than my own; but, beyond that, it seems that I must have been driven by that passion for beauty on which my first lecture also insisted.[6] I suppose my department chairman, needing someone to teach aesthetics, detected this hunger in me when he picked me out as a suitable victim – it may not have been *only* that I was his most junior appointee, and the least able to protest.

Only, what sort of beauty was it that I had a passion for? The concept of beauty has, after all, an uncertain purchase on our minds. Socrates in Plato's *Philebus* remarks that a perfect circle (as defined in geometry) is the very paradigm of beauty, in its flawless elegance and self-containedness; but, even to the most refined taste, circles are somehow lacking in appeal. Hegel observes that the natural beauties of flowers and seashells, however breathtaking, are less deeply satisfactory than the created beauties of art, beauties 'born again' through the mind, in which the Idea takes form. (That is to say: in a mature work of art, the whole culture and civilization of its origin is embodied, expressed, represented; in a flower or a seashell, the shaping forces of nature are demonstrated and exemplified, but not expressed. The natural object, unlike the work of art, has no meaning.)

There is one sort of form, whether it is called beautiful or not, that I find has a special attraction for me. It is exemplified in one of my favourite objects. This is a piece of bone, which I picked up on the shore at Winnipeg Beach. It is clearly a section of a long bone of some large mammal, presumably bovine, near the joint. The curved surfaces of the bone show, I suppose, where tendons fitted: the overall shape reflects lost needs of support and tension. Where the bone has been cut off, the internal form is revealed: the bone is tunnelled to make a cave with two entrances, whose walls are intricately honeycombed for lightness. Like Wordsworth at the leech-gatherer's pool, I have measured it from side to side. It is about three inches each way. I can easily tell you what sort of a shape it is. It is just the sort of bone shape that Henry Moore chose for his carvings. But it is not like anything Moore could have carved. What made it the shape it is was, first, the DNA-directed stresses that made it the functioning support in the leverage system of the bullock's leg; second, the strokes of the butcher's cleaver that cut the three-inch slice that ran through the steak; and, third, when the negligent barbecuer had thrown the bone onto the beach, the long-drawn grinding of waves and wind-blown sand that smoothed edges and rounded corners until it became this entrancingly formed gem that will be my treasure until I die and my heirs consign it at last to the municipal trash.

What these things that so delight me have in common is that the resultant charm of form is, and is plainly seen to be, the outcome of a succession of disparate formative agencies, an accidental and gratuitous interest or pathos. In a way, this is like the special pathos of a ruin in which the quarryman's excavation, the architect's plan, the builders' construction, the besieger's destruction, are all overtaken by earthquake, tempest, and moss. But only in a way. A ruin as an object of romantic reflection typically provokes a pleasing melancholy. To me, that is only a very special case of something more profound: the endlessly complex fascination of the harmonies and dissonances that result from multiple forces working together on the material world.[7]

When I reflect on them now, it occurs to me that many of my shorter poems issue from the same sense of form – in the terms of my first lecture, the compulsion of the same promise of beauty. A poem starts from something seen or remembered, a musical phrase or rhythm, or a verbal phrase. It becomes a poem, not by its own development, but by being caught up with some different impetus, in connection with which it takes on a development toward an implicit completion as a poem, a verbal structure with all that it implies.[8] It is this structure that has to be teased out, waited for, listened for. But when the poem is done, it does not appear as finished, but as a terminal node in the development to which it belongs. It is neither complete nor incomplete, in this world that is inhospitable to the very idea of completion.[9] The status of the poem is equivocal. It is what it had it in it to be, and is what my felt obligation to the poem required me to rest in, but I often have a strong sense that it exists rather as the accidental end of its compromised trajectory. It is almost as if it were like a person, who is, at the end of a lifetime, nothing but what the accidents and projects of that lifetime have arrived at, in the evasive wholeness that people have.

The kind of formal beauty I have in mind, clearly identifiable as a value in the 'beauty' part of my spectrum of operative values,[10] is to be found equally in natural processes and in human creations, in both of which disparate formative and deforming processes intersect and conspire, and very often in processes that involve nature and artifice together.[11] In any case, the resulting process is, in the terms of traditional romantic theory, 'organic' rather than 'mechanical,' a growth rather than a construction. But it is not, as that theory would have had it, like the growth of one beast or plant from a single unfolding stock; it is more like the developing of an ecological unit in which interdependent plants and animals produce their web of interacting life.

I am reminded here of what Aristotle took to be his own great discovery in cosmology (*Metaphysics*, Book I). You can't construct a model of a cosmos like ours, he found, with its constancies and continuous variations, if you postulate only one basic kind of matter, and/or only one kind of process, however much subsequent variation you introduce. To generate a cosmos, you have to have different forces operating independently in relation to each other. The cosmos we know is very different from the cosmos Aristotle thought he saw; but it is still one in which recognizable forms and processes stem from the interaction of forces that resist the efforts of physicists to reduce them to each other.

It now occurs to me, as it should have done from the beginning, that the same sort of procedure that I have traced in my poetry permeates my work in philosophy as well, where it may seem out of place. My books tend to consist of asymmetrical and intractable masses of material only partially ordered. Such order as they have points to the process of their ordering, just as my arguments fade away into accounts of how arguments may be supported and met. Argumentation is, to me, almost a tactile medium. Rigorous demonstration, popular as it is among the most respected enclaves in the philosophical community, has something ludicrous about it: language doesn't and can't work like that.[12] Make no mistake, if one is to do philosophy one has to do a lot of syllogizing and such; it is not the search for formal system that is preposterous, but the pretence that one can rest in it.

The one you are just at the end of represents the intersection of two systems. One is the sequential expansion of that notion, formulated over some decades of reflection but never pursued, that aesthetics as a discipline arises from the persistent convergence and divergence of three radically different lines of inquiry. (Aesthetics itself, as thus interpreted, exemplifies just the sort of imperfect form I have been discussing, in which the eventual form is a transient and unstable outcome of heterogeneous forces.) The other system, in which the first is embedded, is the penetration of layer upon layer of intellectual and cultural structures within which such a discipline can be supported.

The poorly integrated dyad of these intersecting systems has been incorporated here in a double presentation: a more or less consecutive exposition of the material integral to the project, and a mass of annotation, some of it contributing to the project as such, but much of it contributing to my actual project in this book only by being an essential part of it. An essential feature of this material is that it is non-linear. Each note springs up autonomously in its place. The figure in the text from which it dangles shows where that place is, but determines nothing about how that place is to be filled. Within the annotation there are subsidiary, recurrent themes about which I have nothing to say here. But there is more: texts scattered throughout the book hint that it is to be taken as essentially involving and inviting reflection on its own procedures, both as a series of lectures by a stranger to strangers and as a philosophical meditation. And this afterword has invited us to take the book's reflection as a parable of retirement from the university and the world, with an ageing brain's shift of data-processing procedures and a former functionary's disengagement from professional and political participations. But then, finally, such paragraphs as the present invite you to consider all these ramifications as fictions of an author who is partly manipulating and partly imagining them, in a text that may well be perfectly transparent to you and utterly opaque to him.[13]

In this afterword, I have been dwelling on a certain sort of beauty that seems from my early years to have had a hold on my mind and my sensibility. The distinctive nature of this apparent beauty may account for some of the characteristics of my work; the compelling power it shares with other beauties, both perceived and promised, demanding to be brought into being, may account for its unseemly abundance. It is not the beauty envisaged by Baumgarten when he conjured aesthetics into existence; it is not the beauty recognized by Kant in his account of aesthetic judgment; and it is not the beauty stipulated by Augustine as fulfilling the mind's hunger for intactness, completeness, and the radiance of form. But it is indeed beauty, according to the formula of Thomas Aquinas: it is a value fully realized in cognition.

And that is really the last thing I have to say about the future of aesthetics.

Notes

Introductory Note

1 Ferdinand in Shakespeare's *Loues Labour's lost*, I. (All quotations from this play keep to the text of the First Folio, 1623 [New Haven, CT: Yale University Press, 1954].)

I: Aesthetics and the Future of Philosophy

1 Aesthetics was once unambiguously a part of philosophy, but is now interdisciplinary; of the disciplines whose functionaries conceive themselves and are conceived by others as contributing to aesthetics, some belong to what in a more relaxed age counted as domains of philosophy, others do not. This only means that, beauty being ubiquitous and the arts omnivorous, people of many different professional and personal interests wish to discuss beauty and the arts in general terms. It remains true that aesthetics as a distinctive object of intellectual endeavour is rooted in the distinctive concerns and methods of philosophy and sustained by them.

2 It is this cohesiveness that only serious long-term students of philosophy know, because only they know how what is contestable can be debated. This knowledge is called 'dialectic,' and most people take a long time to acquire it. People who have not done so mostly think that philosophy consists of silly people saying silly things, always struggling toward truth and never getting there. It was with this in mind that the proconsul L. Gellius Poplicola in 69 B.C.E. convened the philosophers of Athens and 'urgently advised them to come at length to some settlement of their controversies. He promised his best efforts to aid them in coming to some agreement' (Cicero *De Legibus* I 53). I suppose it was a joke; the proconsul

probably knew that depth in understanding comes from learning what the debatable issues are, and what there is to be said in favour of both sides of them – or, at least, he knew that this is what the philosophers believed. There is, however, a serious point to be made here. We are always sliding back, and each of us as an individual has to start from personal scratch. Since the philosophers of Poplicola's day were almost certainly less intelligent than Plato, the ends of their lives would have found them further behind than he got to be. And there seem to be ages when philosophy slips backward, when the educational ambiance deteriorates to a point where nobody now knows what everybody once knew. Still, the old debates recur in ever new forms, traditional positions are argued from ever new vantage points as new sources of error and obscurity are uncovered. Most importantly, this is what truth and clarity are: the ideal implicit in actual removals of error and folly and ignorance. To know this, one has to understand what it is that has to be known, and this understanding comes only with prolonged, serious, and candid labour in a demanding intellectual field. It is something that Poplicola could never know.

3 Alexander Gottlieb Baumgarten, *Meditationes Philosophicae de Nonnullis ad Poema Pertinentibus* (Halle, 1735), translated by K. Aschenbrenner and W.B. Hoelther as *Reflections on Poetry* (Berkeley: University of California Press, 1954). Baumgarten was twenty-one years old; it was his thesis; he was writing against the clock, his brother correcting his Latin and helping to write out the fair copy. A few years later he published two volumes with the title *Ästhetik*, which established the name of the fledgling discipline. Giorgio Tonelli's brief article on Baumgarten in Paul Edwards's *Encyclopedia of Philosophy* (New York: Macmillan, 1967) is excellent.

4 Seen in this light, Derrida's deconstructionism strikes a deadly blow to the fundamental premise of aesthetics by reducing significance to a play of 'signifiers' without 'signifieds.' Signs refer only to other signs: if you ask someone what a word means, the answer is always a string of words, each of which can be 'explained' only by another string of words. Explanation never escapes from this verbal tracery: contact with the extra-verbal world is for ever deferred, while we proceed through the maze of verbal differentiations. (It's no use showing pictures or examples, because they are unintelligible without verbiage to explain what one is to look at.) But Derrida's trick doesn't work. In Saussure's terminology, on which he is relying, a signifier without a signified could not even be identified as a sign. People sometimes say that Derrida and his compeers have elaborated and sophisticated Saussure's system, but they haven't; they have simply failed to grasp its basics (typically, they confuse a signified with a referent, even

when they pretend to know the difference). Derrida's abiding achievement in this area is his recognition that Saussure himself cannot explain what a signified is (for the reason given above), which leaves his theory of language up in the air. (In the English-speaking world, neither linguists nor philosophers are committed to Saussure, though students of literary theory, unaware of their favourite theorists' rather endearing bias in favour of texts composed in the French language, seem not to know this.)

My linking of Locke and Descartes with Leibniz as movers in the revolutionary new 'way of ideas' may be set against D'Alembert's 'Introduction' to the *Encyclopédie*, which joins the same two philosophers with Bacon and Newton as harbingers of another (and, to his mind, more significant) revolution, that of scientific modernism. But then, Newton could be divorced from Locke (and perhaps from Descartes) and allied with Galileo in yet another revolutionary movement, the inauguration of mathematical/experimental science as we know it.

5 See especially Benedetto Croce's *Estetica come scienza dell'espressione e linguistica generale* (Bari: Laterza, 1902), translated as *Aesthetic as the Science of General Linguistic* by Douglas Ainslie (second edition; London: Macmillan, 1915). This work formed part of an elaborate system, which has been largely ignored in the English-speaking world, and without which it is seriously misunderstood, being equated with R.G. Collingwood's Humean adaptation in his *Principles of Art* (Oxford: Clarendon Press, 1938).

6 Gilbert Ryle himself objected to aesthetics, but ostensibly not on these grounds. His avowed objection was that the study was spurious from the beginning, arising (he affected to believe) from nothing more than the existence of a Greek word (*aisthēsis*) from which the name of a discipline might be coined. Like many Oxford philosophers, though, he really knew (or would admit to knowing) nothing at all about aesthetics; a posture exacerbated in his case by an affectation of philistinism so extreme that he refused in later life to admit that he had ever crossed the threshold of Malloney's Art Gallery, despite our reassurance that the establishment in question was a bar (one of the few in Toronto in 1950, where some of his former students had indeed plied him with refreshment one December night) and entirely unsullied by art of any kind.

7 Aquinas uses the formula *pulchrum est quod visum placet*; or, more precisely, *pulchrum dicatur id cuius ipsa apprehensio placet* (*Summa Theologiae* Ia Iae 27.1 ad 3). Beauty is the sum of those values or satisfactions that are yielded immediately in cognitive operations directed to the object. There is an elegant account of the scholastic theory of beauty by Armand Maurer: *About Beauty: A Thomistic Interpretation* (Notre Dame: University of Notre Dame

Press, 1984). Some Thomist authors – notably Etienne Gilson – call the theory 'callology,' expressly to distinguish it from the theory of artistic beauty.

8 A poem may not be judged a fine sonnet, or even a fine poem; it may simply be found and judged fine, simply beautiful. But the judgment will certainly be made by someone who knows very well that it is a poem, and probably by someone who recognizes also that it is a sonnet, and is in the habit of reading poems and sonnets for such beauty as they may have.

9 Kant's use of his Scottish contemporaries is extensively discussed in the notes to James Creed Meredith's translation of the *Critique of Aesthetic Judgment* (Oxford: Clarendon Press, 1911). (Like most of his contemporaries, Kant seems at best only fitfully aware of the difference between Scottish and English culture.)

10 At the time of writing, state support of the arts is under attack in many countries. The real reason for this may be that such expenditures buy few votes in the elections that preoccupy our governments, but the justification offered is that these expensive arts merely cater to the tastes of a socially privileged class. It is not only that they are not felt to sustain the social order in any way, but rather that there is no such thing as a social order to be maintained. I return to this topic in the third and fourth lectures.

11 There seems to be no real reason to reject the tradition that makes the *Epinomis* a compilation by Philip of Opus from Plato's leavings, but few people rely on its authority. It seems fairly safe to ascribe it to Plato's circle. The relevant placing of the 'arts of imagination' is taken up by Aristotle in his *Poetics*, but without the general classification of arts to which that placing belonged; and it is Aristotle's treatment that has been influential. I return to this topic in Lecture II.

12 I say 'teasingly' because Diotima's speech in praise of love seems to me to be satirically intended, using an overblown version of the kind of language used of 'the good' in the *Republic* without the intellectual context that justifies what is said there. Most people miss the satire because they don't notice the absence of that context, never having realized that it was there. They take the flatulent verbiage in the *Symposium* for philosophy because it is, after all, just the sort of thing they would write if they were Plato. (It is when Socrates starts preaching that they think Plato must be serious. Surely the opposite is the case.)

13 Hippias has been judging a poetry competition – his assignment was to judge which poem was most 'beautiful.' Socrates asks him to define beauty, which he is unable to do. The two philosophers end with a version of the definition of beauty that would be given by Aquinas (see note 7 above), though the reader is hardly likely to believe that this has much to do with

whatever criteria Hippias actually used in judging the contest. Meanwhile, Hippias and Socrates freely use in their conversation the Greek word for 'beauty' itself (*kalon*), which is a common word with many colloquial uses (like 'fine' and 'OK') – uses which their conversation about the meaning of the word completely fails to notice.

In my student days, it was fashionable to think of the *Greater Hippias* as not a genuine work of Plato – apparently for no better reason than that Plato wrote a shorter dialogue, also called *Hippias*, which the pundits preferred. A new translation with commentary by Paul Woodruff (Indianapolis: Hackett, 1982) has planted the ball in the other court; it is those who would deny its authenticity who have to give good reasons.

14 'Enlightenment is man's departure from his self-incurred immaturity. Immaturity is inability to use one's own understanding without the guidance of another' – 'What Is Enlightenment?,' opening words (Immanuel Kant, *Foundations of the Metaphysics of Morals* and *What Is Enlightenment?*, trans. Lewis White Beck [Indianapolis: Liberal Arts Press, 1959]). Note the word 'departure,' *Ausgang*: the implication is that enlightenment is progress, but not indefinite progress – rather, it is an irreversible transition from one stage to another. Note also that enlightenment represents not the substitution of reason for experience, but the substitution of one's own understanding for that of somebody else. People who nowadays use 'enlightenment' as a term of abuse do not seem to mean quite what Kant means: for instance, the rejection of 'enlightenment' as the mask of Terror, popular among French intellectuals who like to think of the specific phenomena of the French Revolution as somehow archetypical for all human history, has nothing to do with independence of judgment and everything to do with ideological paranoia. (Daniel Gordon's argument, amounting to demonstration, that the French enlightenment was a phenomenon peculiar to the *ancien régime* and that the political revolution owed nothing to the *philosophes*, seems unlikely to make headway against this prejudice any time soon – Daniel Gordon, *Citizens without Sovereignty: Equality and Sociability in French Thought, 1670–1789* [Princeton: Princeton University Press, 1994].) The objection to Kant's formulation is rather that the 'somebody else' for whose judgment the individual's autonomous thought is to be substituted is never really another individual, but the accumulated wisdom of mankind or of one's own ancestry – the 'grandmothers' who traditionally bear authority among the Ojibway.

Kant's reference to the present age as an age of criticism is in the preface to the first edition of the *Critique of Pure Reason* – *Unser Zeitalter ist das eigentliche Zeitalter der Kritik, der sich alles unterwerfen muß* (A xi, note).

15 It must never be forgotten that Plato's writings, full of many-levelled ironies which, we feel, are forever eluding us, are dialogues among characters of whom we sense that they are never fully revealed. He is presumably the author of the whole of his dialogues, not only of those parts he assigns to the character 'Socrates.' The world awaits a satisfactory study of the non-Socratic contributions in Plato's dialogues that have played a part in philosophic thought. Meno's contextualization of virtue forms an important part of Aristotelian ethics; Peter Geach has pointed out that there is much to be said for Euthyphro's version of piety; Protagoras makes good points about civic virtue; Thrasymachus is refuted but never eliminated – even Hippias's robust equation of beauty with the beauty of a beautiful woman has more to be said for it than Socrates allows. Simple dismissal of such positions as errors belongs to a quest for dogmatic orthodoxy in credal assertion rather than for philosophical insight (compare note 2, above). Socratic truth emerges only in dialectical relation to the misguided dogmas of his interlocutors, which are refuted but not eliminated.

I say that this oversimplified reading only 'partly' explains the failure to notice the presence of this threefold inquiry in Plato, because a greater part may be played by the unfashionabless of axiological inquiry, which is such that many of today's philosophers do not even notice when such inquiry is being carried on.

16 What 'giving satisfaction' (or 'pleasing') comes down to, and whether there are other values than those definable in terms of satisfaction, is of course also a question (a mind-numbing one).

17 *Tria requiruntur* – 'three things are needful.' Necessary conditions? Necessary ingredients? Necessary aspects? It is a matter for debate, such as medieval scholasticism delighted in.

18 'Three things are required for beauty. The first is completeness or perfection; for anything that is stunted is by that very fact ugly. Also, due proportion or harmony. And, again, radiance; so that things which have a bright colour are said to be beautiful.' – Thomas Aquinas, *Summa Theologiae* I. 39. 8. This formulation seems to be borrowed from Augustine's specification of three requirements of perfection: measure, form, and order (*De Natura Boni* iii–iv). (I filch all this from my book *The Structure of Aesthetics* [Toronto: University of Toronto Press, 1963], chapter 3 – I used to know all this stuff.)

19 *Critique of Judgment*, §59. Theories that 'form follows function' are mostly degenerate variants of this idea. The most significant version, from our point of view, is Francis Hutcheson's contention that providence has endowed humanity with an innate sense of beauty, a tendency to recognize

and prefer the functional to the dysfunctional in both organic and instrumental forms (*Inquiry into the Originals of Our Ideas of Beauty and Virtue* [Edinburgh, 1725]). Hutcheson's innovation was to reconcile the conviction that the innate human sense of beauty relates to perceived functionality with the acknowledgment that this same 'sense' can be educated or perverted to artificially cultivated tastes.

20 There is a tendency to contrast lawfulness with all the others: something is unlawful if a society happens to forbid it, it is a mere matter of opinion, but all the other five are grounded in our experience of reality. This thesis, in the form of a general contrast between nature (*phusis*) and convention (*nomos*), was all the rage when Plato was a young man. It is debatable, but the difference between decreed values and discovered values has an obvious plausibility.

21 See Jerome Stolnitz, 'On the Origins of "Aesthetic Disinterestedness,"' *Journal of Aesthetics and Art Criticism* 20, 1961, 131–43. There was some debate a few years ago about whether the love of beauty could be disinterested: art-lovers are, after all, interested in art. But it was retorted that this was no more than an equivocation: people who spoke of disinterestedness were taking the word 'interest' as we use it in 'conflict of interest,' to refer to some direct or indirect contribution to the agent's advantage. Perhaps we should only say that the value of beauty is characterized by its *apparent* lack of any connection to the agent's well-being; debates about the possibility of this lack of connection, what kind of connection is relevant, and so on, are to be construed as debates about the nature of beauty and its status as an authentic value, not about whether the apparent disinterestedness is the distinctive feature of beauty.

22 Leo Tolstoy, *What Is Art?* (1898), translated by Aylmer Maude, World's Classics edition (London: Oxford University Press, 1930), 87–91. Tolstoy simply takes it for granted that Russian *krasotá* is the equivalent of the words ('beauty,' *beau*, etc.) that it is used to translate in other European languages.

23 That concepts are established by the enumeration and classification of what they are to cover just as much as they initially determine their content is a principle already laid down in Plato's *Philebus*.

24 'O how love I thy law! it is my meditation all the day ... How sweet are thy words unto my taste! yea, sweeter than honey to my mouth!' (Psalm 119, 97 & 103 AV).

25 'Zwei Dinge erfüllen das Gemüt mit immer neuer und zunehmenden Bewunderung und Ehrfurcht, je öfter und anhaltender sich das Nachdenken damit beschäftigt: *Der bestirnte Himmel über mir, und das*

moralische Gesetz in mir ... [I]ch sehe sie vor mir und verknüpfe sie unmittelbar mit dem Bewußtsein meiner Existenz' – I. Kant, *Kritik der Praktischen Vernunft*, opening words. The point is that both of these put me in immediate touch with the infinite and eternal, hence with the sublime (not with the beautiful, in the strict and narrow sense). Plato and Aristotle had no reverence for the infinite, which to them was a shapeless mess; the taste for infinity had to wait for a theology involving a transcendent Creator. The concept of the sublime is introduced in ancient literary theory (illustrated by the injunction 'Let there be light!' in the Judaeo-Christian scriptures ['Longinus' *On the Sublime* ix 9]) to account for what evoked the sort of evaluative response distinctive of beauty in the spectrum of values, without having the characteristics of the finitely beautiful. The association of the sublime with the infinite is to be contrasted with Socrates' superficially analogous encomium on 'beauty itself' [*auto to kalon*] in Plato's *Symposium*, 211E: 'suppose it were to befall someone to see Beauty itself, without alloy, impurity, or admixture' [*eilikrines, katharon, ameikton*]: beauty here is not infinitely great, but absolute, without limitation only in the sense that it is without defect.

26 Cf. *Foundations of the Metaphysics of Morals*, chapter 2 (page 410, note 2 in Akademie edition). The most straightforward presentation of the position is probably the 'Bruchstück eines moralischen Katechisms' ('Fragment of a Moral Catechism') in Kant's *Metaphysische Anfangsgründe der Tugendlehre* (Königsberg: Friedrich Nicolovius, 1797), 168–76.

27 It works like this: the rational component in my reasons for acting as I do is summed up as the 'maxim,' the subjective practical principle, of my action. There is nothing fine or noble about the (tacit) formulation and adoption of maxims as such. What makes my action noble is my realization that this maxim is universalizable as part of the moral law. The moral law, as such, is what moves me to reverential awe.

28 He can, however, say that the spectacle of a person who finds his or her happiness in being good is 'beautiful' (*schön*) (*Critique of Practical Reason* I 1 iii, p. 146). In his earlier 'Observations on the Feeling of the Beautiful and Sublime' (1764) he had said that true virtue could only be grounded on 'a feeling that lies in every human breast ... the feeling of the beauty and the dignity of human nature' (*Gefühl von der Schönheit und der Würde der menschlichen Natur*, Section 2, p. 23) – in which the naturalistic language is much closer to classical thought, though the underlying feeling expressed is the same.

29 Hilde de Haan and Ids Haagsma, *Architects in Competition: International Architecture Competitions of the Last 200 Years* (London: Thames and Hudson,

1988). The account given in the text is of course grossly simplified; but it is not, I believe, misleading.

30 The artist 'earns their gratitude and admiration and he has thus achieved *through* his phantasy what originally he had achieved only *in* his phantasy – honour, power and the love of women' (*Introductory Lectures on Psychoanalysis*, trans. James Strachey [New York: Liveright, 1966], 376–7 – the lectures date from 1916–17). Freud's celebrated dictum must be one of the silliest sayings ever to become famous. No doubt artists do dream of such things, and are unlikely to refuse commissions, prizes, and promising dates. But the part these goodies play in the everyday activities and motivations of most artists is distressingly small. Freud, that paragon of upper-middle-class stuffiness, is not likely to have numbered many creative artists among his associates. Collectors, yes; creators, no.

31 The idea that an incomplete work exercises a compelling attraction on the artist, and the completed work exercises a compelling attraction on the public, is explored by Mikel Dufrenne, in *Phénoménologie de l'expérience esthétique* (Paris: Presses universitaires de France, 1953).

32 The view of aesthetics as a congeries of heterogeneous problems of which any one led ineluctably to all of the others was the principal theme of my *The Structure of Aesthetics* (Toronto: University of Toronto Press, 1963).

33 Aristotle, *Protrepticus*, quoted by Elias; Jonathan Barnes, ed., *The Complete Works of Aristotle* (Princeton: Princeton University Press, 1984), II, 2416 (fragment 51, Rose 3).

34 I say 'impression' because the topic has received so little attention from the 'mainstream' English-speaking philosophy that passes current that there may well be excellent work of which I know nothing. The most substantial body of work known to me is that of the late Robert S. Hartman; but it has made no real impression on my mind. The most familiar writing in this area is probably still that of Sir David Ross, *The Right and the Good* (Oxford: Clarendon Press, 1930) and *Foundations of Ethics* (Oxford: Clarendon Press, 1939), in which he essentially preserves from the classical heritage the dichotomy we observed between the right, which depends on a standard-establishing power, and all the rest, which depend on experience. But this is not enough to ground a general axiology. More ambitious in its scope was G. H. von Wright's much-praised *Varieties of Goodness* (London: Routledge, 1963), but the attempt to educe all positive values from an individual's desire imposed on his work a crippling restriction.

35 The equation of such interests with self-interest is, notoriously, a simple confusion, since the concept of self-interest requires at least the recognition of other individuals with comparable interests.

36 Suspicious-minded people say that the attempt to eliminate all values other than those of self-interest is the intellectual aspect of consumerism. The prevalence of consumerism is itself explained by the alleged fact that the mass media of communication are dominated by commercial interests, which dare not admit the reality of any concern that does not issue in the desire to purchase goods and services. Incidentally, one gathers that in the last few decades cognitive science has taken a long, hard look at the realities of decision-making procedures, and has definitively established that rational choice as economics conceived it is of rare occurrence. It simply is not true that decision makers characteristically act in ways that they conceive will maximize their own interests, rather than in terms of systems otherwise established. Economists will doubtless reply that they knew that all along.

37 The fundamental difficulty in doing value theory today is that we lack any principle to start from – or, more importantly, around which to organize revisions of what has been done already. The most promising line is perhaps one we have suggested already. Start by saying that people want things, then ask what other principles one needs other than that people want to have what they want. The minimum requirements are probably those J.S. Mill uses in his *Utilitarianism*: some sort of ordering principle among desires, and some sort of principle of justice. Satisfaction of these requirements leaves us with three problems: (i) how do we know that the ordering principle we have chosen, and the justice principle we have formulated, are on the right lines (bearing in mind, no doubt, that the rightness of lines is itself a value, hence an object of our inquiry as well as its instrument), (ii) what are we to do next?, and (iii) how will we know when we have finished?

38 See Augustine, *City of God* XIX xxv. I believe the wording in my text is close to something Augustine actually says elsewhere, but I have not succeeded in tracking the passage down.

39 See Anders Nygren, *Agape and Eros* (Chicago: University of Chicago Press, 1982). The word 'Christianity' is being used tendentiously in my text here, to refer to the sort of love-centred theology that has been one central tendency in the Church; in North America recently, the word 'Christianity' is often used to designate a curious pattern of denunciation of sexual and social mores.

40 Love or 'friendship' is one of the main topics in Aristotle's *Nicomachean Ethics* – an examination of it occupies one-fifth of the whole work. Commentators almost never pay it much attention, since it does not fit their own notions of what ethics should be about.

41 Before feminism became so fashionable, a famous text by Raymond

Williams, *Culture and Society, 1780–1950* (London: Chatto and Windus, 1958), extolled the value of solidarity, as opposed to that of service, as a matter of class rather than of gender. Service and altruism as norms of conduct suggest that the agents are in a position to help their inferiors; solidarity aligns one with one's mates. If it is the value of the oppressed, rather than the oppressor, the prevalence of solidarity awaits the emergence of a society without oppressors.

42 Unfortunately, the project did not get anywhere. I am not sure that the generalized euphoria she seemed to have in mind was sufficiently distinguished from the sense of total awareness of a specific world in which one is a participant – 'conscious, somatic, active, transactional,' as Arnold Berleant puts it (*The Aesthetics of Environment* [Philadelphia: Temple University Press, 1992], 18). Her word 'oriental' (even in those pre-Said days) seemed excessively general, perhaps attributing to a variety of different cultural approaches what was more specific to Japanese (and Korean) Buddhism. I am sorry to say that I was unable to offer any useful suggestions for research and reflection.

43 See Arnold Berleant, *The Aesthetics of Environment*. To most people, what is primary in such an aesthetic is perhaps less the positive affect of a sustaining world than the ugliness and horror of a damaged world – in scholastic terms, a world distorted, maimed, and drab. The extinction of species, the homogenization of ecologies, the substitution of mechanism for life, suggest by contrast an ideal of existence that was not noticed when it was mostly realized. Berleant, by contrast, tries to construct a positive account, though chapters 5 and 6 show an imperfectly explained negativity about garbage and skyscrapers.

44 Even where they recognize something that is unmistakably aesthetic value, the practitioners of arts in non-Western societies often centre their value systems around a rather different set of notions, such as truth-to-the-heart or authentic expressiveness. It is by no means clear whether we from our Western perspective should recognize values of this sort as occupying a different domain from that of beauty, or rather as a sort of value (familiar in Western aesthetics) that occupies a location within the domain of beauty itself. Aristotle's concepts of the *philon* (what is dear to one, friendly, one's very own) and the *oikeion* (what is homely, close to one's heart, akin to one) seem to belong to a domain other than that of beauty, and are not associated with the sixfold spectrum of values we glanced at above.

II: Philosophy and the Future of the University

1 See the opening paragraphs of Hegel's 'Introduction' to his *Ästhetik*, ed.

H.G. Hotho, 1842 (repr. Frankfurt am Main: Europäische Verlagsanstalt GmbH, 1965), Bd. I, 13. Hegel's account of what Baumgarten was up to differs from mine, concentrating on what he takes to be Baumgarten's underlying subjectivism and ignoring the philosophical point of his work.

2 We can probably say who they are. And they can probably do the same for us.

3 Fragment B 165, Diels/Krantz. The citation is from Sextus Empiricus (*Adv. Math.* VII 265), whose comment is so silly that one cannot tell from it what Democritus may have meant; Aristotle (*Part. An.* 640b29), if he is referring to the same passage, takes Democritus to mean 'what we can all *see*' – but this seems an improbable rendering of the Greek word for knowledge (*idmen*) used here. Aristotle is probably just guessing that Democritus, as a notorious materialist, must have meant something down-to-earth. So what did he really mean? Who cares? In the absence of a reliable context, I take him to have meant what I want him to mean, that the totality of our direct experience of humanity is such that it cannot be reduced to any formula, being that within which all formulae find their meaning.

4 David N. Livingstone, in *The Geographical Tradition: Episodes in the History of a Contested Enterprise* (Oxford: Blackwell, 1992), says of references to 'the human agent' or 'the human subject' that 'without placing the term in the appropriate conceptual frame it is hard to know whether the user is referring to Augustine's image of God, to Descartes' mind and body sewn together at the pineal gland, to fundamentalist Marxism's flotsam and jetsam of economic history, or to Darwin's trousered ape.' This is clever, and may strike one as shrewd, but it is confused. These theories must all be theories about the same animal, or how could they be alternatives? We understand the theories only because we recognize them as referring to the same animal, the animal we all know, and making claims about that. They are all theoretical claims made *in the face of* and *against* other theoretical claims. Might a feminist complain that all such claims err because they ignore the fundamental gender differences that render all generalizations about human nature suspect? I think not. The human sexes are essentially defined by their differences from each other. The feminist arguments are perhaps best construed as showing that humanity essentially comes in two kinds – or something of that sort.

5 One cannot avoid referring here to Augustine's remark on the question 'What is time?' – 'If nobody asks me, I know; if somebody asks me, I don't know' – *Confessions* XI. ('For what is time? Who can readily and briefly explain this? Who can even in thought comprehend it, so as to utter a word about it? But what in discourse do we mention more familiar and know-ingly, than time? And, we understand, when we speak of it; we understand

also, when we hear it spoken of by another. What then is time? If no one asks me, I know: if I wish to explain it to one that asketh, I know not ...' [trans. E.B. Pusey]. The professorial inversion of this is: 'If somebody asks me, I know; if nobody asks me, I don't know.')

6 The concept of a practice in the sense in question here is introduced and briefly discussed in Francis Sparshott, *Off the Ground* (Princeton, NJ: Princeton University Press, 1988), 113–30.

7 For a long time, Wittgenstein's disdain for definitions and formulae made a lot of philosophers self-conscious about actually *saying* anything. This led to decades of pointless posturing and flopping around.

8 Elsewhere I have favoured a different definition: 'a deliberative inquiry into meaning' ('On Saying What Philosophy Is,' *Philosophy in Context* 4, 1975, 17–27, and 'Philosophy and the Meaningful,' *Philosophy in Context* 4 Supplement, 1975, 12–22; see also my 'Philosophy as a Discipline' (*Canadian Journal of Philosophy* Supplementary Volume 19, 1994, 159–80).

   A critic complains that none of this stuff about what philosophy is can have meant much to its original audience. That is quite true, and it is really what my text says. Philosophy is an essentially contestable notion. The appropriate answer to the question 'What is philosophy?' depends on who is asking whom, and with what perplexity in mind. The audience at a public lecture cannot be supposed to have asked any specific question, or to share any other perplexity than that which my critic expresses: 'What is the lecturer going on about *now*?'

9 The analogies in actual use are nowadays extremely various, because general characterizations of philosophy are often the work of exponents of 'theory' in the humanities, few of whom have seriously come to grips with philosophy as something to be worked at. The result is sometimes rather like what might be produced by a person familiar with ice hockey only from TV broadcasts, who concluded that a hockey game consisted of a series of fistfights interrupted by beer commercials.

10 Here, as before, 'fundamental' does not mean 'foundational.' Philosophy never refuses, in principle, to raise further questions of which the answers are presupposed by the starting point of one's present inquiries; but that does not mean that the furthest reach of one's inquiries should arrive at a position from which all other knowledge might somehow be educed.

11 This is the claim staked out by Plato in his *Republic* V, 474C ff. – a passage still familiar to most students of philosophy – as the implication of Socrates' activities as Plato interpreted them in his *Apology*. Alfred North Whitehead is often quoted as saying that Western philosophy was basically a series of footnotes to Plato; I suppose what he had in mind was mostly that philoso-

phy has consisted of mining this claim. In the same passage, Plato makes Socrates explain that the 'universal scope' to which philosophy aspires is not the accumulation of facts, but the development of theoretical certainties.

12 A different species – but note what Kant's says of an 'age of enlightenment': in such an age, not everyone is enlightened, but the idea of enlightenment is abroad, it is in the public domain and available as the standard by which conscientious judges will judge (see Lecture III, note 47, below). Similarly, Aristotle did not – as people keep saying – say that humankind was 'the rational animal' (zōon logikon – a Stoic locution), but a tame animal 'capable of receiving scientific knowledge,' dektikon epistēmēs. Once the idea of logical deduction from established premises has been formulated and is available for use in the public domain, it becomes the unassailable unique standard of ascertained truth, however few people think logically; and there really is a clear sense in which the availability of this standard makes humanity into a quite new kind of animal.

For Aristotle, who believed in a steady-state universe, humanity always and essentially has the capacity in question, even in historical periods when science is nowhere manifested. The highest actual level of attainment, however seldom achieved, is what defines humanity by showing what it is capable of. In the light of today's evolutionary understanding, humanity at one time lacked any such capacity. At what point would the development of new capacities (presumably dependent on new brain structures) amount to the development of a new species? Zoology cannot say, and resorts to defining species in terms of the possibility of producing viable offspring. But at times when new species are becoming differentiated, no one can say how such lines should be drawn. Taxonomy is in an uproar, and the concept of a species itself is being relegated to the status of folk wisdom. (People capable of scientific thought and people incapable of it are notoriously capable of interbreeding, however little their parents may approve.)

13 Plato, Apology 38A. The Greek verbal adjective or gerundive (biōtos) is not perfectly captured by any English equivalent: such a life is 'not to be lived,' 'not fit to be lived,' 'not livable' – it is not exactly that it ought not to be lived, but that it is unsuitable for living, it just won't do.

14 'Sound like this' in what way? Only experience of philosophy provides the relevant training for the ear. At the annual meeting of the American Philosophical Association (Eastern Division) at Toronto in 1950, Gilbert Ryle was asked how practitioners of the 'ordinary language' school of philosophy could tell the difference between questions in linguistics and questions in philosophy. 'By the smell,' he said. Some of those present felt that his answer stank. (How did they know? By the feel ...)

What our undergraduates (sometimes even our graduates) are taught as philosophy does not have this sort of openness. What we teach is the specific lines of thought that have been profitably opened up when philosophical initiatives are pursued. Some students (even some professors) end up with the idea that philosophy is nothing but the sum of these lines. The more philosophy such students learn, the less they know: a fate that (I used to feel) befell many who attained first- class honours in the old philosophy honours course at the University of Toronto.

15 Throughout this paragraph it is taken for granted that the transition from a philosophy-free world to a world with philosophy is a single irreversible change. The nature of this change is that spelled out by Aristotle in the text that has come down to us as the first chapter of his *Metaphysics*: it is the replacement of memory and experience by active inquiry into causes and explanations.

16 In *Plato's Progress* (Cambridge: Cambridge University Press, 1966), Ryle traces Plato's philosophical decline from the analytic honesty of the early dialogues to the wilfully ambitious speculation of his maturity.

17 The paragons of Oxford 'ordinary language' philosophy, *circa* 1950, actually spent their working days as tutors guiding their undergraduates in the close study of the historical masterworks of philosophy to which their final examinations would be devoted. A contemporary of mine who got a job at Oxford remarked on how someone like J.L. Austin would come to a seminar on Kant or Aristotle armed with the text in the original language and prepared to discuss it in detail.

18 Grant's position, and its biographical grounding, is best seen in William Christian's *George Grant: A Biography* (Toronto: University of Toronto Press, 1994). Grant himself was never a working philosopher; he was a visionary cultural critic who had a dream of what philosophy might be, but he never really tried to do the things such a philosopher would have to do. His mode of agonized pontificating attracted many readers, who presumably thought that this was what it must feel like to be a philosopher.

19 A once-famous article by John Passmore (in William Elton, ed., *Aesthetics and Language* [Oxford: Blackwell, 1954] and other anthologies) attributed 'The Dreariness of Aesthetics' to the fact that it tried to encompass with its generalizing theories the domain of art, in which originality was essential. The circles in which this article was cited as a conclusive dismissal of the supposed discipline never noticed that Passmore's case itself rested on a generalizing theory of art, one of outstanding banality.

20 One of my father's favourite stories had to do with a pastry-cook who was asked how he managed to sell his rabbit pies so cheaply. He admitted that

he did so by adulterating them with horse meat. 'Yes, but how *much* horsemeat?' 'Oh, about fifty-fifty: one horse, one rabbit.'

21 For a consideration of how being a work of fine art depends on the circumstances of an object's use and not exclusively on its properties, see Nelson Goodman, 'When Is Art?' in David Perkins and Barbara Leondar, eds., *The Arts and Cognition* (Baltimore: Johns Hopkins University Press, 1977), 11–19.

22 The function of art surely affects values, or reflects values. And if beauty is a general value area, as our discussion of general axiology suggested, rather than a specific definable value (unless that definition itself provided for alternative interpretations answering to different aspects and kinds of beauty), it could well be that all the fine arts are concerned with beauty in *some* sense, but not in the same sense and not necessarily in the same way. If that were true, there would be some possible maps on which the fine arts would share the same area. Whether it would be appropriate to call such maps maps *of knowledge* is a question we may leave aside until someone does something that calls for an answer.

23 When modern dance was introduced into American colleges, it was at first administered by physical education departments – partly because dance had a prepared niche in the curriculum as a way in which women could satisfy a Phys. Ed. requirement. This affected the way dance was thought of and done in many ways – for instance, in a penchant for stripped-down costume and minimal scenery; though it did not, as it might have, change the status of modern dance in general from art to athletics.

24 See Francis Sparshott, *The Theory of the Arts* (Princeton, NJ: Princeton University Press, 1982). The passage referred to in the following sentences is chapter 3, but the whole book is relevant.

25 Plato, *Epinomis* (see chapter 1, n. 11); and compare Aristotle, *Poetics*. Most of the *Poetics* probably antedates the *Epinomis*, and has been thought by many scholars to relate to the *Republic* and *Phaedo*. The actual authorship of the *Epinomis* does not matter; what matters is the availability of the classification for later use and its attributability to Platonic authority. The classification itself seems to be a reworking of materials from Plato's *Statesman*, to which the text is about to turn.

26 The *Epinomis* (975D) says without explanation that most recreational activities are representational, but none of them are in any way serious (*spoudaia*) – rather than making representation the basic genus, as Aristotle does. This is presumably because the *Epinomis* is in a hurry to dismiss all activities except astronomy as making no contribution to blessedness, and accordingly lumps painting and storytelling in with any other sorts of

amusement there might be (playing draughts, etc.), rather than because the author is beginning to entertain the idea of a non-mimetic fine art.

27 The immediate source of this designation was not Plato, but the classification of 'representations' in the opening chapter of Aristotle's *Poetics*, newly discovered and translated, and enormously influential.

28 The implication of this dialogue and *The Statesman* that only one such classification of the arts and professions can be correct, though consistent with Plato's general epistemological approach, is undefended (and, to my mind, indefensible). Easier to defend is the thesis that a government may find it administratively necessary to opt for a single system of classification, and that there may be only one right way for it to make such a choice.

29 Under the name of 'bad faith,' this idea is developed by Jean-Paul Sartre, most fully in *L'Etre et le néant* (*Being and Nothingness*) (Paris: Gallimard, 1943).

30 In conservative cultures (dynastic Egypt is the classical example), the arts themselves may be congealed in traditions as rigid as the economic structures with which they coexist. But they still stand as wilfully created alternatives to the economic order.

    Since the rise of the Industrial Revolution, the coercions of economic and intellectual power have endowed the 'alternative' status of the fine arts with a new significance. Theorists from J.C.F. von Schiller to T.W. Adorno have found the importance of the fine arts to be that they are the only reliable locus of human freedom. To Schiller, following Kant, aesthetic necessity, akin to what I was calling 'the power of beauty' in my first lecture, opens up a space in which physical determinacy and moral tyranny may be played off against each other (*On the Aesthetic Education of Man* [1795], trans. Elizabeth M. Wilkinson and L.A. Willoughby [Oxford: Clarendon Press, 1967]). Adorno found in the logic of artistic development, ineluctable but freely chosen, the only recourse against the commercialized manipulations of the culture industry (*Dissonanzen: Musik in der verwalteten Welt* [Frankfurt: Suhrkamp, 3d ed. 1963]). At a less sophisticated level, art has been seen simply as a space for subjective freedom through 'self-expression' in a regimented existence; but this view of art, though popular at the level of kindergarten teaching, has not proved rewarding as an account of artistic practice and was vigorously denounced as bourgeois mystification by Marxist critics.

31 On arts of imagination, see my *The Theory of the Arts* (compare note 24, above), chapter 5. Their place on the map of knowledge is the work of Jean LeRond D'Alembert's *Preliminary Discourse to the Encyclopedia of Diderot*

(1751) (translated by Richard Schwab and Walter Rex, [Indianapolis: Bobbs-Merrill, 1963]).

32 A striking way of putting this, devised by the Russian Formalist Victor Shklovskii and popular in recent decades, is to say that the primary work of the arts is 'defamiliarization,' *ostranenie*.

33 Is there always a difference between a work of pictorial art that is used as a political poster, and a poster that has the quality of pictorial art? Is there a difference (in revolutionary China, for instance) between posters that are also works of art and posters that are not art but employ the techniques that art has developed?

34 I touch on this point again in Lecture IV. The point at issue is really the husbanding of energy and resources: the studies mentioned in the text here are so novel, so striking, so little explored, that scholars scrambling for time, funds, and personnel to pursue them are exasperated by the way the institutionally entrenched mini-discipline of aesthetics continues to squander its traditional funding on areas where little of significance remains to be done.

35 How did the phrase get into the argument of this book? It crept in quite casually, in the recapitulation (p. 23) of a passage (on the opening page of the present lecture) in which I spoke of 'the proper place of the fine arts ... among the arts ..., or in the economy of the human mind.' I must have been taking it for granted that places can be identified only as places on possible maps.

36 Quoted by Dorothy Nelkin and M. Susan Lindee, *The DNA Mystique: The Gene as a Cultural Icon* (New York: W. H. Freeman and Co., 1995), 8. The point is a delicate one. In *The Geographical Tradition*, p. 259, Livingstone quotes an earlier author as follows: 'Ignorance of geography produces frequent friction and occasional wars, stupidity in commercial enterprises, hasty and reckless counsel in our journals, and loss of life ... Be it politics, finance or commerce, missionary zeal or the mere pursuit of pleasure or health, an end will be more effectually obtained if we have studied environments' (A.J. Herbertson, 'Geography in the University,' *Scottish Geographical Magazine* 18, 1902, 124–32, at 127). 'That geography should be made to subserve social purposes was not only typical of the era,' Livingstone comments, 'it was a shared assumption that remained inviolate across the ideological reaches of the tradition.' The comment is astonishing. Herbertson, in the passage quoted, is not advocating that either the problems posed or the topics studied by geographers, much less the conclusions they reach or the assertions they make, should be determined by considerations of utility. On the contrary, he is saying that the pursuit of any practical

end whatever may be frustrated by ignorance of what geographers have established. That could be true, obviously, only if the facts in question were true facts, the generalizations sound generalizations.

37 David Buisseret writes of 'the oil company maps that most North Americans keep in their cars, with their studied neglect of most physical features, their exaggeration of the size of roads, their absolute refusal in most cases to take account of historical monuments ...,' and concludes: 'Next time we reach into the glovebox, let us ... reflect upon who made the map, with what interests in mind and with a view to the suppression of what aspects of the actual world' ('Maps and Power, or Something Nasty in the Glovebox,' *Queen's Quarterly* 100, 1993, 861–8, at 867–8). Buisseret presumably does not drive, or he would know why road maps are the way they are. Roads are what drivers drive on; their size is exaggerated so that drivers can see them. The reference to 'oil companies' is presumably intended to make us shudder, but oil companies do not do their own cartography, and the maps they issue are mostly identical with those issued by hotels and government tourist offices.

38 See Roger A. Shiner, 'Sparshott on the Philosophy of Philosophy' (*Journal of Aesthetic Education* 31/2, 1997, 3–8) for a searching critique of my use of the 'map' metaphor in *The Theory of the Arts*.

39 The misgivings referred to in note 36 amount to saying that such world maps do constrain us, but in ways that are not drawn to our attention.

40 My review of F.E. Sparshott, *The Structure of Aesthetics*, drew attention to this pattern and the deviations from it. See 'Up Porphyry's Tree – Where the Nuts Come From,' *Tamarack Review* no. 30, 1964, 69–73.

41 The list in the *Statesman* and *Epinomis* is a sophisticated version of this more general treatment.

42 One is tempted to say that in the age of the manuscript the paradigm map of knowledge might be some research library's catalogue of its holdings, but in the age of print all such particular catalogues are replaced by the encyclopedia, a sort of master catalogue of the possible holdings of an ideal library. But even in Hellenistic and medieval ages, the greatest libraries and the most resourceful scholars contrived to have access to *everything*.

43 The last encyclopedia to do this was, I believe, the *Encyclopaedia Metropolitana* (London, 1817–45). A contemporary encyclopedia is unlikely to have any plan beyond the alphabetical, access to the accumulated data being afforded by multiple indices catering to disparate interests and ignorances. The ingenious expedients to which the fifteenth edition of the *Encyclopaedia Britannica* has had to resort speak to the intractability of the problem.

44 Similarly, any (metaphorical) map of knowledge is bound to combine the requirements of users, the necessities and conveniences of cataloguers, and the strategies of policy makers, and a historical account of any such map must take all three into account – in accordance with the manipulative historian's own agenda, of course ...

45 Who are the 'we' in this sentence? A nebulous consensus of those who have a substantial share in the educational system and communicative community of our civilization? Perhaps, but it might be more honest to say: the people one is usually referring to when one says 'we' in sentences like this, without its either being clear whom we are talking about or in any way puzzling whom we might be referring to. (And who is the 'one' in *this* sentence?)

46 Note that to distinguish the fine arts from each other is also automatically to unite them, as bodies of practice that *need* to be distinguished from each other.

47 Denis Diderot in his article 'Arts' in his *Encyclopédie* (Paris: Lebreton, 1751–72).

48 It is in this situation that the social, political, and economic connections of artistic practices come to be thought of as their underlying reality. Someone who writes a book on the 'real world of ballet' is going to tell you about everything *except* ballet.

49 The reference here is to a paper by Donald Crawford at the Annual Meeting of the American Society for Aesthetics at Montreal, 18 October 1996. But the underlying reality is described in remarks attributed to the physicist Murray Gell-Mann in 1984: 'It is usually said that ours is an age of specialization, and that is true. But there's a striking phenomenon of convergence in science and scholarship that has been taking place, especially in the forty years since the Second World War, and at an accelerated pace during the last decade. New subjects, highly interdisciplinary in traditional terms, are emerging and represent in many cases the frontier of research. These interdisciplinary subjects do not link together the whole of one traditional discipline with another; particular subfields are joined together to make a new subject. The pattern is a varied one and constantly changing' (quoted without reference by Heinz R. Pagels in *The Dreams of Reason: The Computer and the Rise of the Sciences of Compexity* [New York: Simon and Schuster, 1988], 35–6).

50 This durability of established disciplines, familiar to most denizens of the academic world, is repeatedly emphasized by Stanley Fish in *There Is No Such Thing as Free Speech* (Cambridge: Cambridge University Press, 1994).

51 In Aristotelian terms, the 'place' of a thing is determined by its boundaries (strictly: the inside surfaces of whatever surrounds it), and a thing can be in a determinate place without there being any map for it to be on. But its place cannot be *specified* without a map, or a set of coordinates from which a map could be constructed.

52 When I arrived in Toronto in 1950 (from Oxford, which believed itself to be the only real place in a world otherwise composed of outer darkness or – worse – Cambridge), one of the things that struck me most was the constant movement of scholars throughout the English-speaking countries. The movement is not so striking nowadays, where air travel and electronic interchange have made location itself a less salient phenomenon.

53 Note that this alleged pedigree of the myth is an important part of the myth itself.

54 *Berowne*: What is the end of study, let me know?
    Ferdinand: Why that to know which else wee should not know.
    Berowne: Things hid & bard (you meane) from common sense.
    Ferdinand: I, that is studies god-like recompence.

    – Loues Labour's lost I.

55 Martin Bernal made a stir a few years ago with his book *Black Athena* (New York: Rutgers University Press, 1987), arguing that all this myth is a racist deception: in reality, Greece was merely an Egyptian colony, and it was from Egypt that Greek civilization was derived. But the myth does not deny that the Greeks revered Egyptian civilization and relied on neighbouring people for data and doctrines; it claims that what the Greeks did with these data and doctrines was unique. The point is emphatically made in the *Epinomis* (987D): 'Whatever Greeks take over from barbarians, they work it up into a finer completion.' Bernal seems to think that all you can do with data and doctrines is memorize them.

56 It is just this distinction that Aristotle made in the programmatic statement with which he begins what we know as the first book of his *Metaphysics*. (*Metaphysics* A is obviously a general introduction to philosophy as a whole, and has nothing specific to do with the 'theology' or 'first philosophy' that permeates the following books.)

57 For the significance of Aristotle's archive, and the consequent need for a secure repository, see John Patrick Lynch, *Aristotle's School: A Study of a Greek Educational Institution* (Berkeley: University of California Press, 1972) – and consider that the posthumous fate of Aristotle's library was a matter of historical concern.

58 The text here assumes that Cicero was not in any significant way attempting

an original synthesis. This view may be challenged: see Carlos Lévy, *Cicero Academicus: Recherches sur les Académiques et sur la philosophie cicéronienne* (Paris and Rome: Collection de l'École française de Rome, 1992).

59 The same holds true of analogous religions in other long-lived civilizations, notably in India and China, but their traditions of inquiry and pedagogy are so different that it is pointless to bring them into the present discussion. Even the generalization about the 'Religions of the Book' goes too far, since the unique place of the Koran gives Islamic learning a different face from any prevailing in Christendom, and the maintenance of learning in the Jewish diaspora necessarily proceeded by other means.

60 I originally added engineering to law and medicine in this statement. But that would be misleading. Today's basic science is physics, a central discipline in our universities and fundamental to our understanding of ourselves and our world, and physics has been centrally mechanics. Galileo's interest in the trajectories of cannon balls testifies to the close connection between mechanics and practical technologies, and Newton observed that geometry was simply the theory of engineering; but schools of engineering ('applied science') seemed more remote from academic institutions than law or medicine – or, for that matter, divinity. A partial explanation is the distaste among Greek philosophers for 'banausic' occupations, which continues to infect academic tradition. The situation, involving a traditional anti-intellectual stance among engineering students in many American schools, is doubtless related to the practice of segregating 'technical' from 'academic' training at the secondary level on the sole ground of the academic incapacity of those relegated to the former. (Students are not transferred from the manual stream to the academic stream on the sole ground of clumsiness or technical incapacity, and, if they were, their transfer would not be thought of as 'relegation.') But the situation remains deeply puzzling. See, however, the remarks in the next lecture on the 'land grant' universities of the United States.

61 Continuities and discontinuities in the development are a matter of emphasis. Pelikan represents a widespread conviction when he writes that 'the university came into being in the Middle Ages and ... came of age in the nineteenth and twentieth centuries' (Jaroslav Pelikan, *The Idea of the University: A Reexamination* [New Haven, CT: Yale University Press, 1992], 182). It is true that the corporate identity of the university had and preserves this origin; my text at this point refers rather to the idea of unified and unremitting research.

62 This quartet may remind us of what Pelikan identifies as the 'four legs' of the university, 'no one of which can stand for very long unless all are

strong': 'the advancement of knowledge through research, the transmission of knowledge through teaching, the preservation of knowledge in scholarly collections, and the diffusion of knowledge through publication' (*The Idea of the University*, 16–17). Pelikan's fourfold division operates entirely at our fourth level.

63 The medieval distinctions between the primary *trivium* (grammar, rhetoric, and logic, the linguistic sciences) and the secondary *quadrivium* (arithmetic, geometry, astronomy, music – the mathematical sciences as identified in Plato's *Republic),* and between these liberal arts as a whole and the servile arts, fit in here but are, I think, too closely tied to the specifics of pre-modern pedagogy to deserve our examination. In other words: I don't know much about them.

64 The concept of 'post-secondary education,' which figures so largely in political discourse, implicitly denies the existence of this fourth level and risks depriving the university of legitimacy, and even of intelligibility. But the concept has an obvious utility, standing for the fact that students who have completed their secondary education but wish to continue their schooling are confronted with a number of options. 'Post-secondary education' is the appropriate designation for this range of choices (discussed in Lecture III).

65 Pelikan insists (p. 100) that law and medicine are as essential as the arts to the university as traditionally conceived. It may be true (as I said above) that they are essentially hands-on subjects; but they are also essentially learned, with a taxing and definite subject matter that has to be systematically mastered.

66 Universities should be able to assume that new arrivals are able and willing to succeed in the fields of study they take up. What they cannot assume is that those new arrivals will know what fields of study exist, let alone what fields will prove most congenial to them. It makes obvious sense to organize universities in such a way that the consequent selections and transfers can be made within a single administrative framework. In the days before instant electronic communication, that meant having everything close together.

67 See Livingstone, *The Geographical Tradition*, 57–60. It should be mentioned that in Britain the early growth of science took place outside the ancient universities.

68 This model was advocated for the University of Toronto by James Loudon in 1877 (A.B. McKillop, *Matters of Mind: The University in Ontario, 1791–1951* [Toronto: University of Toronto Press, 1994], 156), at the very time when the founding professors of Johns Hopkins were debating the principles on

which they should proceed. The ideal is being strongly promoted by the current president of the University of Toronto, Dr Robert Prichard – except that he tends to state the ideal, not in terms of absolute achievement, but in terms of competition, his own university being assigned the mission of excelling every other. One might be reminded of the young heroes in Homer's *Iliad*, each being egged on by his father 'always to be the champion, and to excel the rest' – *aien aristeuein kai hupeirochon emmenai allōn* – were it not that Dr Prichard is reasonably confident that it is a competition he cannot lose, and there are good financial and political reasons for emphasizing the competitive edge rather than whatever actual values may be involved.

69 Letter to Bishop Mountain of Quebec, 30 April 1795, cited from McKillop's *Matters of Mind*, 5–6.

70 'Shall I tell him to mind his work, and say he's sent to school to make himself a good scholar? Well, but he isn't sent to school for that – at any rate not for that mainly. I don't care a straw for Greek particles, or the digamma, no more does his mother. What is he sent to school for? Well, partly because he wanted so to go. If he'll only turn out a brave, helpful, truth-telling Englishman, and a gentleman, and a Christian, that's all I want' (Thomas Hughes, *Tom Brown's Schooldays* [London: Macmillan, 1857], chapter 4. Puffin Books reprint, 1971, pp. 85–6). This is in 1833 or so. Note, however, that this sturdily lowbrow squire knows that the digamma exists and has recently been a matter of scholarly controversy (see further, Lecture III, note 29). A contemporary Squire Brown might not find it so easy to say what it was he didn't care a straw for.

71 For the conditions at one Oxford college (New College), see William Hayter's *Spooner* (London, 1974). For admission to that college it sufficed to have been a scholar of Winchester School; it was unnecessary to write the university examinations, since New College did its own examining; and the fellows of the college did no teaching, so that an undergraduate wanting instruction had to hire a private tutor. Simcoe had spent two years at Oxford before going into the army. (His college was Merton, but I have no data on Merton comparable to Hayter's account of New College.)

72 Berkeley's title page says it all: *A PROPOSAL for the better SUPPLYING of CHURCHES in our Foreign Plantations, and for Converting the Savage AMERI-CANS, to CHRISTIANITY, By a COLLEGE to be erected in the Summer Islands, otherwise called The Isles of Bermuda*. The text is printed in A.A. Luce and T. E. Jessop, eds., *The Works of George Berkeley Bishop of Cloyne* (London: Nelson, 1955), VII, 335–61. Berkeley obtained a charter for his college, and funds were voted by Parliament, but the money never came through.

73 There is a sequel to *Tom Brown's Schooldays* (note 70, above), in which Tom goes to Oxford. He does so in response to an unexplained summons from unnamed authorities, and no explanation is ever given of why or with what expectations he should be going there, beyond the statement that 'Tom was, in truth, beginning to feel it was high time for him to be getting to regular work again of some sort' (Thomas Hughes, *Tom Brown at Oxford* [Boston: Ticknor and Fields, 1861], I, 2). The author's aim in writing the book seems to be to depict the lives of 'gentlemen commoners,' debauched offspring of the idle rich on whom the colleges depended for much of their income. If *Brideshead Revisited* is to be trusted, this way of life persisted until the Second World War.

III: The University and the Future of Civilization

1 See, for instance, how David Z. Albert's account of the apparent oddities of quantum mechanics keeps insisting that these oddities must be accepted because quantum theory provides all and only correct predictions of the behaviour of particles (*Quantum Mechanics and Experience* [Cambridge, MA: Harvard University Press, 1992]). Obviously, if this is the case, quantum theory cannot be got rid of: if it is not to be retained, its replacement must either incorporate it as a special case or include a paraphrase. The sense in which the theoretical foundations of science are merely hypothetical is a somewhat remote sense.

2 The would-be persuasive word 'surely' here is a danger signal, as usual. Maybe it is not stupid not to be bewildered by *science*. Maybe we should be bewildered already by animal intelligence. All animals that inhabit variable environments must be able to synthesize multiple inputs in unfamiliar combinations and unusual circumstances. Humans (and to a lesser extent all animals whose way of life is so variable as to amount to culture peculiar to specific tribes or hordes) must be able to do the same sort of thing in a more generalized way – to form, divine, and grasp connections of new and recondite kinds. And this ability is already the basis of science, as Aristotle already saw (see the last short chapter of his *Posterior Analytics*, Book I). The development of scientific method and results is nothing other than the cumulative exercise of intelligence and memory – especially, as Aristotle observed, a knack of discovering 'middle terms,' that is, guessing at real but unexpected connections. Two things are necessary: that there should be very many minds engaged in this cumulative enterprise, and that there should actually be unbroken series of links between what is known and what is still unknown. Unless there is some strong reason why these

conditions should not be fulfilled, there is nothing bewildering in the development within the universe of a scientific knowledge of itself, given the initial development of intelligence.

3 Jaroslav Pelikan writes: 'Except perhaps for big-time soccer, the university seems to have become the most nearly universal man-made institution in the modern world' (*The Idea of the University* [cited in Lecture II, note 61], 22). Whether the modern world can be equated with 'our civilization' is a question we will have to consider; equally problematic is the relation between centrality and universality – a problem we will *not* consider.

4 Even in such a society, that order has its shadows and echoes. There is, first, the toughly enduring order of traditional power – feudal, ecclesiastical, aristocratic, squirearchical, military – with its own institutions of schooling and self-maintenance; there is, second, the disorganized world of anarchical desire and intelligence, culturally mediated no doubt, but disavowing all allegiances; and there are, third, the avowedly transpolitical and supersocial orders centred on devotions to God or Nature and maintaining their own more or less ephemeral conventicles. Today's universities contrive to find places for all of these (so long as they don't rock the boat), sometimes by making available physical and organizational cubby-holes, sometimes by turning blind eyes to stowaways. The presence of these others must for the most part be a subtext for my discourse, but from time to time it will come to the surface and breathe.

5 'Schedule of Fall Convocation – 1995,' Wednesday, November 22 – 6 p.m. (University of Toronto, Office of the Vice-Provost and Assistant Vice-President [Planning and Budget]). What are we to say of a university where the convocation is in the hands of the Assistant Vice-President (Planning and Budget)?

6 I once delivered a paper, called 'Aristotle on Underfunding,' to a bunch of department heads and such, in which I pointed out that the concept of '*under*funding' presupposed a consensus as to what level of funding would *not* be 'under': what would be appropriate, and why. No such consensus exists, and no complaint about underfunding that I have ever heard explains how much money would be enough for what purpose, and how that purpose is justified. The title of my paper alluded to Aristotle's little-noticed remark that decisions about what is to be studied, and to what extent, are political decisions (*Nicomachean Ethics* I ii, 1094a28–b2). That does not mean that governments decide; it means that the allocation of resources by the body politic is an allocation by the body politic, no matter how it is made. The assembled dignitaries seemed not to be impressed by my arguments, but they did not say what was wrong with them.

The reason why the concept of 'underfunding' passes without comment where I come from is that it has a definite reference in relation to prevailing practices, even if those practices are themselves undefended (and perhaps indefensible). Ontario universities are said to be underfunded because the cost per student of Canadian universities is 'half to two-thirds that of good quality U.S. state supported universities, and one-sixth that of the leading U.S. private universities' (David L. Johnston, 'Research at Canadian Universities and the Knowledge Based Society,' the 1995 Killam Lecture [Halifax: Killam Trusts, c/o Faculty of Graduate Studies, Dalhousie University], 18); because Ontario grants per student in primary and secondary schools increased by 33.2 per cent from 1970/1 to 1979/80, while grants per student in universities *fell* by 13.1 per cent in the same period, and grants per student in community colleges exceeded those in universities by 8 per cent between 1973/4 and 1977/8 (Paul Axelrod, *Scholars and Dollars: Politics, Economics, and the Universities of Ontario, 1945–1980* [Toronto: University of Toronto Press, 1982]), 180. 'From 1974/5 to 1980/81, Ontario's position declined from seventh to tenth in terms of grants per full-time student, and over the same period the other nine provinces increased their operating grants at a rate "about 65% greater than in Ontario,"' while 'in 1979, Ontario diverted to other purposes $37 million of the $88 million intended for higher education' (ibid, 181). The significance of these last sets of figures is not affected by the fact that 'the wealth generating capacity of Canada has declined in relative terms by over 20% in the last two decades' (Johnston, 'Research at Canadian Universities,' 13). ('Remuneration, O, that's the Latine word for three-farthings' – Clowne in *Loues Labour's lost* III.)

7 The lecture got a laugh at this point, as though the remark had been satirically intended. Academic audiences will laugh at anything, as people drowning in sawdust will grasp at snorkels, but I was not trying to be funny (though I had been prepared for a chuckle). It is not hard to envisage circumstances in which the exotic-sounding combinations mentioned would make sense.

8 The fact that the ideal of comprehensive research is satisfied so long as everything is done *somewhere* may, however, as we shall see, run up against the feeling in political societies that self-respect requires them to adorn themselves in the visible trappings of civilization, of which a 'university' is one. They will have their university whether or not they have the intellectual resources to sustain it, just as suburban householders feel obliged to grow grass between their houses and the street regardless of soil and climate.

9 The situation is not unlike what Diderot noted of the recombination of skills in a technological society, as noted in Lecture II.

10 A striking denunciation of this inhospitability is articulated by Charles J. Sykes in *ProfScam: Professors and the Demise of Higher Education* (Washington, DC: Regnery Gateway, 1988) . His thesis is that what I have called the research university represents the hijacking of institutions of higher education by those who were hired to teach in them but prefer to spend their time amusing themselves in libraries and laboratories. His tirade draws attention to real abuses, though with little regard to consistency. But the main peculiarity of his book is that he nowhere considers *what* should be taught in colleges and universities, or how and where teachable knowledge should be developed. One has the impression that students go to college to have access to some established tradition, neither the substance nor the credentials of which need ever be examined. He invokes the name of J.H. Newman, to whom I shall be referring later, but without any close attention to what Newman was saying.

11 Sykes (*ProfScam*, p. 92) emphasizes this point: 'In the past, of course, people went to college specifically because they *did* believe that when they were finished they would be educated. *That was the point*. That was why they paid so much money for it.' When I first arrived in North America from a very different cultural tradition, I found it very hard to adjust to a world in which this was still true: in which it was a complete explanation of one's not knowing something, or not having read a book, that it was not prescribed in a course one had taken at school. The attitude still survives in some quarters, and I still find it hard to comprehend. But Sykes is quite right to protest against a college course the sole or main value of which is to prepare students for work at more advanced institutions.

12 The university was to be open to undergraduates of any denomination, though my impression is that they were expected to attend the church of their parents' choice. I do not know how effective the exposure to Anglican instruction was expected to be; but in the palmy days of Trudeau a CEGEP instructor told me that he and his colleagues were all proselytising separatists, and would ensure that the next generation of Quebec intellectuals were all indoctrinated.

Strachan was also concerned with the 'useful contacts' mentioned in the text. In a letter to Peregrine Maitland in 1826, he wrote: 'Lawyers must, from the very nature of our political institutions, ... become the most powerful profession ... They are emphatically our men of business, and will gradually engross all the colonial offices of profit and honour. It is, therefore, of the utmost importance that they should be collected together at a university, become acquainted with each other and familiar, acquire similar views and modes of thinking, and be taught from precept and example to love and venerate our parent state' (McKillop, *Matters of Mind*, 66). The 'parent state' was, I suppose, imperial Britain rather than Upper Canada.

13 The energetic Methodist Egerton Ryerson, at the time of the great squabble over the allocation of provincial funds to sectarian organizations, expresses himself as being in favour of 'a Provincial University, furnishing the highest academical and professional education, at least in respect of law and medicine,' together with a 'provincial system of common school education,' both 'conducted upon Christian principles, yet free from sectarian bias or ascendancy; that there should be an intermediate class of seminaries in connexion with the different religious persuasions, who have ability and enterprise to establish them, providing on the one hand a theological education for their clergy, and on the other a thorough English and scientific education, and elementary classical instruction for those of the youth of their congregations who might seek for more than a common school education, or who might wish to prepare for the University, and who, not having the experience and discretion of University students, required a parental and religious oversight, in their absence from their parents ...' (letter to *British Colonist*, 20 Feb. 1846; cited from C.B. Sissons, *Egerton Ryerson, His Life and Letters* [Toronto: Clarke Irwin, 1947], II 106–7). Ryerson assumes that his readers will be familiar with the articulation of studies he describes, but familiarity is not the same as intelligibility and defensibility. At Victoria College in 1841, the arts and science program consisted of (a) the classical languages, (b) mathematics and physics, (c) philosophy, (d) rhetoric and belles lettres, (e) theology (McKillop, *Matters of Mind*, 103).

The song cited in the text goes on to reminisce about 'when I the fearful gauntlet ran'; one has to bear in mind that these students were five or six years younger than today's undergraduates.

14 Compare the passage cited from *Tom Brown at Oxford* (Lecture II, note 73), in which it seems that Tom's sole aim in going to Oxford is to do *some* serious work, no matter what.

15 McKillop, *Matters of Mind*, 112. But I confess I am uneasy about the depth of McKillop's understanding of the relevant theology in relation to faith and reason, and of the contemporary interpretation of the relation between primary and secondary causes. He seems to assume that philistine teachers superimposed a snuffling sanctimoniousness on a scientific instruction to which it was an irrelevant hindrance. But the idea that science unfolded the wondrous ways of the Creator was pervasive in pre-Darwinian days, not only in elementary teaching and not only in Ontario. Scientific research could be motivated by the desire to discover the wonders of nature, the beauties of unity and design (as the scholastic theory of beauty conceived

them). Too many of today's scholars are betrayed by the shallowness and narrowness of their theological understanding.

I take it that McKillop's main point is that science in these little colleges was taught like a dead language, not as an ongoing process of discovery. He is inclined to associate his interpretation of science teaching with the fact that no experiments were performed in class, though he conceded that these tiny impoverished colleges had little money for apparatus. His generalizations are hard to reconcile with such facts as that Faraday Hall, 'the first college building in Canada constructed strictly for the study of science,' was opened by Victoria College in 1878 and equipped with experimental apparatus to the specifications of the science professor, Eugene Haanel (Birgitte Nielsen Worrall in *Vic Report*, Winter 1995/6, 8). But I really wonder what the functions of such 'experiments' are anyway. If my experience is any guide, there is no question of finding anything out: the teacher knows what the results are supposed to be, and the regular procedure is for the student to write down the correct values (as established by previous classes) rather than those established empirically. (After several decades of this, someone may accidentally discover what the number of chromosomes in a rabbit actually is.) What is of scientific value, if anything, is the theory and the mathematical relationships, together with the fact that these have been empirically established; the actual fooling around with Bunsen burners is part of the rhetoric, not part of the science. But I suppose the purpose is to make the students feel that science is *about* something, and that they *might have been* performing real experiments to confirm or disconfirm something that was really in doubt.

16 John Henry Newman, *On the Scope and Nature of University Education* (1852), often reprinted. Newman's argument against the ideal of 'Enlightenment' is that tradition represents the cumulative and corrected wisdom of humanity, hence the best knowledge we have; it must be the function of a university to diffuse this. If new discoveries stand up, they will soon be absorbed into the tradition and change it. One must bear in mind, of course, that what Newman is promoting is a papal initiative to set up a sectarian institution in Ireland, where the extant rival institution (Trinity College, Dublin) represents an alien and intrusive cultural tradition. Defending established truth against untested innovation is a matter of defending Catholic Ireland against the Prods.

17 Pelikan, *The Idea of the University*, 26.

18 J.H. Newman, *Idea of a University* I vii, quoted by Pelikan in ibid., 71.

19 Pelikan, *The Idea of the University*, 48.

20 Ibid., 53. He explores, and maintains against Newman, the strong and

variable connection between research and university teaching (chapters 8 and 9).

21 Sykes, *ProfScam* (compare note 10, above). My interpretation of his relationship to Newman verges on the conjectural.

22 It was as if the publishers were asking us to hate ourselves as much as they hated us. But that was not what was happening. The reality was a shift in the demographics of university attendance. McKillop remarks that university enrolment in the 1960s repeatedly outran predictions, because of the rising expectations of the young – recognized (though McKillop does not mention this) by advertisers as a huge new market with more cash than responsibilities, and accordingly to be flattered and *catered to*, rather than educated. Universities became and remain to a great extent titillation engines.

23 My text throughout ignores mature students, part-time students, and extension courses, whose presence in increasing numbers is modifying the educational landscape.

24 I say lip-service, because I know of at least one protestant seminary where the graduates are not required to know either Hebrew or Greek, the languages in which most of their sacred texts are written, but take courses in 'English Bible' instead.

25 Special attention must be paid to teachers' colleges, intermediate institutions of which the nature fluctuates as the relevant educational levels of instructors and students change.

26 One might say, for instance, that the University of Guelph is the Ontario Veterinary College in wolf's clothing.

27 The standing delusion of government bureaucracies, that their professional concerns are identical with the interests of the nation, is matched by the growing conviction of the ever-proliferating university administrations that *they* are the true university, of which the scholars are the hired help and the students the clientele. The university president as CEO of a huge corporation has natural affinities with his or her fellow executives which may erode any links to the professorate from whose ranks such presidents originally rose (or sank). However, the persistent allegation that the businessmen from whom the promoters and boards of the new universities were recruited have seen them simply as training grounds for their personnel is not borne out by the facts. See for instance the account of York University in Axelrod (*Scholars and Dollars*, 66ff). The board members tended to have agendas, dreams, and ideals of their own – the magnificent fine arts program at York is the outcome of Mrs Eaton's enthusiasm rather than of any economic or academic calculation. Actually, York's founding president, Murray Ross, has

said that the reason for having a big-business board of trustees is not to make the university business-oriented but to secure large lines of credit from the local banks, who would be unlikely to extend them to councils of scholars and students (Axelrod, 76). Axelrod observes that the business press of the 1960s saw no contradiction between the functions of practical and non-practical education, in view of the complexity of today's societies and economies (p. 106).

28 This myth is largely based on my impressions of the talk by Donald Crawford referred to in Lecture II, note 49.

29 Recall how Squire Brown expressed his indifference toward classical learning by saying that he cared nothing for the digamma (Lecture II, note 70). Classical colleges, like Brown's Oxford, trafficked in a sort of residual erudition, a detritus of past research. The prized tradition consists of what squires remember from their schooldays. Today's pundits who bemoan the decline of humanism are really only expressing nostalgia for the days when they thought they knew what education was. Esoteric scholarship flourished back then too, but today's pundits didn't notice it; sound popularization abounds today, but the pundits don't notice that either.

30 The Johns Hopkins ideal was launched in the United States only a few years after the land-grant program, and never really overtook it, since it could not formulate an achievable scenario.

31 Or, to use a hoarier myth: America had been ambushed and risked being scalped. It was time to draw the wagons into a circle.

32 We must not forget, though, the mitigations of the chaos that are also barriers to choice: science labs and Phys.Ed. gyms may impose regimes almost monastic in their exclusive rigour, and institutions interpose filters of varying permeability between departments and specialisms. The office of a college registrar divides its time between imposing (sometimes inventing) such filters and negotiating them. How to exploit the registrar's office is something else the streetwise student learns.

33 I believe, but I am not certain, that this was on that evening in Malloney's Art Gallery in 1950, which Ryle later claimed never took place (compare Lecture I, note 6).

34 My own father did not, in fact, send me to Victoria, of which he had never heard; nor would he have, if he had. He didn't send me anywhere. He would have liked me to be a man, but he gave that up as hopeless when I was quite small. I got to university by sitting for, and winning, a scholarship; my school encouraged me, and I am sure my father was glad of it. I went to the college which offered the most scholarships in my special subject. It was a college of my father's university, which I 'chose' because I

knew of no alternatives, and knew nothing at all about any other universities – how one got there, what one did there, whom one would meet there. My father's father didn't send *him* to Victoria, either. Same reason. Nor did Granddad send my father to Oxford. My father got there on an ex-serviceman's grant after the First World War. I never heard how he made his decision. He was, I think, the first person in our family who had any sort of university education at all.

35 This understanding is continuous with that characteristic of primary and secondary education, in which the less resourceful learn, not how people deal with the world, but how they are dealt with by it.

36 David L. Johnston seems to take the opposite view: 'In my view,' he writes, 'the research university is the key institution in our society to meet the challenge of the information revolution.' But this, it turns out, is a proposal, not a prediction; in fact, having said that 'lifelong learning should be a key design element in the building of the information highway,' he says that 'our recommendations propose we move as quickly as possible to electronic publishing for our scholarship, electronic data bases for our libraries, electronic interactive connections for our teaching and our students' learning. The greatest single obstacle? We professors – especially those of us over 40 – who won't explore whether and how these new tools can help us and our interactive audiences.' He has seen the enemy, and it is me. So really, he agrees with me after all: the university as he would like it to be is to replace the university as it actually is (David L. Johnston, 'Research at Canadian Universities and the Knowledge Based Society' [compare note 6, above], 7, 12–13). Johnston is a former principal of McGill University, the current chair of the Canadian Institute for Advanced Research, and chairs the federal government's Advisory Board on the Information Highway; he has also served on the boards of such companies as Seagram, Domtex, and Southam. (His academic specializations are 'securities regulation, corporation and labour law, and law related to the environment and sustainable development.') His use of the expression 'we professors' almost verges on the tendentious; his career has mostly been in administration.

37 That the future of the university is, as they say, up for grabs becomes clear when we reflect that my favoured word 'archive' translates nowadays as 'data base,' and that a data base is a somewhat equivocal and ethereal entity. The whole business of acquiring, storing, and accessing information is changing almost by the week, under the control of technical and economic forces that are not clearly identified but are only loosely related to the system typified by the research university.

38 The concept of 'relevance' as deployed in these discussions is an interesting

one. 'Relevant to what?' is the obvious question. But I am not sure it is the most *relevant* question. I suppose the underlying appeal is to a Deweyite view of education, and can be most fairly put by saying that worthwhile educational procedures must surely justify themselves *either* by the way in which they arise out of interests the students already have or can be made to have, *or* by the ways they contribute to the solutions of real problems. What sort of teaching would be 'irrelevant' to both of these? It could only be something that was traditionally inculcated for no known reason (or for entirely spurious and factitious reasons). This way of looking at things leaves equivocal the relevance of studies set in motion by unmotivated but real curiosity in the student, or conduciveness to the solution of problems which nobody really needed to have solved. However, given the openness of the future, we never know what may turn out to be useful or fruitful, so that perceived relevance is a dubious value in education.

The threat represented by the uncontrolled growth of the university archive, referred to in the text, is perhaps no more of a threat than the equally uncontrolled paving and steamrollering of the so-called information superhighway; but this, governments may feel, is a commercial affair, and the market can take care of that. Meanwhile, there is something terrifying in the mendacity with which the commercial media are promoting the electronic apparatus in which fortunes of their owners are invested.

When my friends tell me of the wonders of e-mail and the Internet, I am reminded of Ivan Illich, who in pre-computer days was already asking: why go to school, instead of just calling experts on the phone when you want them? (See Ivan Illich, *Deschooling Society* [New York: Harper and Row, 1971].) But we have all learned the answer to that one: all you will get is the great man's answering machine, and he will not call you back. However much information there is out there, none of us has any more hours in a day to process it than our ancestors had.

39 The most powerful exposition of this aspect of Canadian origins remains Donald Creighton's *The Empire of the St. Lawrence* (Toronto: Macmillan of Canada, 1956).

40 The settlers were, indeed, confronted with models of intricately functioning social structures, those of the indigenous peoples with whom they variously interacted. But the models were too remote from their experience of the authoritarian regimes from which they had fled to be useful, or even intelligible.

41 Paul Axelrod observes that the Ontario cutbacks in university expenditure in the 1970s proceeded from the same principles as the expansion of the 1960s: 'Higher education was valued *not* for its ideals, but principally for its products – skilled professionals who would contribute to economic prosper-

ity. So long as they seemed to be fulfilling this function, universities remained an important social priority. But once they produced surplus manpower, redundant programs, and a burdensome addition to the public debt, they no longer appeared to be such profitable social investments' (*Scholars and Dollars*, 4). Social scientists get a charge out of this 'realistic' sort of talk, but the truth it expresses is misleadingly slanted. At no time was professional training rather than general education the exclusive goal (compare note 27, above). Part of the motivation seems to have been that an advanced economy in an international marketplace needs to function with a generally well-informed and sophisticated personnel. The expansion of universities in the 1960s had no clearer intention than to accommodate the postwar 'baby boomers' who would be expecting university education to be provided. Axelrod (p. 90) observes that the Ontario government between the wars had *no* university policy, referring university affairs to committees that merely served as clearing-houses for plans emanating from the universities themselves. Until 1951, the Ontario government had no bureaucrat working full-time on university affairs.

Lack of educational policy in Ontario has not been confined to the post-secondary level. Consider the way in which W.J. Dunlop, the Ontario Minister of Education in 1957, ended the merging of history with geography in 'social studies' in the lower high-school years, according to the deputy minister, Dr F.S. Rivers:

> 'Dr Dunlop was invited,' Dr. Rivers continued, 'to speak to what he thought was to be the Executive of the Ontario School Trustees' Council at the General Brock Hotel. When he got there, he discovered that it was the annual convention of the trustees, and that there were several hundred people in the auditorium and he had no prepared speech. He figured he had to say something of substance, so he announced the end of social studies in grades 9 and 10. Just like that.'
>
> Dunlop considered a lot of people including those who even *talked* about social studies as 'progressives' in education. In fact, all people in the Department during his tenure in the fifties were forbidden to use the expression 'philosophy of education' in public speeches, since Dunlop associated that expression with progressive education. He didn't like progressives ... (J.R. McCarthy, Deputy Minister of Education, 1967+, in interview with Bob Davis, 8 May 1990 [Bob Davis, *Whatever Happened to High School History* (Toronto: James Lorimer and Co., 1995), 26].)

Devotees of the TV program *Yes, Minister* will observe that what one had taken for light-hearted satire would, in an Ontario setting, be a whitewash.

To return to the university scene, in a context particularly germane to these lectures: Trent University was sparked (in 1958) by a suggestion from the local president of the Quaker Oat Company, and the land was donated by General Electric: the Ontario government in 1960 refused to support the venture. Tom Symons, the first president, expatiated on how much the university would do for the local economy (Axelrod, p. 61); but Axelrod says nothing at all about what any of these people, or their fellow promoters in other communities, thought a university was for.

42 McKillop, *Matters of Mind*, xviii–xix.

43 Michael Skolnik, 'Balancing Drift and Design: Ontario Universities Need Firmer Direction,' *University of Toronto Bulletin*, 9 December 1996, p. 12: '[T]he most striking thing about the Ontario university system is its lack of diversity of institutional types. For example, unlike other countries or provinces, we have no open or distance university, no private university, no liberal arts institution, no institution that is specialized by mission or branch of knowledge or application, nor anything like the university colleges in British Columbia. Rather we have an exclusively public system of institutions of similar standards and similar aspirations. All institutions strive for comparable standards, curriculum breadth, graduate programs and involvement in research.' He contrasts the elaborate differentiation within the systems of American states such as California.

44 For a depressing account of how this worked out in Ontario between the world wars, see McKillop, *Matters of Mind*, Part IV. He relates (p. 407) that in 1927 Emma Goldman said that in her experience Toronto was unique among universities in the extent to which it had had to withdraw from the city in which it was situated. In later years, universities were allowed and even encouraged to burgeon (Premiers Davis and Robarts were enthusiasts for education); but under the last two regimes governments have started to think (always a dangerous tendency in politicians) and have concluded, not surprisingly, that they purely hate universities. It is dizzying to feel these blasts of cold air directed from the standpoints of, successively, the op-ed page of a campus newspaper and a country club locker room. In fairness, though, one must add that the Ontario universities, faced with the huge increases in student numbers in the 1960s, proposed to deal with the influx by the foundation of junior colleges; it was the government director of education, J. G. Althouse, who protested in 1955 that 'a junior college cannot attempt specialized and professional training; the best it can offer is a sort of second rate general education. The professional schools must remain in the universities' (cited in Axelrod, *Scholars and Dollars*, 85). So the positive hatred of universities (if it exists at all – but those who deny its existence must find some way of accounting for the familiar statistics cited in note 6, above) is not a continuation of unresisted extant trends.

45 Who is it who proclaims, and is complacently quoted by Canadian politicians as proclaiming, that Canada is such a happy country? Opinionmakers, poll-takers, international bureaucrats. What they mean is that Canada is a good place to be if you are the sort of person who becomes a maker of opinions and rules and a taker of polls. But are the oppressed, the impoverished, the marginalized, really happier in Canada than the corresponding groups elsewhere? Well, perhaps they really are, if they can keep warm. But how sound are the values of the kind of people who make their living taking polls, conducting surveys, making opinions, and ruling roosts?

46 T.H.B. Symons, *To Know Ourselves: The Report of the Commission on Canadian Studies* (Ottawa: Association of Universities and Colleges of Canada, 1975). Robert D. Chambers's entry 'Trent University' in *The Canadian Encyclopedia* (Edmonton: Hurtig Publishers, 1988) reads, in part: 'Trent embodies the academic objectives of its founding president, Prof. Thomas H.B. Symons. The five residential colleges provide excellent small-group teaching in the traditional arts and science disciplines and in a number of interdisciplinary programs, including administration and policy studies, Canadian studies, computer science, cultural studies, environmental and resource studies, comparative development studies and native studies ... Graduate programs in special areas include anthropology, freshwater science, Canadian heritage and development, and watershed ecosystems.' Symons's basic insight is that such a university does well to base its research on local problems and conditions, using this special experience to arrive at results of universalizable significance. The weakness in his position is that he ignores the investigative dynamics generated by the actual personalities and interests of the local professorate, as opposed to superficial and journalistic conjectures as to what the local situation has to be (cf. my 'National Philosophy,' *Dialogue* 16, 1977, 3–21).

47 'If we are asked, "Do we live now in an *enlightened age?*" the answer is, "No," but we do live in an *age of enlightenment*. As things now stand, much is lacking which prevents men from being, or easily becoming, capable of correctly using their own reason in religious matters with assurance and free from outside direction. But, on the other hand, we have clear indications that the field has now been opened wherein men may freely deal with these things and that the obstacles to general enlightenment or the release from self-imposed tutelage are gradually being reduced. In this respect, this is the age of enlightenment ...' ('What Is Enlightenment,' in *Foundations of the Metaphysics of Morals*, trans. Lewis White Beck [Indianapolis: Bobbs-Merrill, 1959], 90–1). See also Lecture II, note 12, above.

48 To some extent, civilization is a matter of degree. Some peoples are called

uncivilized because their ways of life are judged to lack most of the characteristics I mentioned. Some cultures are not identified as civilizations
because their distinctiveness and cultural autonomy are in doubt.

49 Quoted by Andrew Wheatcroft, *The Ottomans* (London: Viking, 1993), 208,
from Lord Kinross, *Atatürk: the Rebirth of a Nation*.

50 I quote this in all innocence. But it occurs to me to ask: in what language
was this speech delivered? If in Turkish, as one might suppose, what are the
connotations of whatever word is being translated as 'civilization'? If it is
the same word, is it perceived by speaker and audience as a loan word? If
so, from what language? Is the understood thought-world that of France, or
Germany, or Britain? It makes a big difference. And by the way: what did
the speaker actually say the head covering was called? He can hardly have
used any Turkish vernacular word, or his point would have been lost. Did
he say *hat*, or *chapeau*? Or what?

The remarks in the text on Turkish civilization and Mahmoud II should
be weighed against other accounts, notably that of Timothy Mitchell's
Colonising Egypt (Cambridge: Cambridge University Press, 1988), and, more
generally, Samuel P. Huntington, *The Clash of Civilizations and the Remaking of
World Order* (New York: Simon and Schuster, 1996), who would no doubt
argue that Atatürk was confusing westernization with modernity – and
who, incidentally, remarks that 'in the post–Cold War world flags count and
so do other symbols of cultural identity, including crosses, crescents, *and
even head coverings*, because culture counts ...' (p. 20, my emphasis).

51 James Boswell, *Life of Johnson*, Everyman Edition, ed. S.C. Roberts (London:
J.M. Dent, 1949), I 414.

52 Someone once said that in such conversations more recently the difference
between culture and civilization is the difference between the Germans and
the French, between rurally centred attitudes and cosmopolitan views. That
makes a lot of things horribly clear, satire beats sociology any day, but it
belongs to the seamy side of discourse analysis and cannot be countenanced
on a respectable occasion like this. Let it be incarcerated in a note, thus.

53 Jean Starobinski, 'The Word Civilization,' in his *Blessings in Disguise: or, The
Morality of Evil*, trans. Arthur Goldhammer (Cambridge, MA: Harvard
University Press, 1993), 1–35, elaborating on work done by Lucien Febvre in
a 1930 article, 'Civilization: Evolution of a Word and a Group of Ideas' (in
Peter Burke, ed., *A New Kind of History, from the Writings of Febvre* [London:
Routledge and Kegan Paul, 1973], 219–57). The quotation is from page 3.

54 He quotes (p. 2) a definition from Léonard Snetlage's *Nouveau dictionnaire
français* (Gottingen: J.C. Dieterich, 1795): 'The tendency of a people to polish
or rather to correct its mores and customs by bringing into civil society a

luminous, active, loving morality abounding in good works,' and says that
the word is first used in this sense by Mirabeau in *L'Ami des hommes* (1756).

55 Starobinski, 'The Word Civilization,' 2–7. He goes on to say that in the
revolutionary period the idea of civilization became associated in France
with humanitarianism, beneficence, and civic spirit, and ultimately with
French nationalism (pp. 17–20).

56 This was the last edition whose editors could and did feel that their major
articles were in some sense authoritative. The fourteenth edition put a brave
face on it, but without much conviction; the fifteenth edition has given up
(cf. Lecture II above, especially note 43).

57 For Aristotle's world-view, see my book *Taking Life Seriously* (Toronto:
University of Toronto Press, 1994), 363–8.

58 The error is analogous to Socrates's assumption in Plato's *Republic* (485–501)
that the philosophic rulers who specialize in scholarship and administration
are not only different from everybody else, but essentially *better people* – that
the good qualities they need amount to overall human superiority. The
error is bound up with what is really a threefold view of such people as
carpenters. A carpenter is regarded in the *Republic* sometimes as a person
with a skilled function to perform in society, sometimes as a person whose
view of life is confined to joinery, and sometimes as a person who, functioning only in the economic sphere, is essentially a servant of the desirous part
of the soul. In the ordinary course of their daily lives, carpenters responsibly carry out a valuable service to their cities – and this, as Socrates admits,
is more than you can say for real-life philosophers.

The *Britannica* article also seems to make two careless assumptions, which
I have silently corrected in my text: first, that civilization is a worldwide
phenomenon culminating in a single way of life; second, that civilization
once perfectly achieved is stable. The 'cultural complacency' implicit in the
text becomes explicit in the claims that used to be made, that the British
empire conferred benefits on its subject people by bringing them 'civilization,' identified with the specific customs of the intruding administrators.
This way of thinking is often satirized as 'dressing for dinner in the jungle,'
and was complicated by the apparent tendency of some Protestant mission-
aries to identify civilization with Christianity, and Christianity with the
sartorial customs of their own tribes.

59 A complicating factor is the contrast between the country and the town.
Driving into an urban environment after a rural excursion, one may greet
the first scatter of industrial detritus by saying (presumably with irony, but
are we sure?) 'Civilization at last!' I think part of what is going on here is
that rural vacations allow the middle classes to substitute informal dress

and manners for those that town life and office employment require. We unthinkingly confuse this contrast with that between savage and civilized cultures.

60 Starobinski writes, rather optimistically: 'The historical moment in which the word *civilization* appears marks the advent of self-reflection, the emergence of a consciousness that understands the nature of its own activity, that believes it knows how collective reality develops and ought to be regulated. This self-reflection is not self-absorbed: the moment that Western civilization becomes aware of itself reflectively, it sees itself as one civilization among others' (p. 32).

61 For Kant's remark that his age was the age of criticism, see Lecture I, note 14.

62 'For ... though we scarce see a man whose fancy agrees with another in the many hands and paintings, yet in general when the cabal is over ... the public always judges right ... So that the gentleman who follows his caprice may undo himself. But he who either fixes his taste, or buys according to the universal judgement and public taste and confession of painters in the work of the deceased, will never be abused or come off a sufferer when he parts with his effects' – Anthony Ashley Cooper, Third Earl Shaftesbury, 'Plastics' (1712), in his *Second Characters*, ed. B. Rand (Cambridge: Cambridge University Press, 1914), 124.

63 See Mary Mothersill, *Beauty Restored* (Oxford: Clarendon Press, 1984), for a profound discussion of this sort of security in relation to Kant's notion of 'necessary pleasure.'

64 This concept is explained and explored in my *Concept of Criticism* (Oxford: Clarendon Press, 1967). See also *The Theory of the Arts* (Princeton: Princeton University Press, 1982), 234–40.

65 The idea of a distinctive function for art, in this sense, has most powerfully been harnessed to Baumgarten's original idea of the true work of art as being a meaningful but unanalysable image. This entails that neither description nor interpretation is ever possible, so that the foundation of critical discourse is left problematic. But other general functions may be plausibly assigned – some concerned with what art can do for us as individuals, some with what it can do for connoisseurs as such, some with what it can do for societies or classes, some with what it can do for humanity as a whole. In general, we might reflect that the arts as we know them have at least three rather obvious functions, which may conflict with one another, or may reinforce one another – how they could, or whether they should, is matter for debate. First, the arts enlarge and reinforce the bounds of imagination, perception, experience, formal order, and what not, and in

doing so clear a space for human freedom; second, they enhance and adorn our physical and mental surroundings; and, third, they commemorate and honour what deserves not to be neglected and forgotten. All these three together, it should go without saying, with their elaborations and negations.

66 Aside from the vague claim to esteem mentioned in the text, assigning a phenomenon to 'art' functions most practically as distinguishing it from 'craft' and from 'entertainment' – compare R.G. Collingwood, *Principles of Art* (Oxford: Clarendon Press, 1938). 'Craft' in this context means whatever can be produced by using set means to achieve predetermined goals; the meaning of 'entertainment' has been the object of less careful exposition, but roughly it means a way of passing the time that enjoyably engages a spectator's attention without demanding any outlay of intellectual or spiritual energy. Of course, most actual works of art are also works of craft. The significance of the distinction is that whatever can be assigned to craft cannot play the cognitive role that Baumgarten assigned to the unitary aesthetic image. This accounts for Collingwood's denigration of 'craft' as epistemically nugatory – but does not excuse it, since Collingwood has no argument to show that the structural articulations of works of art can have no distinctive cognitive value of their own. Actual works of art may also be entertaining (as the protestations of such stage virtuosi as Shakespeare and Balanchine insist, they'd better be), but the relationships here are complicated.

67 This is bound to happen when museums acquire new works. Since directors and curators spend their lives in the study and appreciation of art, their understandings and delights are inevitably ahead of those of the public, whose appreciation can only be based on what museums and galleries have *previously* brought before them. To complain that one dislikes such new work is merely silly, even if one may *suspect* that the taste involved is one that one will never acquire. A notorious case in point is the National Gallery of Canada's purchase of a big painting by Barnett Newman in 1989. A recent collection of materials relating to the subsequent furore seemed to me to show two things. First, as the editors insist, how responsibly the gallery officials acted throughout the purchase and how irresponsibly and dishonestly the mass media fomented the fuss. Second, as the editors seem not to have noticed, how disingenuous was the gallery's public promotion of its new treasure, and how right the public was to suspect that the purchase represented some personal agenda of the gallery officials rather than the rational pursuit of a defensible public policy. See Bruce Barber, Serge Guilbaut, and John O'Brian, eds., *Voices of Fire: Art, Rage, Power, and the State* (Toronto: University of Toronto Press, 1996).

68 That unfamiliar works may impose different sorts of demands on criticism can appear from Hume's essay *On the Standard of Taste,* which will be considered in the next lecture. The 'standard' of Hume's title is the perennial consensus of the best critics, which is assured because the criteria of the 'best critics' are really uncontroversial. This consensus establishes inductively a list of aesthetically good qualities and procedures. A new work imposes on the critic a double challenge: to determine whether it possesses or lacks the consensually established excellences and, if the judgment it actually evokes from the best judges is at variance with its conventional merits and demerits, to decide how the judgment and the convention are to be harmonized and if necessary corrected. One could object to Hume that none of this will work unless the consensus appealed to actually prevails, which it is unlikely to do except in times of cultural stability. Otherwise, the critic may feel called on to determine who the judges are to be and what the relevant comparison classes are, on what can only be a hypothetical basis, leaving the ultimate reconciliation to history. Hume could no doubt retort that in times of cultural turmoil there can be no standard of taste and no recognized critics.

69 Adequate performance of this function does not require that reviewers have more knowledge or better taste than their readers. (Tellingly, reviews are often attributed to the newspaper that prints them, rather than to the reporter who composed them.) Readers readily develop the skills necessary to judge whether the reviewer will share the reader's taste, whether the reviewer is good at estimating whether a new work is 'the sort of thing that will be enjoyed by those who enjoy this sort of thing,' and whether the reviewer is likely to have discerned what is relevantly going on. Miners who judge that methane has reached a dangerous level when the canary dies do not necessarily credit it with any considerable mental capacities.

70 The following discussion rests on, and partly repeats, my paper 'Aesthetics and the End of Civilization' (compare 'Introductory Note,' above).

71 This is an oversimplification, for reasons that may be gathered from Walter Cahn's *Masterpieces: Chapters on the History of an Idea* (Princeton, NJ: Princeton University Press, 1979). Starting from the medieval artisan's demonstration of technical skill to secure admittance to a guild, the idea of a masterpiece proceeds through the metaphorical notion of humankind as God's crowning achievement in creation, through the idea of a canon of supreme works and artists, to the idea of art history as establishing a sort of ideal museum, admission to which amounted to success in an unrestricted competition. This idea, once established, lays the foundation for exaggerated claims about the status of new and untested works (Cahn specifies

Rosa Bonheur's *Horse Fair*). Cahn concludes that 'masterpieces in a time which has not yet become a past will be masterpieces of publicists and seers' (p. 155).

72 I allude here to the basic idea of Baumgarten, mentioned in my first lecture, as developed early in the present century by Benedetto Croce and R.G. Collingwood (compare notes 65–6, above).

73 How fruitful this method can still be may be seen from Richard Wollheim's subtle use of it in his *Painting as an Art* (Princeton, NJ: Princeton University Press, 1987).

74 Plutarch, *Life of Pericles* XIII 3.

75 It has been suggested that the Van Gogh *Sunflowers* referred to was not in fact a genuine Van Gogh, but the work of one of his students (see Thomas Hoving, *False Impressions: The Hunt for Big-Time Art Fakes* [New York: Simon and Schuster, 1996]). The argument is unaffected: the people to be impressed had to agree that the painting *might* have been by Van Gogh ...

76 Alan Bowness, *The Conditions of Success: How the Modern Artist Rises to Fame* (London: Thames and Hudson 1989), cited by Peter Watson in *From Manet to Manhattan: The Rise of the Modern Art Market* (London: Vintage Books, 1993), xxvi.

77 Questions from the floor when this lecture was delivered suggest that it is necessary to emphasize that the phrase 'high art' is not a coinage of my own, designed to convey my esteem for the institutions and practices to which it is applied. It is a phrase quite commonly used in the literature to pick out those among the fine arts (and analogous arts in other cultures) that are officially cultivated and awarded esteem *ex officio*. Not all works of the 'high arts' are masterpieces. A masterpiece is a work accorded special esteem within any of the arts (though perhaps it must belong to some art or other, since the word 'masterpiece' [*Meisterwerk*] seems to carry with it connotations of cultivated skill within a recognized training system). But it seems obvious that it will be easier for a work to be, and to be recognized as, a masterpiece in the high arts, which are already singled out for attention and are able to recruit and reward the best and most ambitious talent.

Feminist critics have drawn attention to the way in which the recognized 'high' arts of a civilization have tended to be those practised by males, as opposed to those (for instance, fabric arts such as quilt-making) conventionally practised by females. Emphasis on this obvious tendency has rather obscured the significance of the singling-out of 'high' arts in the first place.

78 I was on a committee once where a distinguished town planner, of Indonesian origin, startled us by saying that, for him, the Dutch language had been 'the way out of the village.' Today, of course, Indonesia has become a great

empire of its own, but one that displays the malfunctions of imperialism more conspicuously than the functions of empire (compare Lecture IV, note 39).

79 It was refurbished and promoted as such, as a matter of conscious policy, by Indira Gandhi's Congress Party. The result is viewed with mixed feelings, to say the least; but I am not competent to deal with the cultural politics of this intricate issue.

80 'Ethnic' and 'folk' mean very different things. What is ethnic is what belongs intimately to (or 'expresses') a group so closely knit that it regards itself as an extended family, whether it is genetically a tribe or not. But what is ascribed to the 'folk' is being ascribed to the inarticulate and unselfconscious populace, in contrast with the works of individual artistry. Folk art enshrines two overlapping sets of products: works of unsophisticated artists, and artefacts of utility on which aesthetic properties have been incidentally (even if deliberately and painstakingly) bestowed. The concept of 'folk art' at one time was thought to involve humble anonymity, but this has been abandoned as mere ideology. The concept has also been thought to imply a dynamic relation to some more sophisticated artistic tradition, from which the 'folk' art derives or to which it contributes, or both; but this relationship is generally supposed to be an empirical matter, not a defining property. (I will have a bit more to say about 'folk' in Lecture IV.)

81 Significantly, Kapila Vatsyayan, a dominant figure in the artistic life of Indira Gandhi's India (she founded the Indira Gandhi National Centre for the Arts in New Delhi in 1985), identifies the characteristic movements of ethnic dances as embodying and expressing the characteristic work movements of the tribe (see her *Traditions of Indian Folk Dance* [New Delhi: Indian Book Co., 1976]). This effectively dissociates them from the universalistic theological implications of the classical dance.

The way the ideological pattern of empire works in the United States was shown by E.D. Hirsch, Jr, in his book *Cultural Literacy* (New York: Vintage Books, 1988). There are a lot of things, he explained, that Americans need to know before they can understand a newspaper or engage in conversation about public affairs, and without which they are confined to relatively menial employment in a narrow sphere. Somewhat naïvely, Hirsch supposed that the wider sphere into which cultural literacy initiates one must be an intrinsically superior reality, rather than merely a domain of public mobility and potential power of which the public educational system is the official doorkeeper. The idea of 'cultural literacy' attracted a good deal of attention at the time, but seems not to have attained lasting or general currency. It has become fashionable in some circles to pretend that Hirsch was equating cultural literacy (which involves knowing such things as the fact that *Romeo and Juliet* is a play about young lovers frustrated by a family feud) with the content of a general education – as if being literate were the same as being well read.

82 See Thomas A. Sebeok, *A Sign Is Just a Sign* (Bloomington: Indiana University Press, 1991).

IV: Civilization and the Future of Aesthetics

1 As I revise these words, the prevalence of the emphasis on masterpieces is attested by James O. Young's review of a new journal, *Film and Philosophy*: 'It is fair to say that philosophy of film is in its infancy compared, for example, to philosophy of music. If the papers in this journal are a representative sample, the contrast between the philosophy of film and philosophy of music is striking. Philosophers of music primarily concern themselves with musical masterpieces' (American Society for Aesthetics *Newsletter* 15/3, Winter 1996, 3). Note the unargued and indefensible assumption that the preoccupation with masterpieces is a sign of maturity, not of superficiality or corruption.

2 Canadians are singularly well situated to be sensitive to the nuances of imperial and colonial structures. In addition to the various hierarchies mentioned in the text, we are exposed to an assortment of apparent hegemonies with divergent bases: Quebec versus 'The Rest of Canada,' Newfoundland versus the older provinces with less biting nostalgias, the 'colonized' prairies versus the financial power of 'Eastern Canada' where the bankers bloom. All these relationships, vivid when politicians vie for power, tend to slip out of mind in everyday life.

3 Schumpeter offers the following definition: 'Imperialism is the objective disposition on the part of a state to unlimited forcible expansion' (Joseph Schumpeter, *Imperialism and Social Classes: Two Essays* [New York: Meridian Books, 1955]), 6. Schumpeter is entirely concerned with the expansion process itself, and says nothing at all about the organization and administration of the peoples and territories taken in by such expansion. His formulation invites two comments. First, though imperialism as he defines it must result in empire, it is not clear that empires are usually the outcome of imperialism rather than of actions undertaken to protect frontiers (as often in the Roman empire) or trading interests (as in the British conquests in India before Disraeli, or in Rupert's Land). Second, it is not clear that any state's disposition to forcible expansion has ever been unlimited: patriotic songs and jingoistic rhetoric ('Wider still and wider shall thy bounds be

set ...') are not descriptions of policy. In the Roman empire, Trajan's expansionism was followed by Hadrian's retrenchment.

The concept of imperialism is difficult and contested. The root idea could have come from Anchises' famous injunction to Aeneas in the *Aeneid*: The Roman people, he says, will never excel in sculpture, oratory, or astronomy:

> Tu regere imperio populos, Romane, memento;
> hae tibi erunt artes; pacisque imponere morem,
> parcere subiectis, et debellare superbos.

The Roman art will be, not to conquer the 'peoples,' but to rule them once conquered, and to rule them by (untranslatable word!) *imperium*, the sort of power that is delegated to a military commander; the people are to be spared, presumably to live their own lives (for nothing is said about Romanization), except that the habit of peaceable living is imposed on them; and the recalcitrant are to be warred down. For centuries, these lines formed part of everyone's education, and some vague impression of their implications must have been left on many minds.

People often say 'imperialism' when they mean no more than 'empire.' But an extant empire, even one maintained by force, is not to be mistaken for a manifestation of imperialism, if the latter be identified as a policy of *extending the bounds* of empire. There are other common uses of the word, too, that are outrageously tendentious. For several decades, imperialism was understood neither on the Virgilian model nor on Schumpeter's, but was equated specifically with the European grabbing of colonies, not for incorporation within a political structure, but as alien subjects to be economically exploited. Imperialism was construed economically as the last stage of capitalism, the disappearance (or failure to appear) of the proletariat as Marx conceived it being accounted for by its being (as it were) shipped overseas. (The emphasis on *overseas* expansion was necessary because Czarist Russia and the Soviet Union confined their vigorous and ruthless territorial depredations to expansion across their land frontiers; this redefinition of imperialism was a determined and largely successful manoeuvre to make militaristic expansionism conceptually inseparable from capitalist economy.) In the present age of the international corporation, it is increasingly obvious that these sorts of market distortions, common as they are, do not correlate closely with actual colonialism, or empire, or imperialism, but have a more complex dynamic. Fortunately this can of conceptual worms did not need to be opened too widely in my text, which is concerned with empire as I defined it, and not with imperialism as *anyone* defines it.

4 In addition to these native cultures and the official educational/cultural system that forms the imperial *lingua franca*, a close-knit administrative group will no doubt form its own idiosyncratic cultural understandings as a by-product of its cooperation – fads and fashions have their own dynamics which intersect the cultural patterns we are accustomed to think of as more basic.

5 *Prima facie*, imperial power has three aspects: military and police force, to impose and preserve the structure against noncompliance and rebellion; bureaucracy, to flesh out the organization and specify the implementation of its policies; and economic power, the organized flow of goods and services. All of these facilitate some actions and relations and preclude or inhibit others, in ways that are perceived as variously advantageous and disadvantageous to different individuals and groups on different occasions. To reduce all these to terms of violence uniformly exercised by a dominant group against all other groups in its domain, though it may often correspond to one's general impression, is to ignore the facts about the nature of power and the ways it operates referred to in the next paragraph.

6 The Canadian 'imperialism' expressed by G.R. Parkin in the late nineteenth century involved the British empire (including the Canadian ruling class) imposing not only its political institutions but its civilized way of life on the peoples fortunate enough to be incorporated within it (see Carl Berger, *The Sense of Power: Studies in the Ideas of Canadian Imperialism, 1867–1914* [Toronto: University of Toronto Press, 1970]). Imperialism in Canada generally had nothing to do with militaristic expansionism (though Berger cites Lenin and others in a way that shows that he recognizes that this is how the word is generally used), but signified the belief that Canadian nationhood was most effectively pursued within the existing structures of the British empire, rather than independently or in subservience to the United States. One recalls the controversies surrounding Quebec sovereignty (with the scarcely disputed contention that what the Québécois really want is an independent Quebec in a strong Canada) and the union of the Scots and English crowns in 1704 (some arguing that an independent Scotland would be doomed to perpetual poverty and weakness, others that a Scotland in union with England would be for ever alienated and marginalized). The debates continue.

7 One advantage of a boarding-school education (another one being that early in life one learns not to expect justice or encouragement or understanding from this world) is that one learns to make a life in the interstices of an indifferent organization, or to ride its stormy waves, evading or dodging what one cannot use or enjoy. People more humanely nurtured are often

curiously inept in this, and adopt absurdly unproductive attitudes to the presence of an environment that has to be negotiated. One used often to hear would-be writers complaining of how they had to express their precious private thoughts in the words of a common language, a language that had actually been *already used by other people* – like a child complaining at having to blow its nose on Mummy's hanky. One knows the feeling; but without a language one obviously couldn't communicate those private thoughts and (only slightly less obviously) wouldn't *have* the private thoughts in the first place. Real writers make their own uses of a common language and make it their own.

8 Inclusion of the term 'economic' perhaps needs more formal attention than I gave it in note 3. Raymond Williams, for instance, equates imperialism with exploitation of the proletariat in late capitalism, an exploitation that transforms the relation of colonizer to colonized into that between town and country by reducing the colonies to primary producers (*The Country and the City* [London: Chatto and Windus, 1973], chapter 24). It should be obvious that this relationship is quite different from the 'restless seeking of power after power,' and is dynamically quite independent of it – it may be manifested, for instance, in the relation between Great Britain and the Scilly Isles, or even between Ontario and Alberta. No doubt military expropriation, bureaucratic integration, and economic exploitation encourage and facilitate one another in many circumstances, but to equate them with one another would be absurd, even if observation had not made their separability evident. (Aristotle had already pointed out the difference between a trading network, with its ad hoc arrangements for specific marketing relations, and a political community, with its many-sided organizational structure.)

9 Marxists used to use the word 'comprador' as a term of contempt for representatives of a local or 'colonial' population who entered into (complicitous) relations with the central or imperial power. But the term derives from international trade, which (unless one is to undo one's corded bales on the beach and leave it at that) requires that the party traded with have a representative who can carry on intelligible negotiations with the trader – it being assumed that the trader is making the rounds of a large number of settlements or customers.

10 The appearance of oppression may often arise from the simple fact that in any encounter and exchange of information the participant with more resources is more advantaged. This is not because of any exploitation, but because having more resources means that one can do more with whatever one gets. If an ignorant audience member asks a lecturer a dumb question

and gets a brilliant answer embodying all that needs to be said, the questioner is unlikely to learn anything much, not having the sophistication and information necessary to put the answer to good use; but the lecturer is likely to learn a lot from the bare fact that just this dumb question was asked at just this point, being able to see all the aspects of the issue to which it might be relevant. That is the truth that lies behind the lecturer's slogan 'There are no stupid questions, only stupid answers.'

Edward Said claims that the French publication of the twenty-three-volume *Description de l'Égypte* in 1809–23 represented a 'great collective appropriation of one country by another' (*Orientalism* [London: Routledge and Kegan Paul, 1978], 84). This is daft. Publication is the opposite of appropriation. Anyone at all, including Egyptians, could borrow and study the work – provided they wanted to. Nor did the French publication prevent Egyptian scholars from forming their own organizations to study their own history and antiquities on their own terms – provided they were prepared to take the trouble. To speak of appropriating a country by writing about it is like saying of a man who leers at a woman that he 'undresses her with his eyes' – the point being that he does not undress her at all, he only looks as if he might like to. In the same vein, writers on geography sometimes relate the discipline to conquest and imperialism, simply because it makes them possible, and because it might not be possible to get money for extensive mapping, the mounting of exploratory expeditions, and so on, without some such intentions (compare David N. Livingstone, *The Geographical Tradition* [see Lecture II, note 4], especially chapter 7). One sees the point of all this stuff easily enough, but I do not see how one can take it seriously; it indulges in paranoid thought-patterns without the excuse of being actually clinically insane.

11 Schumpeter's account explicitly recognizes this. Of the Persian empire, which did not exploit its subjects, left intact the social organizations of the conquered countries, elevated their leading men to the highest ranks of the imperial aristocracy, and used many languages for official communications, he remarks that it was 'a case of "pure" imperialism, unmixed with any element of nationalism' (*Imperialism and Social Classes*, 29).

Effective power in the Roman empire was in the hands of the imperial secretariat, which was manned by Greeks; in fact, the official culture of the empire was Greek or based on Greek models. As Horace observed (and Juvenal later complained), Greece in captivity held Rome captive. The information system was perpetually being co-opted or resumed by the brute force of Rome, but ineffectively, because the information system is itself the means of control.

12 E.P. Thompson writes of late eighteenth-century Britain that 'the polite culture was an elaborated code of social inclusion and exclusion ... These accomplishments both legitimated and masked the actualities of brute property and power, interest and patronage' (*Witness against the Beast* [New York: New Press, 1993], 110). But this is not credible as it stands. Legitimation and masking are unnecessary. Direct and overt exclusion from political power on the basis of descent and property is not only feasible, but common. And polite manners conjoined with a classical education could work in the way that Thompson suggests only if in fact they correlated with power and property, which they never did. Elaborated codes have to be acquired, whatever social class the aspirant was born into.

The fact that functional mandarinates are regularly subverted by racism, nepotism, ageism, sexism, favouritism, and the like is neither here nor there. The world is badly run, and all its institutions are in fact designed to be badly run – designed, that is, so that their functioning is not prevented by obstructionism and incompetence. Besides, the fact that empires are usually set up by conquest almost guarantees that the dominant culture will indeed *begin* by being that of the conquerors; it is only when the imperial structure is established and operative that it will acquire the mandarinate necessary for its operation, and it is this mandarinate to which ethnic mores are irrelevant.

If the truth be told, however, the description of nepotisms, favouritisms, and the like as perversions or malfunctions is an overstatement, if not a downright error. The running of an empire as of any other organization depends on effective communication. Such communication requires common education, but it also requires mutual reliance and personal understanding; and the people I can rely on not to get me wrong, to understand *me* and not just my words, are my close family, my tribe, my schoolfellows. It is obvious why such preferential reliance is an abuse, but it should be no less obvious why it is ubiquitous and in its own way deeply functional.

13 That a mandarinate may not be the same as a ruling clique of any sort, ethnically based or not, is shown in detail by Daniel Gordon's examination of the 'polished society' of pre-revolutionary France. So far from the egalitarian society of the salons being a manifestation of the spirit of the new regime, the latter was intolerantly exclusionist. It was the absolutism of the French court that required conceptual uniformity, hence linguistic uniformity, and inaugurated the academic movement that standardized the French language. But this movement superseded the traditional class-based society of the separate estates, establishing a sociable grouping that supported a 'new service elite' but was itself non-political and egalitarian

(Daniel Gordon, *Citizens without Sovereignty* [Princeton, NJ: Princeton University Press, 1994], 29–46). A mandarinate as such is not a hereditary ruling group, but a group constituted by its members having acquired eligibility to participate in imperial affairs, whether they do so or not.

14 See Lecture III, note 68.

15 This identity seems not to have been generally noticed. But an early essay by John Rawls points out the significance of just these criteria for moral judgment, though I do not recall that he mentions their origin in Hume's essay (John Rawls, 'Outline of a Decision Procedure for Ethics,' *Philosophical Review* 60, 1951, 177–97 [§§ 2.3–2.4]).

16 Hume's argument for the stability of artistic judgment was that the qualities necessary for good judgment in general are established by experience; that the artistic judgments of such judges establish a consensus on the merits of familiar works in established genres; that the principles implicit in these consensual judgments can be elicited and used to evaluate unfamiliar works; but that these last evaluations remain inferential and subject to reversals which lead to the revision of the implicit principles. Other thinkers have derived arguments from working out the relation of beauty to goodness (beauty is the promise of goodness); from examining how the development of an art represents the successive discovery of its possibilities; and from the possibility (exploited by contemporary auction houses) of developing, in an endlessly beautiful world, new ranges of discrimination within which appreciation can be secure even if the range itself is arbitrary. (All these are supplemented by the discovery that the development of a range of positive values automatically makes it possible to generate an equally complex and stable interest in their detailed denial.)

17 Somewhere in his voluminous lucubrations on musicology, in which he argues that the only *serious* music today is that written to Schoenberg's recipe, T.W. Adorno sneers at 'the young people and their jazz.' It is obvious that what he means by jazz is not precisely jazz; he is using the word vaguely to cover a wide range of music-making about which he has never bothered to inform himself. He has not inquired into the classifications, discriminations, styles, conventions, affiliations, and criteria recognized and explored by those conversant with this field, and is thus not entitled to an opinion as to the possibility (or actuality) of a legitimate connoisseurship in it. But he is, of course, entitled to reject the whole field as one that he regards as socially, culturally, and musically beneath his notice, and into which he does not think it worth his while to venture.

18 Anyone inclined to pontificate about the spread of British power in the Indian subcontinent might profit from reading and reflecting on Garry

Alder's *Beyond Bokhara: The Life of William Moorcroft, Asian Explorer and Pioneer Veterinary Surgeon, 1767–1825* (London: Century Publishing, 1985). Moorcroft's quest for a reliable source of cavalry mounts took him into a world of trade, conquest, and espionage that is unlike anything of which the usual ideological narratives give one an inkling.

19 Compare the Canadian situation, as sketched in note 2, above, and the situation Moorcroft thought he perceived (see preceding note) in which British suzerainty might protect the local farmers from enslavement by the rival powers of Nepal and the successors of the Mogul empire.

20 Tennyson, in 'Locksley Hall' (1842), already envisioned 'the Parliament of man, the Federation of the world,' but as a sort of international consortium (rather like the United Nations, in fact) set up after a destructive world war dominated by air power, itself the outcome of massive airborne commerce – 'magic sails ... dropping down with costly bales' (possibly of heroin). Writing before our information explosion and intercommunicational interweaving, he could not imagine the intricacies of instant exchange on which the actualities of an effective world-order would construct itself.

21 Which critics are these? I am not sure; the memo on which I recorded the observation merely ascribes it to 'Doran.' This is probably Robert Doran, author of *Theology and the Dialectics of History* (Toronto: University of Toronto Press, 1990), but I do not recall reading this book.

22 Except, of course, to the extent – the very important extent – that any such system generates a quasi-culture of its own, as suggested in note 4, above.

23 Information transmission in an empire is not a one-way affair. Gamelan groups are formed in the United States. The question is not whether such things exist, but how they are related to the central cultural organizations of an imperial order. Readers are invited to consult their own judgment and experience as to how far an international system of high-art practice prevails and how its hegemony operates.

24 'But isn't science merely the way that Western and westernized societies establish their beliefs? Science *is* one of the major ways that people in Western and westernized societies establish their beliefs, but it is neither the only way nor merely the way that they do so. What science has in its favour is that it beats all other ways hollow. There is no contest ... Success in the knowledge game is hardly an incidental feature of *Homo sapiens*. It is our chief adaptation' (David L. Hull, *Science as a Process* [Chicago: University of Chicago Press, 1988], 26). For further discussion of the supposed limits of science, see Ronald Munson, 'The Human Limits of Science,' *Philosophic Exchange* 17, 1986, 43–57.

Samuel Huntington (cited in Lecture III, note 50) envisages a world-order in which the most culturally diverse and opposed civilizations will maintain their separate coexistence, in ways suggested by the reaction of pan-Islamic 'fundamentalism' against 'Western' secular corruption. If that comes about, a civilization in which the prevalent science and technology are not indigenous will have to choose between doing without it and somehow segregating its bearers. Neither policy seems very promising. Huntington gets round the problem by distinguishing westernization from modernization, and neglecting the distinction between an imperial mandarinate (with its own culture) and indigenous ethnicities. The issue is shrugged off in a pronouncement by Heinz Pagels (*Dreams of Reason* [New York: Simon and Schuster, 1988], 172): 'What distinguishes scientific theories from the picture of reality provided by religion, culture, or politics is the intention of their creators that they be useful theories independent of their user's religion, culture, politics, sex, race, personality, feeling or opinions. This is perhaps the most socially and culturally distinguishing feature of science – it is universal in the sense that its truths are true for *everyone*.' But in a later chapter Pagels insists that science stems from instrumentation and technology; his own science, high-energy physics, cannot be practised without machinery of immense sophistication and vast expense and cannot be understood without massive training in quantum mechanics and mathematics. Nor does one see how his theories could be useful independent of culture – how they could be understood and applied within the cultural contexts of New Guinea, for instance. I prefer the position stated in my text, that modern science and technology are indeed 'for everyone,' but are inseparable from an educational system and the civilization that sustains it.

25 The discipline of aesthetics, as it has originated and grown, is likewise indigenous to that educational system and nowhere else. An aesthetics conference in Peterborough could be addressed by a speaker from Australia, or Russia, or Japan, without anyone noticing the difference; the only kind of speaker who would be exotic would be one from outside the world university system.

26 The most sophisticated and far-reaching study known to me of the dynamics of technological expansion and of imperialism worldwide is Jared M. Diamond, *Guns, Genes, and Steel: The Fates of Human Societies* (New York: W.W. Norton, 1997). Of particular value is the way Diamond's knowledge of the Pacific island cultures enables him to break free from our usual fixation on the familiar range of examples, and his suggestion of the way in which the practical intelligence of individuals may vary inversely with the technological sophistication of their societies.

27 The equation of power with oppression, to which I have already objected,

and the association of brutal violence with imperialism, tend to obscure the prevalence of gratuitous and murderous violence between groups of all sorts. For a complex and horrifying case in point, compare the breakdown of civic order and the spread of incomprehensible violence in the Lebanon civil war, as described by Robert Fisk (*Pity the Nation: Lebanon at War* (London: André Deutsch, 1990).

28 I essayed some jejune remarks on this theme in *The Structure of Aesthetics* (1963), 135–41. But I am not aware that the relevant categories have ever really been established. What is meant by 'folk' art, for instance? I gave one answer in note 80 to Lecture III, but what I said there had more to do with textbook artifice than with actual usage. The idea of folk art seems to imply spontaneity as against self-consciousness, naturalness as against artificiality, traditional practice as against school theory, ethnic specificity as against international convention, aesthetic poverty as against elaboration, and/or this or that specific set of 'folksy' traits romanticized nostalgically by a jaded bourgeoisie. I once heard someone say that Tam Kearney's annual New Year's Eve party attracts 'everyone in the folk community from this end of [Canada and the United States]. One chap even comes up from M.I.T.' It would take a long time to explain just what is meant by 'the folk community,' and what M.I.T. has to do with it; but it is, at least, certain that nothing the textbooks tell you about folk music will be much help.

29 The distinction between what is known as gossip and what is known as history is important in principle, if not always easy to make in practice. Much of Calvin Tomkins's art columns in *The New Yorker* is on the same level as *TV Guide*, purveying the glamour of a world to which we suburban readers have no access, and presenting the people who do have such access as neither pleasant nor admirable.

30 For further discussions of these relationships and their significance, see the article 'Art and Culture Today' referred to in my introductory note. Relationships of this sort are complicated by a factor that David Hume allowed to modify his own examination of a 'standard of taste': that variations in artistic practice and preference are systematically related to differences in gender, age, and temperament. We are accustomed to allowing for this variability in all the affairs of life, and should not let it bother us here. Hume did not let it bother *him* – a fact that bothers many students and some professors, who think that when one enters the sacred groves of academe one should wipe from one's feet the dust of the workaday world, and don the wingèd sandals of *docta ignorantia*. In Hume's defence, should that be necessary, we have to remind ourselves that he is writing an essay for the

general educated public, for whom theory is an extension of experience, not for besotted victims of indoctrination.

31 Though the issue was not terminological, it is worth nothing here that an Ontario minister for Multicultural Affairs gave great offence, while gracing an ethnic celebration with his presence a few years ago, by referring to the dancers as 'the girls with the pink booties.' This was rightly judged to show disrespect for the trained skills of the dancers and for the art form that they were practising. On the other hand, what may have been even more offensive, the minister was recognizing that the dancers were really not so much engaged in an artistic display, in an artistic milieu, as helping to demonstrate the ethnic solidarity of an émigré community. The red boots were not more important than their skill, but for some of those most directly concerned they were almost certainly more important than their level of artistic achievement.

32 The final cultural empire in which this would be realized is what Hegel's absolute idealism divined. His system articulated a process whereby research science and scientific history would inevitably, by their own dialectical impetus, make all their competitors irrelevant (their errors exposed, their successes subsumed), so that a world cultural community would attain unassailable authority. The imaginative expression of this complex spiritual unity would be world art; it was the task of the philosophy of art to articulate the development and establish the hierarchy of fine art within the hierarchy of the manifestations of mind. Art as such is obsolete, its imaginative presentations inadequate to the articulation of theoretical truths; but the introduction to the published version of Hegel's lectures on aesthetics ends by telling us that the concrete mission of art will take ages to fulfil: 'It is as the external actualization of this Idea ['the self-unfolding Idea of beauty'] that the wide Pantheon of art is rising. Its architect and builder is the self-comprehending spirit of beauty, but to complete it will need the history of the world in its development through the millennia' (*Hegel's Introduction to Aesthetics: Being the Introduction to the Berlin Aesthetics Lectures of the 1820s*, trans. T. M. Knox [modified] [Oxford: Clarendon Press, 1979], 90). The obsoleteness means only that artists cannot now be leaders of world thought, as an Einstein or a Hegel can.

33 Note how this finite idea of rational correction becomes swallowed up in the indefinite notion of evolutionary improvement embodied in the old *Encyclopaedia Britannica* article on 'civilization' described in Lecture III.

34 The program sounds unexceptionable. But there is a problem. A system of error-removal may lead to a system incorporating what the removal

procedures have to treat as ineliminable error, whereas a different procedure might have turned up more errors that could be eliminated. (A related
point was made in Lecture III (page 59) in discussing the idea of civilization.) The enlightenment idea implies a program, essentially progressive
rather than conservative, which allows no room for alternative ways of
identifying error. But does this make sense? If such a program includes all
possible ways of identifying all *conceivable* errors, it does not correspond to
any realistic policy; but if it enumerates and classifies everything it recognizes as error or correction, it is merely one method among others. This
supposed objection, however, may be factitious. It may be met by saying
that the enlightenment idea as such does not imply any program, but only
the principle that errors are to be sought and corrected by whatever means
can be devised. In that case, the real difficulty may be that to treat an
opinion or a procedure as erroneous is to identify it as an attempt to solve a
specific problem. But suppose it was not designed to solve that problem but
some different problem that the reformers are unaware of, or was not
functioning as a piece of problem solving at all? Are such misgivings merely
paranoid?

35 See Thompson, *Witness against the Beast*, as cited in note 12, above. The most
striking manifestation of this intransigence may be the widespread recru-
descence of 'Islamic fundamentalism,' a leading component in which seems
to be a combination of resentment and repudiation directed against the
intrusion of an alien rationalism into lives already organized on other
principles. But, as we have seen, a more neutral way of putting the matter is
to say simply that one civilization is protecting its own culture against an
alien culture: self-correcting science and technology do not validate the
lifestyles that appear to support them but may only be associated with them
by custom.

36 The simultaneous achievement and discrediting of world civilization may
remind us of the simultaneous implementation and disintegration of the
research university, as noted in Lecture III. But the cases, though in a way
parallel, are very different. What went wrong with the university idea was
that the possibility of its institutional implementation showed that its
ramifications were infinite and could not be institutionally controlled. What
is said to be going wrong with the civilization idea is that the prospect of its
fulfilment causes revulsion.

37 Contrast Cardinal Newman's objection that the achievements of individual
reason are to be measured against the cumulative and constantly corrected
knowledge enshrined in tradition – especially in theologically guided
tradition (cf. Lecture III, note 16). The present complaint is that the tradition

itself is an entrenchment of error, protected from correction by the fact that research is guided by ideology in the first place. Doubts of this sort about the scientific establishment are reflected in the current controversy about the human genome project, which is alleged to attract disproportionate political support and funding because it combines two aspects of patriarchal prejudice, the preoccupation with single-point causality and the prospect of profitable manipulation of human beings.

38 It is this superimposed official-industrial reality, not the substance of the lives people live, that Jean Baudrillard has identified as contemporary experience in which images are substituted for reality. That so many readers find Baudrillard irresistibly titillating shows that his vision is a recognizable caricature rather than an informative likeness.

39 These scientifically based intrusions are not to be confused with the sheer brutal and incompetent meddling of which governments (especially, perhaps, military dictatorships) are also capable – as amply illustrated, for instance, by Norman Lewis in *An Empire of the East: Travels in Indonesia* (London: Jonathan Cape, 1993), and exemplified by the Canadian government's repeated resettlement of Inuit communities in localities that do not provide the wherewithal for their way of life. An illustration of the kind of presumably expert intervention I have in mind in the text is the Three Gorges Project in China, the controversy about which has been widely reported. For the case against the project, see *Yangtze! Yangtze!*, by Dai Qing (London: Earthscan, 1994).

It is perhaps unfair to mention the environmental havoc caused by mega-projects without remembering what was at one time more often mentioned, the havoc caused by the implementation of unsophisticated technologies by large numbers of individual agents, whether they be an excess of indigenous population or an invading horde – the felling of trees, the grazing of sheep, the burning of cover.

40 'So Studie euermore is ouershot,
    While it doth study to haue what it would,
    It doth forget to doe the thing it should' – *Loues Labour's lost*, I.

41 That only good science can remedy bad science is a thesis by which I have long been comforted. But it is profoundly ambiguous. What is this good science that is being invoked? Is it simply more of the same sort of focused research and massive intervention that got us into trouble in the first place? If so, the scepticism expressed in the text is in place. Is it a different kind of science, one guided by modesty and caution in its generalizations and applications? If so, well and good, but one suspects that the alleged merits

of this 'good science' are precisely what is least scientific in it, its departure from the actual procedures and paradigms of the scientific professions.

42 It has been objected to this familiar argument that in it 'power is conceived abstractly, without any real social foundations or systemic origin. In fact, it has become part of this dominant discourse to *deny* the systemic origins of power, and therefore also to deny its contestability. Where power has no identifiable cause but just *is*, where in fact there *is* no causality but only contingency, there can be no resistance and no contest' (Ellen Meitsis Wood, 'Edward Palmer Thompson: In Memoriam,' *Studies in Political Economy* 43, Spring 1994, 31; cited from Davis, *Whatever Happened to High School History?* [see Lecture III, note 41], 206). Wood's polemic is specifically directed against the excesses of Foucault's later writings, but it applies *mutatis mutandis* to much environmentalist rhetoric. A somewhat different approach to the same argumentative style is taken later in the present lecture.

43 This line of thought has become so familiar that we do not always stop to ask what is meant by 'disaster' here. From what point of what observer is what outcome deemed disastrous? And how does that viewpoint come to be privileged by such a judgmental term? What is referred to is, I think, the final degradation of the biomass. All but unicellular organisms, perhaps, would be wiped out. Some billions of years of biological development in a self-transforming ecosystem would be cancelled. It would be possible to dismiss the judgment that such a catastrophe would be disastrous by calling it something like 'speciesism,' but such dismissal would surely be heroic to the point of imbecility.

44 One of Xerxes' generals, foreseeing the disaster of the Battle of Plataea, said: 'Of the agonies in human affairs the most hateful is this, to have understanding of many things and power over nothing' (Herodotus IX 16).

45 'And therefore welcome the sowre cup of prosperitie, affliction may one day smile againe, and untill then sit downe sorrow.' – *Loues Labour's lost*, I. This post-catastrophic condition might rather be like that of the innumerable small-scale self-sustaining economies that (as I am constantly assured by the charitable organizations that solicit my support) continue to flourish, when left alone, in the interstices of empire. My text fastens on the stage in the development of our civilization fastened on as basic (and hence, in a sense, innocent) in Aristotle's *Politics* and in the country of the Cyclopes in the *Odyssey*: an economically stable and prepolitical situation in which self-sustaining farmsteads maintain themselves. This assumes that existing staple foodstuffs will not vanish in the nuclear night, or whatever; daydreamers usually make this assumption, imagining that wheat, maize, and so on were developed by bountiful nature rather than agricultural selection.

46 David Schmid, 'PC with Pride,' *Oxford Today* 5/2, 1993, 54. Cf. Stanley L. Katz, 'The Humanities and Public Education,' in *The Humanities in the Schools*, ACLS Occasional Paper no. 20, 1991, 7: '[A]s recently as a generation ago, the humanities focused on old, elite (and largely Euro-American) cultural texts and problems. It was the case in every field from music to philosophy. But now every aspect of human life seems suitable for serious humanistic studies – all social classes, all the areas of the world, all periods of time (including the present), and all activities.' But that everything is suitable for serious *study*, by someone, in some circumstances, for some purposes, is not news. What is missing from Katz's statement is the possibility that our own civilization might have a cultural tradition to which we belong, by which we are formed, and to which we contribute.

47 The Stanford advocate's appeal to equal rights for previously disadvantaged groups seems so evidently just that the obscurity of his argument may escape our attention. Is the Western intellectual tradition being condemned solely on the grounds that its contributors were mostly white males? Or are white males being condemned because they contributed to the Western intellectual tradition? (I omit the advocate's term 'upper class' because the contributors in question were mostly members, not of the nobility, but of the middle classes, and anyone who gets to make a recognizable contribution to intellectual life becomes, ipso facto, a member of the middle class.)

48 The point of view is that presented in Jean Genet's play *The Balcony*, in which it is assumed that judges and generals are identified by their uniforms, not by the information systems and power structures in which they regularly function and which they have learned how to operate (Jean Genet, *Le Balcon* [Décines, Izère: Marc Barbezat, éditions l'Arbalète, 1956]). In the world of *The Balcony*, impersonation is both easy and impossible – easy, because anyone can pretend to be anything; impossible, because if nobody really *is* anything there is nothing for anyone to pretend to be.

49 Typically, a bare announcement of the verdict by the announcer is followed by an extensive rebuttal delivered on camera by the lawyer for the defeated side. Nothing is done or said to remind viewers that this 'rebuttal' is not a response to the finding of the court, but a mere rehash of one of the two opposing positions that the court had to take into account in reaching its verdict. A similar pattern prevails in the radio newscast I most frequently hear. After the announcement of a scientific pronouncement or policy decision, the announcer will regularly say 'Not everyone agrees,' and state a contrary opinion. But it is obvious that not *everyone* agrees with *anything*; one can always find some nutter to endorse any opinion, however foolish or ignorant. The announcer does *not* say 'Not all informed people agree,' or

'A few people disagree,' and seldom says what reasons have been given or might be given for either side. Any opinion, to a newscaster, is just as good as any other opinion.

I note, however, that this democracy of mere opinion, which I have attributed here to the levelling force of the electronic media, is no such novelty. Referring to a correspondence in *The Times* in November 1881, an essayist of the day writes: 'No! I am not surprised. I am surprised at nothing in controversy. Talk about the invention of printing or of the steam-engine. What are these discoveries when compared with the simplification of dialectics which this generation has arrived at, whereby a disputant can always cut the ground from under those who stand upon statistics, by blowing their statistics into the air with the mighty explosive of a flat contradiction?' (Augustus Jessopp, D.D., *Arcady: For Better For Worse* [London: T. Fisher Unwin, 6th edition, 1892], 104). In considering the significance of this comment, one must ponder the use of the correspond-ence columns of *The Times* as a means for the exchange of opinion among the favoured readership of that organ (like a postprandial chat in a Picca-dilly gentlemen's club, where any member who has paid his dues is entitled to his say). In justice, one must add that neither of the correspondents cited by Jessopp supports his opinion by any statistics – or by anything else, except that one of them has a knighthood and the other does not.

50 No doubt this is just another of those silly jeremiads against television for which print-oriented savants are notorious. Bob Davis (*Whatever Happened to High School History?*, 61–2) has another: 'It seems that the government of Ontario no longer needs history and civics as core curriculum because their main function of yore, that is, teaching that we have the best of all political and economic systems, is now being carried out more directly and more cheaply by television. Loyalty-training has been privatized. Why go at loyalty with the roundabout route of history and civics classes when students will "voluntarily" pick it up through the commercials, i.e. the goodies you get from a good society and, secondly, from the sit-coms, soaps and game shows which show the life-style you will enjoy when you own the goodies?' It is perhaps unfair to point out that TVO, the only television network funded by the Ontario government, does not have commercials. Even so, Davis seems not to have observed that the products most often featured in TV commercials are such as disposable diapers, panty liners, underarm deodorants, toilet cleaners, cold medicines, and hair dyes, 'goodies' unlikely to bewitch adolescent viewers; that the most popular shows on network television tend to be set in hospital emergency depart-ments and police homicide squads, which may or may not 'show the life-

style [they] will enjoy when [they] own the goodies'; and that young viewers have a special penchant for shows depicting star-ships careening through unknown regions of place and time.

51 Stanley Fish (as cited in Lecture II, note 50), commenting on the furore aroused by the Stanford reform, claims that in fact the existing course was not deleted from the curriculum: the new course was merely an option added to the existing structure. The fact remains that the change could have been proposed and might have been accepted, and no doubt would then have had the significance that so many people ascribed to it. The fact that it never happened, if it never did, is also significant, in ways that my text suggests.

52 This contradicts Marshall McLuhan's dictum that '[w]e don't know who discovered water, but we do know it wasn't a fish.' But a fish out of water soon learns at least what water *isn't*, and it is notorious that newcomers to universities feel like fish out of water. (A fish that has never been out of water has no need to know what water is.) An alternative to the claim in the text would be that a civilization does not have a basis that can be separated from the particular studies that the undergraduates are already undertaking, and that what is really needed to supplement those studies is the diffuse experience of the lived world that they already have – a quite different sort of foundation than anything that any course of college instruction could supply.

53 Hans Andersen's fable has a lot to answer for. We all know that emperors do not really parade in the nude, and that kids who pretend to see them naked should have their mouths washed out with soap. A fairy story should not blind us to the ugly truth that anyone who succeeds has to be doing *something* right.

54 Carol S. Gruber, *Mars and Minerva: World War I and the Uses of the Higher Learning in America* (Baton Rouge: Louisiana State University Press, 1975). The original offerings were 'war issues' courses, she tells us, and '[a]fter the war was over, the theme of absolute good versus evil was retained by simply putting the Bolshevik in place of the Hun as the menace to democracy everywhere' (p. 241). The prototype of compulsory 'Western civilization' courses was introduced at Columbia in 1919, and promoted as a bulwark against radicalism.

55 This is in line with the idea I traced to the Socrates of Plato's *Apology*, that the critical self-examination of life transforms humanity into a new species. Beginning students who come (as many do) from unintellectual homes and inferior schools find, when they come to college, that they belong to the wrong species, and must struggle to transform either themselves or their

new environment. (In Plato's *Euthydemus*, 283C–D, a sophist confronts Socrates with the paradox that educating people is a way of destroying them: '"And you people," said Dionysodorus, "want him to become wise, and not to be a dunce? ... Then you wish him to become one that he is not, and no longer to be one that he is ... Since you want him no longer to be one that he is now, you want him to be destroyed, it seems."' Socrates shrugs the paradox aside.)

56 Arguments to this effect are widespread, notably in the writings of Edward W. Said. Some people are genuinely wounded by such insinuations, some are offended by them, others brush them aside. It depends, I suppose, on one's assurance of one's own human worth, and on the practical implications of the put-downs in the context of one's life.

Note that the text at this point suggests that the old-style courses implied that incoming students are excluded from the mandarinate by their insufficient basic education, and are to be brought up to speed. But if there really is such a content to be imparted, in which the professors are adept and the beginning students are not, the implication of the replacement course can only be that the incoming students will never be brought up to speed, are for ever cut off from the mandarinate, and will never be able to take part in public life. (In much the same way, secondary schools in rural and impoverished areas may actively discourage students from preparing for university, whatever their talents and ambitions, on the assumption that they are predestined for a disadvantaged existence.) But if a Stanford undergraduate is excluded from participation in the mandarinate, who on earth is *not* excluded?

57 'How well hee's read, to reason against reading' – *Loues Labour's lost* I.

58 A television program (in the series *Dancing*) on a multicultural dance festival in Los Angeles presented that city as an epitome of global multiculturalism, with its national groups from all over the world: the festival was to be a meeting place for ethnicities. To the dispassionate viewer, however, it was obvious that the festival was being organized by Americans using the resources of the international educational and cultural network of the super-empire, and that the ethnic dances themselves were adapted and packaged for display in this context. Nothing in the program made any reference to the logistics or organization of the festival itself. The disingenuousness of the proceedings was underscored by the fact that the brilliant dancing was interspersed, not with comparable contributions from the host country, but with satirical shots of the more depressing aspects of Los Angeles life. There were, of course, no corresponding shots of the downside of life in the homelands of the dancers. A prominent part of the

program was repeated denunciations of 'the white man' by members of the dancing groups.

It is interesting to compare such multicultural festivals from a post-colonial age with the displays of colonial culture at international exhibitions in the palmy days of colonialism, as commented on by Edward Said: 'These subaltern cultures were exhibited before Westerners as microcosms of the larger imperial domain. Little, if any, allowance was made for the non-European except within this framework' (*Culture and Imperialism* [New York: Knopf, 1993], 112). Apparently, such exhibitions differed from their successor in that the latter falsified the context of its own presentation, and the former did not. The international exhibitions were open to whoever came along; since they were held in Western capitals, the people who came along were almost all Westerners. What would Said have considered an improvement? Obviously, nothing would have pleased him. At first, one may be inclined to take this indiscriminate determination to find fault as a reason for not taking him seriously. On reflection, however, one recognizes that this is his whole point: everything done by a colonial power was imperialism, and imperialism was an unrelieved evil, so denunciation needs no justification. The sillier Said can be, the more obvious it is that his judgment has been impaired by the horrors of imperialist oppression. To speak judiciously would have been a tacit admission that his being colonialized has not left him unable to think.

59 Can frameworks *generate*? Yes, of course they can; a political framework is not an inert scaffolding, but a patterned set of actions that combine in a framing function. Such sets always generate a cultural reality, because the attitudes necessary to maintain the necessary degree of cooperation in common action amount to what Aristotle (the pioneer of this discourse, in *Nicomachean Ethics* VIII–IX) calls *philia*, 'love' or 'friendship' or 'camaraderie.'

The essential point about this aspect of empire is made by Starobinski: 'The historical moment in which the word *civilization* appears marks the advent of self-reflection, the emergence of a consciousness that thinks it understands the nature of its own activity, that believes it knows how collective reality develops and ought to be regulated. This self-reflection is not self-absorbed: the moment that Western civilization becomes aware of itself reflectively, it sees itself as one civilization among others' (Jean Starobinski, *Blessings in Disguise*, 32). Certainly; but some champions of Western civilization suspect that it may be the *only* civilization that sees itself as one civilization among others – or that it may align itself with the one super-imperial super-civilization to whose mandarinate all first-order civilizations are 'one civilization among others,' with the proviso that it is uniquely from the technical side of Western civilization that the super-imperial order emerges. Thus Starobinski goes on to say that we need a new, more complex conceptual model, 'if critical reason can recognize that it is a product of the very civilization against which its polemic is directed, if it is willing to admit that civilization-as-value can be formulated only in the current language of civilization-as-fact' (p. 33). Indeed; but critical reason cannot recognize anything, only critical reasoners can do that; and among which reasoners is a unified 'language of civilization-as-fact' current?

60 This substitution is what the nightmare of Foucault's *Surveillir et punir* is all about. The history of the 'residential schools' imposed by church and state on the aboriginal peoples of Canada is exemplary: the brutal regimes that (it is now being revealed) prevailed in those institutions were simply a projection of the basic brutality of the whole enterprise. One recalls the tale of the visitor from a different culture who had been shown round a Western school: 'Are you sure it's a good idea to shut the children up in a building all day? That is just the age at which they should be learning something.'

61 Carbon dioxide is a greenhouse gas, we are told, so it is wicked to emit it – as, of course, we do every time we breathe out. The word 'environment' is often used to mean 'the world as it would have been if human beings had never existed' – as if we could be pure observers of a world untouched by our observing presence, rather than organisms interacting with a world in mutual transformation.

62 For serious reflection on the possibilities and probabilities here, one has to read science fiction. For anthropologically sophisticated but technologically unrealized imaginings in this area, see especially Ursula K. LeGuin's *Always Coming Home*, and her more recent 'A Man of the People' (in her *Four Ways to Forgiveness* [New York: HarperCollins 1995], 93–144). But such fictions never speculate helpfully about the main problem that confronts us, namely, just *how* advanced methods of information handling can be maintained in an environmentally sustainable ecology. Such methods need repair and upkeep, which in our experience require a technical and institutional infrastructure of considerable elaboration.

63 See Lecture II, with note 34. But the immediate point being made there was rather different: that the resources being wasted on the diminishing returns of the exhausted research program of aesthetics were badly needed to investigate the newly opened and endlessly rich fields of communication and information research. At issue now is not the intellectual poverty of aesthetics, but its supposed elitism.

64 Inclusion of this theme is less arbitrary in this context than my text has

made it seem. We have just seen that talk about the end of civilization is, in its own way, equally apocalyptic. Both discourses belong to the same anxiety, and lead to much the same sort of resolution.

65   To circumvent this tiresome word-play, one usually says that one will be talking about, not what the future is now, but what the future timelessly is. That is, one is using what has the form of a present tense as though it were an aorist. But sturdy commonsense languages to do not have distinctive aorist tenses: the wisdom that generates grammatical forms baulks at committing itself to timeless being.

66   Frivolous philosophers point out that, on this account, nothing ever happens. The past has happened already. The future has not happened yet. And the present, strictly speaking, is a dimensionless instant (the interface of past and future) within which there is no time for anything to happen.

67   To this one may retort that, in aesthetics as in everything else, there is of course a *real* future: it is what will turn out to *have been* the past of some present yet to come. And the observed and remembered, simply as such, are intentional objects, no less than the anticipated. But this caveat is, in the last resort, mere sophism. It makes an important point, but the difference it glosses over remains as real and important as ever.

68   Please do not object that 'to die' in the last of these three cases is a different form of the verb – the infinitive – than 'die' in the other two. The same form, 'die,' figures as indicative, infinitive, and imperative. To make it clear which was being referred to, old grammar books added an exclamation point ('die!') for the imperative and the particle ('to die') for the infinitive. The 'to' was not part of the verb; it was the grammarian's indicator. Pedantic boneheads who had learned their grammar from others of the same tribe failed to understand that, and generated the myth of a compound infinitive which would be 'split' if one intruded an adverb between the 'to' and the verb.

69   The very idea of grammar was borrowed by students of the English vernacular from the old grammarians who had elaborated a grammar for the learned language of Latin. (And, originally, of Greek. The Greek word *grammatikē* originally meant 'the art of writing,' the point being that in writing one is no longer using language unselfconsciously, so one has to stop and formulate the rules one would be automatically following if one were talking in one's native language.) The original grammarians of European vernaculars mainly worked by using the Latin categories and stating what vernacular forms corresponded to them. The practice was useful, in two ways. First, since all vernacular grammars followed the same practice, it made comparisons between languages vivid. Second, it provided

the grammarians with a ready-made system that was highly sophisticated. What was wrong with the system was that it neglected the procedures actually followed by the language supposedly under study. The practice has accordingly been abandoned by linguistic science, but it is still the only one most people know if they know any, and is still clung to by primary school teachers and some professional copy-editors.

70 The example, and the controversy, are from Aristotle, *De Interpretatione.* Aristotle's solution to the problem of the truth-value of statements about future contingencies is wildly at odds with the preferred practices of modern logic, and is sturdily realistic. It probably goes something like this. The present reality is such that there may or may not be a battle tomorrow, and that is the present truth of the matter. Tomorrow evening, the truth will either be that there has been a battle or that there hasn't been; but neither of these truths affects the truth of what we were saying yesterday, because yesterday's statements are no longer around to be affirmed or denied. I mention this, not because I think Aristotle's way of doing things is work-able, but because he helpfully refuses to allow his thinking about present and future reality to be befuddled by the free-floating timeless truths with which the symbolic logic of the early twentieth century found it easiest to operate.

71 The reason astronomy is an exception is not that the heavens are unchang-ing, as people once thought. Irregularities and unpredictabilities are not absent from the skies: in a few billion years, something will happen to Mercury, though there is no telling what or when – but the time-scale on which these occur is so vastly greater than human lifetimes that the patterns seem immutable.

72 This is the basis of the sophism mentioned in note 67, above.

73 That is to say: 'events' and 'situations' are selections from states-of-the-world (space/time segments) made in the light of interpretations. What constitutes them as distinct entities is the determinate part they are assigned in narrations.

74 Donella H. Meadows and others, *The Limits to Growth: A Report for the Club of Rome Project on the Predicament of Mankind* (New York: Universe Books, 1972). This was by no means the first such warning to receive public attention. See for instance *Natural Resources: A Summary Report for the President of the United States,* by the Committee on Natural Resources of the National Academy of Science (Washington: NAS-NRC, 1962), where the world outlook is summed up in the following terms: 'Within this decade and continuing for at least the remainder of this century, we may expect a world wide total resource demand which many qualified observers doubt

can be met' (p. 21). (I remember quoting this to a class in ancient philosophy that year, in connection with Lucretius's comments on the exhaustion of the soil in the first century B.C.E.) But the prestige of the Club of Rome gave the predictions of Meadows and her colleagues a special panache.

75 H.S.D. Cole and others, *Models of Doom: A Critique of* The Limits to Growth (New York: Universe Books, 1973). Prepared by the Science Policy Research Unit of the University of Sussex. For the whole controversy, and a review of all such predictions from the earliest times to the present, see now Joel E. Cohen, *How Many People Can the Earth Support?* (New York: W. W. Norton, 1995). The critique of *Limits to Growth* is on pages 121–8.

76 A resource is, in fact, to be defined as such relative to the current conditions of extraction, production, and availability.

77 Cohen (see note 75, above) gives full weight to the fact that agents in later years will be acting in situations other than those the prophets took into account, but does not explicitly attend to the likelihood that the situations will be construed by those in them, not as later phases of the same problematic, but in terms that the prophets may not have foreseen at all. (See further note 81, below.)

It is hard to believe that this radical mutability of perspective could escape the notice of our prophets; but it usually does. The reason may be that theorists assume that either one has a grand system or theory, explaining everything in terms of a single cause or set of causes, or one is a 'positivist,' simply enumerating the succession of events. 'Chaos theory' has partly cured us of this delusion; but too little attention has yet been paid to what seems the obvious truth, that large-scale events and situations are precipitated by the mutual adaptation of innumerable individual choosers. Their choices are made in situations that are all different, but have strong common elements that are interpreted (because the choosers are in communication with one another and given to cooperation and structured competition) on similar lines. The resulting actions generate identifiable trends and large-scale causal patterns, which themselves become the new (and unpredicted) common elements in the situations that constitute the reality in relation to which the next round of choices is made. This would be the pattern of Hegelian dialectic, except that Hegel's theory of *Aufhebung*, in which a totalizing movement preserves the force of the original situations through each successive development, imposes (for theological reasons) a unity on the course of history, and precludes novelty: Hegel writes as if new historical situations, though unforeseen, should have been foreseeable, and are bound to seem rational in retrospect.

78 Note that the same linear extrapolation that leads the futurologist astray is

what gives us all the assurance we have about the future. Predictions are reliable when they rest on commitments made by individuals in contexts within which they have control over their actions (when, for instance, they have established careers in stable institutions) – but not when they rely on the interactions of many independent individuals, each of whom has her or his projects and predicaments.

79 As we review the history of philosophy and culture, general history, and the conditions of life wherever we know them well enough to say, we may wonder whether there has ever been a period in which people could go for their whole lives without experiencing radical change. Certainly not in modern Europe; but consider also the periods 500–450, 450–400, 400–350 B.C.E. and so on. Each such fifty-year period is strikingly unlike at the end what it was at the beginning. The type of radical change may differ, so that we can contrast a present instability with a stable past – but that past will prove to have had its own instability, in some other respect. There are important constancies on the scale of the intimate rhythms of individual life, imposed by the narrow limits within which human physiology (including brain physiology) varies; but the overall patterns and organizations that the historian sees keep changing. (Old-fashioned books tell us that 'primitive' peoples have remained unchanged for millennia, and show us how our remote ancestors lived; but there is no evidence for this cultural fossilization – it is just that the culture *looks* primitive, and does not think of itself as a historically changing entity.) *Tempora mutantur*, though there are limits to the extent in which *nos mutamur in illis* (of course, the converse is true too: in a social situation that remains stable, the ineluctabilities of age and the vicissitudes of fortune are constantly changing the ways in which each individual relates to that situation).

80 Although the text here is written as if it concerned individuals diversely acting and reacting independently of each other, it is not intended to imply a positivist elimination of class and group dynamics of any kind. Classes and groups can rather be expected to redefine, reorient, and realign themselves in unforeseeable ways as their world changes, the inertia of class consciousnesses being itself one sort of factor. Consider how Marx's 'proletariat,' the supposed universal class, has been repeatedly replaced by successive reorganizations of work.

81 Dr Don Chant, doyen of Canadian environmentalists, writes: 'When, as a practising ecologist 35 years ago, learning from my own research on insect population dynamics, I first became aware of the problem of human overpopulation, I came to believe that there was a chance, albeit faint, that rationality and logic would prevail and solutions would emerge and be

implemented on a global scale. I no longer hold that belief ... My own, now thoroughly jaundiced view is that there will be some global tinkering that may buy a bit of time, perhaps a few decades, before biosphere collapse really is upon us – and by then it will be too late' ('Opinion,' in *Delta* 4/2, Summer 1993, 13). Dr Chant is an expert in this field, but I note that he thinks of solutions 'emerging' on a global scale and being 'implemented' in the passive voice, governed by 'rationality and logic' operating on the overall condition of the biosphere. In zoology, Dr Chant's specialism is in creepy-crawlies (mites or ticks, I believe), and he lacks the concept of individuals acting in and on the situation they find themselves confronted by. Such actions have massive unforeseen consequences (such as flooding of the Yangtze), but we really do not know what the specific forerunners of 'biosphere collapse' will be, or how people will react to whatever they are. (It is interesting to note, by the way, that so recently as 1993 one could write on these matters without mentioning the possible effect on overpopulation of the devastating spread of AIDS in some of the most densely inhabited regions.) It is important not to take lightly the real point that Chant is making: after a process has reached a certain point, it may have its own momentum, so that it no longer matters how people interpret or redefine it or change the direction of their attention. Chant thinks that biosphere collapse may involve such a process. However, I must admit that I do not know exactly what 'biosphere collapse' means (despite note 43, above). Is it a condition in which *no* organisms of any sort can survive, so that a new range of life forms can never become established? Or is it merely a change in terrestrial conditions (temperature, atmospheric composition, chemical components of oceans, radiation levels, etc.) so radical that most existing species will be wiped out, to be replaced eventually by a different fauna and flora? If it is the latter, this will be just one more change in a changing world, good from some points of view, bad from others, but mostly conceivable as just *different*. It is hard to think of a reasonable standpoint from which, for instance, the elimination of *Homo sapiens* and all other hominids would be either an unmixed blessing or an unmitigated curse.

82 This impossibility of prediction is not to be confused with the difference between linear and non-linear phenomena, as I understand that (see Heinz R. Pagels, *The Dreams of Reason* [cf. Lecture II, note 49], chapter 4 – if Pagels is wrong, I am wrong; but if he is right I may still be wrong, because I am really out of my depth here). Non-linear phenomena, like the weather, are unpredictable because the solutions to the relevant equations do not sum: their upshot is chaotic (see James Gleick, *Chaos* [New York: Viking Press, 1987]). But the weather, chaotic as it is, is still weather, and the solutions to

non-linear equations are still solutions to sets of equations. In the practical contexts to which I am referring, by contrast, where we have to do with how real people are indirectly deciding how to live their whole lives by directly deciding what to do next, in whatever they make of their immediate situations at the time, what chiefly changes is the terms of the equations themselves. The problem that the Sussex critics of *Limits to Growth* set themselves prevented them from taking this into account.

The projections of pop futurologists tend to overlook, not only the way tendencies dissipate themselves and are superseded, but the invariances in human physiology alluded to in note 79 (above), which set limits to tendencies that technology seems to promise. The processing capacities of the brain, the muscular strength of the limbs, the requirements of food and drink and the elimination of wastes, and who knows what detailed tolerances in all kinds of specific areas, are likely to impose limits on the unrecognizability of future ways of life. The fact that we cannot predict what these limits will be does not mean that there will be none. In a once-famous passage of his *Autumn Journal*, Louis MacNeice contrasts the schoolteachers' idealized picture of the ancient Greeks with the crooks and deviants – not to mention the slaves – actually encountered in their literature, and concludes: 'And how one can imagine oneself among them / I do not know; / It was all so unimaginably different / And all so long ago' (*Autumn Journal* [1938], IX; in his *Collected Poems, 1925–1948* [London: Faber and Faber, 1949], 139). Different indeed, and perhaps unimaginably so – but MacNeice has no difficulty in recognizing the human types characterized in those ancient texts, and relaying the characterizations to his readers.

83 See also my 'On Metaethics: A Reverie,' in Jocelyne Couture and Kai Nielsen, eds., *On the Relevance of Metaethics: New Essays on Metaethics* (Calgary: University of Calgary Press, 1996), 31–50.

84 This is not because coroners are self-important busy-bodies ignorant of how the world's work is done. The duty of making recommendations is laid on coroners by law (*Revised Statutes of Ontario*, 1990, chapter C37).

85 Trades unions are exploiting this fact when, unwilling to call an actual strike, they institute a campaign of 'working to rule.' By complying with all management rules and statutory requirements, they ensure that no job can ever be completed on time.

86 'Anything but commonsense,' that is, unless 'commonsense' is taken to mean 'based on ignorance of the relevant facts,' as it often does.

87 David Hume, borrowing a theme from Plato's *Protagoras*, observes that human beings 'are always much inclined to prefer present interest to distant and remote'; and this is so obviously true that Jeremy Bentham included

proximity as a factor in his calculus of pleasures. But it must not blind us to the yet more obvious truth that humans will *in every case* prefer *what is most forcibly present to their minds*, whether this be a present interest, a remote interest, or something that is not an interest at all – such as an accepted obligation, a continued resolve, or a recognized demand. Of course, a remote interest will not guide action unless it dominates present motivation. But it may well do so. What is taken for the weakness of a remote interest is often the belief that it can be no less certainly satisfied if it is postponed in favour of a present opportunity that may not recur. That such beliefs are often delusory (and may involve self-deception) is not to the present point.

88 To say that people always act in the light of the pressures they experience as impinging on them at the time of decision and action is not to endorse behaviourism. Behaviourism is a theory about what will impinge: namely, what belongs to a pattern that has been reinforced by reward. That may or may not be true, but it is far from being a tautology. My proposed tautology really is one: it has no predictive force, it only requires us to look at moments of decision as they are and see what factors are operative.

89 We all know that different people have different views about law and morality. Even if they have the same principles, they may have them in different forms and have different styles of compliance. Moral philosophy has tended to assume that things should not be this way: that styles of principledness can be ranked as more or less mature, for instance. (Compare the work of Lawrence Kohlberg, according to whom Kant's ethical theory is a mere sign of his failure to grow up, and could have been cured in any good secondary school by the average graduate of any American college of education.) Similarly, we tend to suppose that people should all be consistently law-abiding, though we know perfectly well that in fact people differ in what laws they keep, and in how selectively, how rigidly, and how conscientiously they keep them. But law-enforcement agencies do not in fact expect perfect compliance, and in less formal contexts we take it for granted that not everyone keeps deadlines, pays debts, answers letters, and so on, and accommodate our lives to this understanding. I suspect it is a mere superstition that things would be better if everyone did what they should. The real world in which the uptight and the slipshod rub along together is probably the only workable world – even if it is a world in which a pretence has to prevail that perfect compliance should be sought or imposed. (One of the ways in which this applies to political regimes I have commented on in note 12, above.) Anthropologists have long differentiated between the formal codes of behaviour to which a society pays lip-service

and the operative codes by which its members really expect one another to live, but in a complex society like our own there are many more distinctions to be made, as the troubles surrounding contemporary attempts to legislate for 'zero tolerance' are showing us. Heinz Pagels (*Dreams of Reason*, 330) points out that an equilibrium state for mendacity in a society is one in which most people mostly tell the truth, but not all and not always; this would keep the society in a condition both wary and honest. I want to go one step further and say that a truth-telling equilibrium implies rather a widespread understanding of who is likely to be lying, and when, and how. Being deceived is a subtle and intricate business, perhaps even more so than deceiving is.

The variations in compliance I am referring to in this note, by the way, are not the same as the various 'forms of subjectivization' of moral codes brilliantly distinguished by Michel Foucault in his *Use of Pleasure* (New York: Vintage Books, 1990), 26–31.

90 This contradicts the breezy confidence about the future of historical entities expressed in Lecture I. What sort of thing *can* have a future? The suggestion underlying the statement in the text is that it can only be a continuant separable from its own history (as a human being has a body separable from the actions that constitute its biography). The argument would have to be that a history, a sequence of events and conditions united by their being placed and interwoven by a common narrative, does not determine the narratives into which other narrators will weave it in time to come. But one could perfectly well stipulate that the term 'aesthetics' properly belongs to *any* philosophical inquiry in which the three problematic areas I have identified are allowed to interact, and in that sense aesthetics has a future that is constituted by any and all future occasions on which such interaction significantly occurs (if there will never be any, the future of aesthetics is that it has no future). The objection to this way of talking is that nothing in the history of aesthetics guarantees that the idea of such an inquiry will even make sense in time to come, so that the stipulation is vain.

91 For this suggestion, compare note 67, above.

92 This is not always uncontroversially true. Consider Zeno's paradoxes, so challenging when first propounded. Some people still find them philo-sophically challenging, other people think they have been definitively disposed of, if not by Aristotle, then by modern mathematics; and what seems obvious and decisive to the one group seems incredible or irrelevant to the other. But no one in modern times has managed to make sense of the fragmentary texts which are all that remain of what Zeno himself actually wrote.

93 I was taking them to the theatre. I found I had forgotten our tickets. I left my guests in the foyer while I drove home (not far; plenty of time) to get the tickets. Next thing I knew I was on foot, alone in a dark wood ...

94 I also knew I would use the dream in an epilogue, like this. But not quite like this, because I did not yet know how dark and dense the wood would prove to be.

95 C.B. Williams, 'Le Petit Salvié,' *Poems New and Selected* (Newcastle upon Tyne: Bloodaxe Books, 1995), 189.

Afterword

1 Søren Kierkegaard, *The Point of View for My Work as an Author: A Report to History*, trans. Walter Lowrie (New York: Harper Torchbooks, 1962).

2 This is the converse of the movement implied in what young Stephen Dedalus (like many children) writes on the flyleaf of his geography book, starting with the Class of Elements, Clongowes Wood College, and ending 'The World / The Universe' (James Joyce, *A Portrait of the Artist as a Young Man* [New York: Modern Library, 1928], 11–12).

3 My first book, *An Enquiry into Goodness* (Toronto: University of Toronto Press, 1958), mostly written before I was thirty, was concerned with how we can argue with other people who can also argue with us – that is, how one can place one's own arguments advantageously within frameworks that also accommodate other arguments, appealing to the framework itself for differential legitimations.

4 William Langland, *The Vision of William Concerning Piers the Plowman*, Prologue.

5 Is it just a coincidence that we owe our first definition of political authority to Aristotle, a career academic? A city, he says, is a community of which all members are equal before they assume office and after they relinquish it. While they are in office they have authority but, unlike aristocrats and monarchs, this authority carries with it no suggestion of personal superiority.

6 That must also be part of what has made me a lifelong practitioner of the art of poetry in its most dandified form, the production of verbal structures in which an internal autonomy (like it or not) is achieved and an impetus of verbal becoming has reached its implicit end. It has made me in my last years an accumulator of seashells and fragments of driftwood, as small children often are, and a restless photographer of whatever in my visual reach seems destined to come to rest in a two-dimensional frame.

7 Such formations and deformations may be contrasted, not only with the special pathos of ruins (for which see Rose Macaulay, *Pleasure of Ruins,*

illustrated by Roloff Beny [London: Thames and Hudson, 1964]), but with the satisfaction of achievement celebrated by John Dewey in his *Art as Experience* (New York: Minton, Balch, 1934). The aesthetic moment, for Dewey, is that at which a problem is resolved and tension released. Beauty is the sign of this release. The beauty of ongoing life, on this view, would come from the fact that living is a dense ramification of overlapping problems arising, faced, and resolved, and of problems that are never perfectly realized too; life thus involves endless concatenations of complete or partial or adumbrated tendencies to resolution, and is beautiful through-out. What I am singling-out in my own experience is rather the observation of apparent terminations produced by the intersection of processes none of which by itself looks to that termination as its proper completion.

8 These are all familiar themes in discussions of the 'poetic process.' I discuss the matter in an essay called 'Every Horse Has a Mouth,' *Philosophy and Literature* I, 1977, 147–69 (reprinted in D. Dutton and M. Krausz, eds., *The Concept of Creativity in Science and Art* [The Hague: Martinus Nijhoff, 1981], 47–73).

9 A dear friend of mine has long been obsessed by the imagery of paradise: a perfect world of divinely guaranteed nature in which nothing sickens, ages, or dies, and in which everything spontaneously fulfils the perfection of its own nature while somehow contriving effortlessly to be as if it were a park designed for our delight and convenience. To be native to such a world, we would ourselves need to be deathless and ageless, exempt from sickness and injury – and, I suppose, birthless too. The image of paradise has no deep appeal for me. In my world, the only world I can imagine myself loving, things are born and dying, vulnerable, fragile, transitory, bearing the marks of their births and destinies. It is a world into which I was born, from which I must die, in which there will never be time for everything.

10 For the spectrum of values, see the remarks on axiology in the first lecture. The relevant point here is that general value theory has suggested that any adequate analysis of values must assign a place to the general sort of value that the English word 'beauty' and the ancient Greek word *kalon* pick out, but that that place may not coincide with the idiomatic meaning of any word in any natural language.

11 All artificial processes involve nature, which provides the whole basic repertory of materials and processes. The cases envisioned by my text here are those in which the conspicuously distinct and interactive components are of both kinds, as when the butcher's cleaver slices what grew as bone.

12 The 'ordinary language' philosophers I grew up among wrote witty and elegant prose, but were not habitual writers and readers of poetry. In

consequence, they had no conception of how languages worked, of what one would say and wouldn't say. The nadir of the movement was the jaunty paraphrase by the young Frank Ramsay of the concluding sentence (Proposition 6) in Wittgenstein's *Tractatus*: 'What you can't say you can't say, and you can't whistle it either.'

13 In the oracle of Apollo at Delphi, the god's message was delivered by a priestess while she was unconscious. The priests (male, naturally) wrote down her utterance and handed or recited it to the suppliant, but did not explain it. The priestess said it without knowing it; the priests knew what she said (or what they said she said), but did not understand it. Only the god knew what she meant – or what was meant, wittingly or unwittingly, by what the priests said she said. But everyone, except possibly the god, knew pretty well what was going on.